Beyond Schizophrenia

Beyond Schizophrenia

Living and Working with a Serious Mental Illness

Marjorie L. Baldwin

ROWMAN & LITTLEFIELD
Lanham • Boulder • New York • London

Published by Rowman & Littlefield
A wholly owned subsidiary of The Rowman & Littlefield Publishing Group, Inc.
4501 Forbes Boulevard, Suite 200, Lanham, Maryland 20706
www.rowman.com

Unit A, Whitacre Mews, 26-34 Stannary Street, London SE11 4AB

British Library Cataloguing in Publication Information Available

Library of Congress Cataloging-in-Publication Data

Baldwin, Marjorie L., 1949-
Beyond schizophrenia : Living and working with a serious mental illness / by Marjorie L. Baldwin.
pages cm
Includes bibliographical references and index.
ISBN 978-1-4422-4833-5 (cloth : alk. paper) -- ISBN 978-1-4422-4834-2 (electronic)
1. Mentally ill--Employment. 2. Schizophrenics--Employment. 3. Discrimination against the mentally ill. I. Title.
HV3005.B346 2016
331.5'94--dc23
2015032341

Printed in the United States of America

For David
Whose courage, determination, and faith are
the heart and soul of this book

Contents

Preface

For the majority of civilized history, our treatment of persons with serious mental illness has been misguided at best, cruel and inhumane at worst. Thankfully, the psychiatric hospitals of 2015 are nothing like their predecessors of one hundred years ago. Today we have laws that establish the rights of persons with mental illness to live in the community, to make decisions about their treatment, and to work in jobs for which they are qualified. Unfortunately, for too many persons with serious mental illness the laws have translated into the right to live in a jail cell, or homeless on the street; the right to continue experiencing symptoms of psychosis, although effective treatments are available; and the right to work in a low-paid, low-skill job, dependent on government support. Today, persons with serious mental illness are no longer incarcerated in mental institutions for life, but they are still bound by low expectations, negative stereotypes, and the belief that they will never live a normal life.

In spring 1999, I was abruptly thrust into the world of mental illness when my younger son was diagnosed with schizophrenia. I was better prepared than most parents would likely be. As a health economist who studies discrimination against workers with disabilities, I was knowledgeable about the laws that protect my son's rights. I had connections to the psychiatric community, and the means to ensure he received the best possible care. Still, my encounters with the mental health services system often left me angry, frustrated, and feeling that I was on my own in caring for my son.

This book evolved from the dual perspectives of researcher and parent. As a researcher, I understand the sources of the intense stigma against persons with mental illness. As a parent, I have experienced that stigma first-hand. As a researcher, I realize that disabilities are disruptive to a person's education. But my son wanted to return to college, and I saw no reason why he should not. As a researcher, I know that vocational rehabilitation pro-grams place most persons with serious mental illness in low-wage, low-skill jobs. As a parent, I wanted more for my son. Hence, each chapter begins with a story from my experience dealing with my son's illness, then continues with current research that informs the story.

In the research sections I have tried to present an unbiased view of current scholarship. However, I am aware that I cannot completely eliminate the bias that comes from my personal interactions with the mental health system. That experience has left me with a number of beliefs that appear as recurring themes throughout this work: that persons in their rational mind would not choose to be mentally ill; that persons with serious mental illness whose symptoms are in remission can make rational choices for themselves, and most would prefer to work; and that, with informed public policies, an un-known but substantial proportion of this population are capable of supporting themselves in competitive jobs.

Today, schizophrenia is a disease unlike any other in the *intensity* of stigma it evokes, the *acceptability* of that stigma, and the *havoc* it creates in the lives of patients and their families. All too often, the burden of the illness is exacerbated by a chaotic and unresponsive mental health system. I have written this book as a message of hope—that with more rational mental health policies, more people will be able to move beyond schizophrenia to have fulfilling and productive lives.

Acknowledgments

This project was jump-started with a sabbatical leave from Arizona State University (ASU) in 2013–2014. I thought I might wrap it up in a year, but I am now working long hours to meet my mid-2015 submission deadline. I am grateful to ASU for funding the sabbatical. Herb Schaffner was instrumental in forging my connection with Rowman & Littlefield, and Regina Herzlinger was instrumental in forging my connection with Herb.

I owe a special debt to Rebecca White for essentially coauthoring chapter 8 and for her skill and insight in helping to organize and conduct the interview survey. Colleen Healy greatly assisted with chapter 6, where her knowledge of the law and its bewildering terminology saved me countless errors. I benefited enormously from the thoughtful comments and criticism of Patrick W. Corrigan, Larry Davidson, Benjamin G. Druss, Danielle Freeman, Katie Greeno, Trevor Hadley, Mark S. Salzer, and Mark Olfson. Their valuable insights have surely enriched the final product.

I have benefited from the encouragement of many friends and family members—so many that I will not try to name them all—as the work took shape, but my gratitude is not diminished by my poor memory. Thank you, CJ O'Connor, not just for your optimistic encouragement, but also for your buoyant attitude and ever-present inspiration in my life. Thank you, Fred Baldwin, for helping to fill in the gaps in my memory, and for always being there for our son.

And thank you, Steven Marcus, my research partner of twenty-five years and counting. You are never short on insight, creativity, and kindness. Without your persistence, the data reported in chapter 10 would not exist. Indeed, the entire project would not exist. Finally, thank you, Allan, for believing in me and my work, for your insights that have shaped so much of this work, and for assuming the role of stepfather with grace, compassion, and love. Most of all, thank you for adopting my dream as your own.

Part I

Living with Schizophrenia

Chapter One

A Disease Unlike Any Other

EVERYTHING BAD IS GOOD AGAIN

Spring 1999

On the day my twenty-one-year-old son was admitted to the psychiatric unit at University of North Carolina (UNC) hospital, my overwhelming emotion was relief. At least I knew where he was: He was safe; and he was with people who understood what was wrong. I was too numb, then, to appreciate how irrevocably our lives would change after that day.

I had noticed something wrong with my son's behavior for months, maybe even years. During a weekend visit home in the fall of his sophomore year, he talked nonstop. The words fit together in sentences, but the sentences didn't fit together into coherent thoughts. When he finally finished rambling, I was not sure what he had said, if anything at all. Parents, however, have an uncanny ability to explain away unusual behavior in their children, and I am no exception. I told myself that David was just excited about all the new ideas he was being exposed to at the university.

When the incessant talking gave way to angry emotional outbursts and verbal abuse, it was no longer possible to find an innocent explanation. I recalled all the warnings about behavioral changes associated with illicit drug use, all the signs indicating that your teenager is using drugs. I assumed David was experimenting with marijuana, cocaine, or something worse. I confronted him about the dangers of drugs and lectured him about the permanent effects that drug use could have on his brain. I encouraged him to seek help, to just say "no." I expect that most parents would come to the same conclusion I did. The possibility of mental illness never crossed my mind.

Given the warning signs, I cannot say that I was surprised when the break occurred. David's college friends called to say that he was in the emergency room; they had notified the police because he was talking about killing himself. Nonetheless, I was stunned at the diagnosis of *schizophrenia*, and shocked to find David almost completely delusional when I finally could talk with him. What do you say when your son tells you, in all seriousness, that he thinks he is God? I asked if he had enough clean underwear for the hospital.

Schizophrenia turns your world upside-down. David was admitted as an inpatient and remained hospitalized for nearly three weeks, a lengthy and expensive stay that would have been impossible without health insurance. As I visited him over those weeks I discovered that my naïve perceptions of psychiatric units, shaped by popular films such as *One Flew over the Cuckoo's Nest* and *Girl, Interrupted*, were not at all representative of current reality. Clinical staff on the psychiatric unit at UNC hospital were some of the most caring, compassionate, and patient people I have ever met. On one afternoon a patient passed the time walking in circles round and round the room. An aide walked beside him, round and round. Why he needed to be accompanied on these circuits I do not know, but he needed to walk, so she walked with him. Round and round and round.

A modern psychiatric unit is, in fact, a relatively safe place for the parent of a young adult with mental illness. The bizarre behavior, intermittent outbursts, and incoherent talk that are so confusing and embarrassing in the "real" world are completely acceptable here. I can recall one afternoon when David put a pencil between his toes and began writing on the wall. I was embarrassed and asked him to stop, but he just continued to write, and no one seemed to care. In a psychiatric unit, the abnormal is normal. In schizophrenia, some things you thought were bad, like psychiatric hospitalization, turn out to be very good indeed.

Drug use is an example of a bad that appears good (or at least *relatively* not so bad) through the lens of schizophrenia. When David was first hospitalized, one of the clinical staff commented that it would be useful to know what kinds of drugs, if any, he had been taking before he became ill. Eager to help in any way I could, I grilled David's college friends to get the information, and relayed it back to a nurse. She said, "Dear, I know you wish this could be drugs, but it is not." When would a parent *hope for* a diagnosis of drug abuse? If the alternative is schizophrenia, you wish the problem was "only" drugs.

Smoking is another example. The psychiatric unit had a balcony set aside for patients who wanted to smoke. Given the health hazards associated with smoking, I was surprised that a hospital would allow patients to smoke on site. I later learned that the prevalence of tobacco smoking is higher among persons with schizophrenia than among the general population; and some research suggests that nicotine improves measures of cognitive functioning among this population. I do not mean to suggest that smoking is good for persons with serious mental illness, but when David was acutely ill, smoking appeared to be the lesser evil.

Schizophrenia also makes some good things appear bad, or at least not so good. On my daily visits to the psychiatric unit David often spent the entire time talking about Jesus and the path to salvation. Throughout his illness, religion was a principal theme of his delusions. One day another visitor commented on how nice it was that my son had such a strong faith. I told her no, the religious talk was a symptom of his illness; I would know he was getting better when he talked about religion less.

I should not imply that the psychiatric unit insulated me from the horror of mental illness; there is no such escape. On various occasions when I visited David he would tell me that the television commercials were sending messages to him, or that a former friend of his was stalking the halls, or that he had watched his roommate "shrink and grow" all night. Sometimes he was angry at the doctors, or suspicious of other patients. Sometimes he called me at work, telling me nothing was wrong with him and begging me to get him released. When he asked me to take him out for Easter dinner on a "day pass," I panicked, wondering how I would get him back to the hospital.

I should not have worried. Midway through dinner, he said we had to be sure to be back by 7:00, because they were going to color Easter eggs. Schizophrenia turns your world upside-down.

THE INCIDENCE AND IMPACT OF SCHIZOPHRENIA

Schizophrenia is not a rare disease. The lifetime risk of developing schizophrenia is approximately 0.7 percent; its prevalence at any point in time is approximately 4.5 per one thousand persons.[1] Schizophrenia appears among all populations, in all regions of the world, with pockets of relatively high or low prevalence. Prevalence is higher within developed versus less-developed countries; and among lower versus higher socioeconomic classes.[2] Schizophrenia has been reported in the medical literature only since the mid-nineteenth century, but there is evidence that the illness appeared long before then.

History and Speculation

Historical records of illnesses that resemble schizophrenia are worthwhile for consideration not only because the accounts are interesting, but also as a reminder that so much about the disease remains unknown. At least since the medieval period, there are case records of individuals with schizophrenia-like illnesses.

Opicinus de Canistrus (1296–1350) was an illustrator and scribe employed in the papal offices in Avignon, France. At age thirty-eight he developed a sudden illness that left him unconscious for several days. By his own account, when he awoke his "right hand [was] weak in worldly work, but strong in spiritual endeavors."[3] The physical symptoms suggest that Opicinus suffered a stroke, from which he gradually recovered. Nonetheless, over the seven years that followed the "event," he produced more than fifty large drawings and maps on parchment, a manuscript with nearly two dozen additional maps, and an accompanying commentary. The maps are examples of what could be called "interpretive geography," in which Canistrus depicts various European countries as parts of his body; the commentary associates aches and pains he is feeling with current or impending events in the corresponding regions of Europe.[4] Eventually, Canistrus withdrew from papal employment to devote his time fully to these endeavors.

The thought patterns revealed in Canistrus's writings suggest that his illness is a "historical case of possible schizophrenia."[5] Persons who have read the commentary say the language is often incoherent and the reasoning illogical, at times becoming mere verbiage. Many of the features of Canistrus's illness (disorganized thinking, grandiose delusions, incoherent writing, and prolonged duration of symptoms) are typical features of schizophrenia, although no such disease had been identified at the time.

Franz Xaver Messerschmidt (1736–1783) was a talented sculptor and artist who was appointed to the Academy of Fine Arts in Vienna in 1769. When he was denied academic promotion in 1774, the responsible minister noted (emphasis added) that:

> The most important objection . . . is the fact that for three years he has shown signs of some *confusion*. . . . Although [the confusion has] subsided . . . it occasionally is still evident . . . in that he believes all other professors and directors to be *his enemies*.[6]

Despite his considerable artistic talent, Messerschmidt's career came to a near screeching halt. He was no longer entrusted with students and soon moved on to Munich. He spent the last three years of his life in near-total isolation in Bratislava because "it seems that all Germany feels obliged to persecute me."[7] Messerschmidt claimed, during this period, that demons made nocturnal visits to his rooms to torture him. One demon, in particular, envied the perfect proportions Messerschmidt achieved in his sculptures.

At the time of his death, more than sixty sculpted heads were found in his studio. Their expressions ranged from blank faces to contorted screams; some have been interpreted as self-portraits captured during his attempts to ward off the demons. Speculation aside, Messerschmidt unquestionably experienced hallucinations, along with delusions of grandeur and persecution. Whatever afflicted him seriously hampered his quality of life.

Recent History

The disease concept that we now call schizophrenia first appeared in the medical literature in the mid-nineteenth century. At the end of the century, Emil Kraeplin labeled the disease, "dementia praecox," and described its characteristic features to be onset in late adolescence, with a course of chronic and permanent deterioration of mental functioning.[8] Kraeplin distinguished dementia praecox from "folie circulaire," an illness characterized by acute and episodic dementia, no chronic deterioration of mental functioning, and a more favorable prognosis, which he labeled "manic depressive insanity."[9] Thus, Kraeplin's early distinction between the two disorders laid the groundwork for our current classification of schizophrenia and manic-depressive (bipolar) disorder. Recent genetic research, however, has identified genes that appear to be implicated in both schizophrenia and bipolar disorder, as well as evidence of shared genetic susceptibility to the two disorders. These findings have called into question the sharp dichotomy of two identifiably distinct mental disorders.[10]

It is currently believed that, around 1911, Eugen Bleuler conceived the name "schizophrenia" for the illness Kraeplin had called dementia praecox. In describing the disease, Bleuler placed particular emphasis on the *loss of association* or *splitting* of various psychic functions that patients exhibited, hence the name schizophrenia ("split mind").[11] According to Bleuler, the fundamental symptoms of the disease, crucial for a diagnosis, were inappropriate affect, loss of attention, lack of motivation, ambivalence, and autism; delusions and hallucinations were considered accessory symptoms, secondary for a diagnosis.[12] Bleuler viewed schizophrenia, not as a single disease entity, but as a heterogeneous group of mental disorders. The disorders had common clinical features, but different etiology, development, and clinical outcomes. For some patients, the clinical course might be more favorable than that which was postulated by Kraeplin, but complete remission of symptoms was unlikely.

Today, in contrast to Bleuler's characterization of fundamental and accessory symptoms, delusions or hallucinations are considered characteristic features of schizophrenia, and among the most useful clinical factors in arriving at a diagnosis. Current research does, however, support Bleuler's view that schizophrenia is not a single disorder but a syndrome with "multiple disease entities, multiple etiological factors, multiple relevant pathophysiological processes, multiple symptom dimensions, multiple protective and pathoplastic factors."[13] The different clinical manifestations of the syndrome, in combination with currently available treatments, yield different courses of illness and wide variance in patient outcomes.

Symptoms

Schizophrenia is generally diagnosed based on the presence of *positive* and *negative symptoms*, when other factors, such as substance use or another neurological illness, cannot account for the psychotic (positive) symptoms of the disease.[14] Positive symptoms may involve delusions, hallucinations, or other distortions of reality.[15] *Delusions* are implausible beliefs that are unfounded in reality (such as David's belief that he was the risen Christ, or Canistrus's belief that his aches and pains were signals of events occurring in Europe). The most frequent are delusions of persecution, and delusions that seemingly innocuous events have special meaning or significance (such as David's belief that the television was talking directly to him). *Hallucinations* are abnormal sensory or perceptual experiences that are unrelated to real stimuli (such as David seeing his roommate "shrink and grow," or Messerschmidt feeling demons torturing him). Hallucinations can be related to any of the five senses, but auditory hallucinations (hearing voices) are most common. When an individual is experiencing positive symptoms, they may also exhibit increased emotional arousal or emotional reactivity.[16]

The negative symptoms of schizophrenia create the opposite affect—a lack of emotion or impulse. Negative symptoms may manifest as a *lack of drive* to perform activities or pursue goals; a *lack of will* or ability to act decisively; a *lack of interest* or enthusiasm; or, a *lack of ability to experience pleasure*. Other characteristic negative symptoms include *poverty of speech*, a *flattened affect*, and *difficulty focusing attention*. In the first few months after David was released from the hospital, I came home every day to have lunch with him. I was worried and anxious, he was indifferent. Our conversation was strained. He was mostly silent and expressionless, I chattered on about anything to fill the void.

Other symptoms associated with schizophrenia include: cognitive impairments, such as disorganized thinking and behavior; a slowing, or acceleration, of psychomotor activity; mood symptoms, such as anxiety or depression; and a lack of insight into the illness. A "significant majority of patients with schizophrenia either believe that they do not have any disorder, or acknowledge symptoms but misattribute them to other causes, or deny any need for treatment."[17] This denial or disbelief is critical, because insight is strongly correlated with functional outcomes in schizophrenia. Indeed, lack of insight may be one of the most frustrating aspects of the illness for family members. How can one convince an individual to seek treatment, when they do not believe they have an illness at all?

Yet schizophrenia is most definitely an illness. It is not an assortment of odd behaviors that an individual could control if they made an effort to do so. Recent studies, using new imaging and neurophysiological techniques, as well as postmortem examinations, have revealed that schizophrenia is associated with alterations in brain functioning, abnormalities in brain structure and brain chemistry; and changes in the electrical activity of the brain.[18] Through these studies, we have made amazing progress in identifying the ways the brain is affected in schizophrenia, but the exact causes of the disease remain more elusive.

Causation

Manfred Bleuler (son of Eugen Bleuler and also a psychiatrist) discussed the causes of schizophrenia in a 1968 address to physicians at the University of Zurich. Describing his findings from a twenty-three-year longitudinal study of 208 patients with chronic schizophrenia, Bleuler concluded that,

> Neither heredity alone nor environment alone is sufficient to explain the morbid development into a schizophrenic psychosis. We must assume a collective activity, an interplay of both.[19]

Half a century later, we have amassed mountains of evidence on the genetic and environmental correlates of the disease, but the exact physiological process whereby genes and environment interact to bring on acute symptoms of schizophrenia is still unknown.

Genetic factors, by themselves and through interactions with environmental factors, contribute about 80 percent of liability for developing the disease.[20] The lifetime risk of schizophrenia increases, from an average of 0.7 percent in the general population, to 10–15 percent if a sibling has the illness, and to 40–50 percent if an identical twin has the illness. Several specific chromosomal abnormalities have been linked to schizophrenia, but none have been identified as a necessary or sufficient indicator for the illness. At most, the presence of an individual genetic abnormality increases the lifetime risk of developing schizophrenia to only 1.5 percent.[21]

A number of environmental factors have been linked to increased liability for developing schizophrenia. Some of these occur before or immediately after birth, including: maternal infection or malnutrition, older age of father at conception, complications during pregnancy or delivery, and birth during late winter or early spring (especially in regions where winters are severe). Other environmental risk factors occur during childhood, adolescence, or young adulthood. Migration, residence in an urban area, and the use of marijuana or stimulants are each associated with a higher risk for schizophrenia, but the exact relevance remains unknown. A number of other environmental factors have been linked to liability for developing the disease, so many that one expert cautions, "our field at large runs the risk of being buried under a plethora of unrelated and undigested findings."[22]

One popular model that attempts to make sense of the disparate findings is the stress-vulnerability, or diathesis-stress model. The model posits that development of schizophrenia is a function of interactions between three categories of factors, namely: *genetic vulnerabilities*, *environmental stressors*, and *protective factors*.[23] According to the model, genetic abnormalities determine the vulnerability (diathesis) of individuals to developing psychosis; environmental stress precipitates the onset of illness (or relapse) in vulnerable individuals; and protective factors mitigate symptoms or reduce the probability of relapse. Thus, individuals with equal vulnerability to schizophrenia may or may not develop the disease, depending on their exposure to risk or protective factors. Similarly, individuals experiencing equal levels of environmental stress may or may not develop the disease (or experience relapse) depending on their underlying genetic vulnerability and the presence or absence of protective factors.

Two psychologists propose a version of the diathesis-stress model in which a hormone, cortisol, is the mechanism whereby genetic vulnerability and environmental stress interact.[24] According to this model, environmental stress causes the release of cortisol to the brain. The elevated cortisol levels exacerbate brain abnormalities in individuals who are genetically liable to schizophrenia. In this way, stress triggers the onset of psychotic symptoms. If the stress is chronic, the response is cumulative, causing permanent changes in brain structure that enhance responses to future stress.

Another version of the diathesis-stress model is the "two-hit" model. This model posits that genetic risk, together with abnormalities in early development, constitute a "first hit" that increases the vulnerability of individuals to environmental risk factors occurring in later development. When those risk factors occur, the "second hit" leads to onset of the disease.[25]

In concluding this section, it is important to emphasize the positives over the negatives. The positive view is that, since Manfred Bleuler gave his lecture, research into the causes of schizophrenia has made enormous progress. The progress is multidimensional in terms of both understanding possible genetic abnormalities associated with schizophrenia and identifying a host of environmental risk factors for the disease. Genetic and neurological research continues to investigate hypotheses suggested by the diathesis-stress model, as well as models of schizophrenia focused on developmental abnormalities, mechanisms of the brain, or clinical expressions of the illness.[26] The negative view is that Bleuler's blanket reference to the interplay of heredity and environment still characterizes the vastness of what we do not know about schizophrenia. We do not yet have a definitive explanation of the cause of the disease, or know how to prevent it. And no cure is on the horizon. It is even unclear if schizophrenia is a single, complex disease that manifests in different ways, or a continuum of diseases with overlapping symptoms. However, one reason for emphasizing the positives is that, despite our limited understanding of the etiology of schizophrenia, the disease has become more and more treatable over the last fifty years.

Treatment

At present, the only treatment for schizophrenia with proven effectiveness in clinical trials, is a regimen of one or more antipsychotic drugs, all of which chemically alter dopamine activity in the brain.[27] The first generation of these drugs, the most powerful and most successful of which was haloperidol, were developed in the 1950s.

Haloperidol was synthesized by Janssen Pharmaceutica in 1958.[28] Clinical evidence on the efficacy of the drug, as well as its adverse side effects, was published in the medical literature the following year. Those results are still valid today: haloperidol can control the positive symptoms of schizophrenia (hallucinations, delusions, agitation) in many patients, at dosages far lower than the dosages required of other first-generation antipsychotics. However, the drug's side effects, predominantly motor disorders, can be severe. These include restlessness, Parkinsonism (tremors, rigidity, and instability), involuntary muscle contractions, and tardive dyskinesia (involuntary movements, usually of the lower face).[29] Haloperidol is still in use for the treatment of schizophrenia, but today it has largely been replaced by a second generation of "atypical" antipsychotics with less severe side effects.

The first of the atypical antipsychotics, clozapine, was introduced for treatment of schizophrenia in the late 1960s. Clozapine represents a significant improvement over first-generation antipsychotics with regard to both efficacy and the absence of motor side effects. In particular, clozapine is effective in treating the positive symptoms of schizophrenia among some patients who are not responsive to first-generation drugs. The elimination of motor side effects is another important plus, but clozapine is associated with other negative side effects that limit its usefulness in clinical practice. Most importantly, patients who take clozapine over long periods have an increased risk of developing agranulocytosis, a potentially fatal blood disorder characterized by a dangerous reduction in white blood cells.[30]

Since the early 1990s, more than a dozen other "second-generation" antipsychotics (e.g., olanzapine, quetiapine, risperidone) have been approved for treatment of schizophrenia. The drugs have proven efficacy in treating the positive symptoms of the disease, but are less consistently effective in treating its negative symptoms. Moreover, large-scale clinical trials indicate that the second-generation drugs are no more effective than first-generation drugs in treating either positive or negative symptoms (except that clozapin superior for treating patients who are not responsive to other drugs).[31] The primary benefit of the newer drugs is a more tolerable side-effect profile.

That is not to say the side effects of the atypical antipsychotics are negligible. Patients taking second-generation drugs have an increased risk of developing metabolic syndrome (weight gain, high-blood pressure, excess body fat around the waist, high blood sugar levels, abnormal blood cholesterol levels) and its related conditions (diabetes, heart disease).[32] Individual antipsychotics differ in their specific side-effect profiles, but other common side effects include sedation, low-blood pressure, cardiac arrhythmias, sexual dysfunction, and anticholinergic side effects (e.g., dry mouth, drowsiness, blurred vision, confusion).[33] Collectively, the side effects amount to more than a nuisance; they are the reason why many patients stop taking the drugs that provide their only bridge to a normal life.

Despite the potential for adverse side effects, the discovery of effective drug therapies for schizophrenia was one of the factors that enabled the movement of patients out of mental hospitals and into the community. Prior to the 1950s, there were no effective treatments for schizophrenia, and the most severely ill patients had little hope of life outside an institution. Since the advent of haloperidol, clozapine, and the other antipsychotic drugs, physicians are able to alleviate the most bizarre symptoms of the disease for many patients, offering them a realistic hope of leading a productive and meaningful life. The curious fact is that the tremendous advances in treatment of schizophrenia over the last fifty years have done little to reduce the economic and social burdens of the disease.

Postscript

A recent study estimates the total costs of schizophrenia in the United States in 2002 to be $62.7 billion.[34] The costs include direct expenditures associated with inpatient and outpatient medical care, housing and other social services, and involvement with the criminal justice system; as well as indirect costs associated with disability and premature mortality. Of these cost factors, the single largest component is the loss of productive output attributed to unemployment of individuals with the disease.

The large employment losses associated with schizophrenia are not surprising, given that onset of the disease typically occurs around the time a young adult is ready to enter the labor force full time. What *is* surprising is that improved treatments for the disease have had so little impact on employment outcomes for patients. Persons with schizophrenia fare poorer than almost any other disadvantaged group in the labor market. Employment rates and wages are lower for persons with disabilities than for nondisabled persons; lower for persons with mental disorders than for persons with other types of disabilities; and lower for persons with schizophrenia than for persons with other types of mental disorders.[35] Patients, providers, and families have a right to ask why, with improved treatments that are effective in controlling the symptoms of the disease for many patients, there has not been a parallel improvement in employment outcomes.

Chapter Two

The Mark of Schizophrenia

THAT COULD BE MY SON

In *The Scarlet Letter*, Nathaniel Hawthorne tells the story of Hester Prynne, a Puritan woman sentenced to wear a scarlet letter A upon her breast as punishment for adultery. The letter was symbolic of the sin that purportedly set Hester Prynne apart from others in the town. The townspeople cooperated in her punishment by shunning her:

> It had the effect of a spell, taking her out of the ordinary relations with humanity, and enclosing her in a sphere by herself. [1]

This is what it feels like to be the object of stigma—to be set apart, to be alone, to be different. Until you experience it, stigma is only a word. Once you encounter it, you become a different person; stigma changes you; you begin to view the world as less kind, less friendly, less safe.

Spring 1999

Shortly after David was released from the psychiatric unit, we were scheduled to attend the wedding of my husband's niece. The most conspicuous positive symptoms of David's illness were controlled by olanzapine, but the negative symptoms were perhaps heightened by its side effects. I was skeptical about his ability to cope with a large social event, when he could barely carry on a short conversation with me. But David wanted to attend, and both his doctor and social worker encouraged us to take the trip, believing it would be good for his recovery. It was not so good for me.

During the wedding ceremony, which required little social interaction, everything appeared normal with my in-laws. At the reception, we were seated at a large table with extended family. David was quiet and withdrawn, but no one seemed to notice. Soon after dinner, however, I became aware that everyone had drifted away from the table, and no one was coming back. We sat there alone, David and I and one perceptive sister-in-law (to whom I will be forever grateful), while groups of relatives mingled a "safe" distance away. Fifteen years later, I still feel the anger, hurt, and humiliation of sitting there with my son, hoping he wouldn't notice that everyone was avoiding us.

Since that early experience of being shunned, I have become more sensitive to the nature of stigma against mental illness. It is pervasive, enduring, and so *acceptable*! Even in a world of hypersensitivity, in which derogatory terms once used to describe women, racial or ethnic groups, and persons with physical disabilities have been eradicated from politically correct speech, the term "schizo" remains acceptable. The word stings me, like Hester's scarlet A burned through her clothes.

Summer 2005

The pervasive stigma against serious mental illness causes many patients and family members to conceal diagnoses of schizophrenia or other psychotic disorders. An example caught me unawares while visiting Amsterdam's Van Gogh museum several years ago. I enjoy art history and pay close attention to the artist notes that appear next to each painting. According to the notes, Van Gogh's behavior exhibited classic symptoms of psychosis, but the captions bore no mention of any diagnosis of schizophrenia or bipolar disorder. Upon reflection, I realized that I had never seen such a diagnosis mentioned in my readings on the artist's work. A close friend and art history teacher unraveled the puzzle. After Van Gogh's death (from a self-inflicted gunshot wound), his family vigorously promoted his legacy, but insisted that no mention of mental illness should ever appear in art catalogs or museums displaying his work.

For many years, I too avoided telling people about David's illness. Although I was researching the subject, lecturing to community groups, and teaching about mental illness in my classes, I avoided discussing my personal connection. I do not know why my attitude changed, but I remember exactly when I first told my story in public. In October 2006, I delivered a keynote presentation on job accommodations for mental illness for the Mental Health Association of Arizona. At the beginning of my talk, without any advance preparation, I briefly told my son's story. The talk was well received, but I was apprehensive about how *I* would be received afterward. It was a revelation to me how many people came forward to tell *their* stories of loved ones with mental illness.

Fall 2013

Today, I lecture on mental illness in many of my classes, and I usually weave David's story throughout the presentation. It is a vulnerable position, opening up to students about such a personal trauma. However, I have been rewarded by hearing my students' stories of friends and relatives with mental illness, and by their comments on the lectures. One student remarked, "I will never look at a homeless person the same way again."

I do not always have the courage to speak out when I should. One morning, several years ago, I was walking with a colleague to a meeting in Washington, D.C. As we waited to cross the street, I found myself standing next to a man, dressed in disheveled clothing and carrying a large plastic bag over his shoulder. He was having an animated conversation with himself. His words were incoherent and rambling, but I recognized the disorganized speech pattern of the monologue. I suppose my colleague thought I was uncomfortable or uneasy, because he suddenly moved to stand between us and quietly said, "You don't want to be next to *that*." I was not uncomfortable or uneasy. I thought, *that could be my son*. I wish I had said it.

STIGMA

The word "stigma" comes into English from a Greek word meaning a mark or brand made by a pointed stick or other sharp instrument. By the seventeenth century, it had acquired negative associations of evil or subjugation, and by the mid-nineteenth century it was being used in medical texts in reference to drug addiction and mental illness. Today, *stigma* has evolved to mean "a mark of disgrace or infamy; a sign of severe censure or condemnation."[2] Many physical disorders are stigmatized, epilepsy and cerebral palsy being good examples, but serious mental illness is different. The intensity, pervasiveness, and acceptability of stigma directed toward schizophrenia makes it a disease unlike any other.

Social Distance

Numerous studies have documented the intensity of stigma against mental illness relative to physical illness, and against schizophrenia relative to other mental illnesses. The typical study measures intensity of stigma by the degree to which average people prefer to maintain *social distance* from individuals with a particular "mark," or stigma. The concept of desire for social distance as a measure of intensity of stigma originated in the work of Emory Bogardus in the 1930s. Bogardus developed a *social distance scale*, using brief descriptions of social relationships that connote increasing degrees of familiarity. For example, regarding a particular stigmatized group, is the average person willing to "marry" a member of the group, to "work beside them in an office," or "to have them merely as a speaking acquaintance"?[3]

Thirty years later, Erving Goffman provided a theoretical explanation for the link between stigma and social distance. Goffman suggests that stigma is evoked by negative stereotypes which devalue an individual "from a whole and usual person to a tainted and discounted one."[4] Goffman identifies three potential sources of negative stereotypes that generate stigma: physical disability or deformity (e.g., blindness, paraplegia); deviant behavior (e.g., mental illness, crime); and tribal identity (e.g., race, nationality). He theorizes that discomfort involved in social interactions with a stigmatized person generates a desire to minimize such interactions, in other words, to maintain social distance.[5]

When social distance is used to measure the intensity of stigma directed toward alternative health conditions, mental illness *always* ranks among the most stigmatized. A good example of these types of studies is one conducted with a multiethnic sample of health practitioners in Australia. Participants were asked to rate the acceptability of twenty chronic conditions, within their community, on a scale from 1, representing no acceptance ("people would prefer a person with this disability be kept in an institution or out of sight") to 5, representing full acceptance ("people would accept a person with this disability marrying into their immediate family").[6] Psychiatric illness received an average ranking of 2, representing low acceptance ("people would try and avoid a person with this disability").[7] Only AIDS elicited stronger stigma.

Similar studies indicate that the stigma directed toward persons with mental illness is equivalent to that directed toward ex-convicts, alcoholics, or drug addicts.[8] The hierarchical rankings of health conditions are remarkably stable across populations (racial or ethnic groups, employers, health care providers, etc.), age groups (children, university students, adults) and over time (1970–1993).

More recent research compares the intensity of stigma directed toward persons with different types of mental disorders. One study team compared alcohol dependence, cocaine dependence, major depression, schizophrenia, and a "troubled" person (described as nervous, sad, and worried).[9] Subjects were presented with vignettes describing the symptoms of each disorder and asked to rank their willingness to interact socially with the individual described in the vignette. Subjects were least willing to interact when the vignette described symptoms of alcohol or cocaine dependence. Among the three types of mental disorders, schizophrenia elicited far greater stigma (63 percent unwilling to interact) than major depression (47 percent) or the "troubled" person (29 percent). Other studies, investigating social distance responses to vignettes describing schizophrenia or depression, consistently find that schizophrenia elicits more intense stigma.[10]

Some of the most intriguing social distance studies of mental illness have been conducted by psychologist Marc Weiss, among Chicago schoolchildren. In 1986, Weiss reported the results of a study in which he assessed the attitudes of 577 children, grades kindergarten through eight, toward persons with various types of mental disorders.[11] Weiss later conducted a follow-up study with thirty-four of the original kindergarteners, then in grade eight.[12]

In both studies, students were given a series of abstract drawings that were said to represent a person who was: "normal," "mentally retarded," "mentally ill," "crazy," "emotionally disturbed," "physically handicapped," or a "convict." Students were asked to draw stick figures representing themselves at a distance where they would feel comfortable being around the other person. The outcome measure, social distance, was literally a measure of the linear distance between the two figures.

Weiss's results suggest that negative attitudes toward persons with mental illness are well established by the time a child enters kindergarten, and fairly stable through eighth grade.[13] Eighth graders distinguished five groups with significantly different social distance rankings: (1) normal (most accepted); (2) physically handicapped; (3) emotionally disturbed, mentally ill, or mentally retarded; (4) convict; (5) crazy (least accepted).[14] Thus, by grade eight, the attitudes expressed by children mirror the attitudes expressed in social distance studies with adult subjects. The intensity of stigma directed toward a "crazy" person is on par, or greater than, the intensity of stigma associated with criminal behavior.

Stereotypes of Mental Illness

The remarkable cross-cultural and intertemporal consistency of societal attitudes toward mental illness begs for a rational explanation. To be sure, the negative associations are partly the vestiges of superstition, wherein mental illness was once associated with demonic possession. Stories are passed from one generation to the next and children adopt negative attitudes toward mental illness at an early age. Social scientists, however, have devoted considerable effort to move beyond folklore and superstition in our understanding of the genesis of stigma.

Two prominent social theories of mental illness stigma, labeling theory and attribution theory, proceed from Goffman's idea that stigma is evoked by negative stereotypes associated with a disfavored group. Labeling theory identifies the specific stereotypes (or labels) that generate feelings of fear and uneasiness around persons with serious mental illness (SMI). Three of the most prominent stereotypes label persons with mental illness as *dangerous*, *incompetent*, and *unpredictable*.[15] Attribution theory investigates the circumstances under which the negative stereotypes associated with a "marked" group elicit more intense stigma. In particular, the theory suggests that stigma increases with the degree to which others attribute *responsibility* for a mark to members of a stigmatized group, and the degree to which others perceive the mark to be *stable* (i.e., impossible to escape). [16]

My purpose here is not to assess the relative merits of the two theories, but to focus on the inferences that can be drawn from the vast array of empirical work they have spawned. Accordingly, I shall consider all five characteristics as factors that help to explain the intense and pervasive stigma against persons with SMI.

Responsibility

The degree to which an individual is perceived to be responsible for a stigmatizing mark, or any negative outcome, is a key factor in determining how others respond to that individual. Consider, for example, a college student who fails a calculus exam. If the student has attended class and completed all assignments, the failure is ascribed to a lack of mathematical ability (for which the student *is not* responsible). A visit to the professor's office is likely to elicit sympathy and help. If, on the other hand, the student is obviously bright but has skipped classes and ignored homework assignments, the poor exam performance will be ascribed to lack of effort (for which the student *is* responsible). In this case, the professor is likely to respond with blame and disapproval.

Bernard Weiner applied the responsibility attribution to conceptualize differences between "disease" and "illness." [17] According to Weiner's paradigm, a disease (e.g., pneumonia, meningitis) occurs because the body is invaded by a bacteria or virus, for which the unfortunate individual cannot be held responsible. Such conditions elicit little stigma and often considerable help (e.g., neighbors prepare meals, others assist with child care, the mother-in-law arrives). In contrast, an illness occurs because of behaviors an individual can control (e.g., chronic liver disease caused by alcohol abuse). Such conditions elicit stigma and condemnation, rather than sympathy and help.

Stability

The degree to which negative outcomes are perceived to be *stable* over time also affects the way others respond to a marked individual. If a negative outcome is perceived to be unstable (i.e., if it can change or be reversed), others are likely to offer help toward recovery. If it is perceived to be stable, and the outlook for the future appears to be hopeless, helping responses are perceived to be a waste of time. [18]

When David was first diagnosed with schizophrenia, I remember being struck by the cynicism of some of the people whom I encountered in family support groups. They told stories of evicting children from home, of siblings estranged from their brother, of fathers who simply walked away from their family. I expressed surprise that someone could abandon a loved one who was seriously ill. One mother responded, "You're new to this dear, wait until you've been dealing with it for years." Over the years I have come to understand why family members may distance themselves from a relative with SMI, when the prognosis appears hopelessly stable and the only reprieve is avoidance.

Incompetence

One of the most common stereotypes associated with mental illness is *incompetence* or helplessness: the perception that persons with mental disorders are incapable of making rational decisions, of handling responsibility, of managing a career or family.[19] The stereotype of incompetence is so pervasive that some type of discrimination against the mentally ill is codified into law in nearly every state.[20] As of 1999, forty-four states restricted the right of persons with mental illness to serve on a jury; thirty-seven states restricted their right to vote; twenty-four states restricted their right to hold elective office; twenty-seven states allowed parental rights to be restricted solely on the basis of mental illness. Between 1989 and 1999, as pharmaceutical treatments for mental illness were *improving*, fourteen states *expanded* legal discrimination against persons with mental illness, while none removed restrictions already in place.

There is a sinister irony in associating incompetence with mental illness: Persons with mental illness are perceived to be incapable of making responsible decisions as parents or citizens, at the same time they are perceived to be *responsible* for their behavior and symptoms.

Unpredictability

Another common stereotype of SMI is unpredictability. Although mental *illness* is perceived to be stable, with predictably negative long-run outcomes, the *behavior* of persons with mental illness is perceived to be erratic from day to day or moment to moment. In other words, persons with SMI are perceived as unable or unwilling to follow predictable social norms. The perceived unpredictability generates apprehension that a person with SMI will say or do something unexpected or inappropriate (like writing on the wall with a pencil between his toes). The emotional response is insecurity and uncertainty, which translates to anger, avoidance, and stigma.

Dangerousness

If perceived unpredictability evokes feelings of uneasiness, the perception of danger magnifies the uneasiness into fear. Numerous studies show that persons with mental illness are perceived to be dangerous and prone to violence.[21] Persons with schizophrenia or psychotic disorders are perceived to be even more dangerous than persons with other types of mental disorders, with the possible exception of persons who abuse alcohol.[22] In the presence of perceived danger, fear provokes instinctive avoidance, in other words, stigma.

Empirical Studies of Mental Illness Stigma

To what extent do the various stereotypes of mental illness explain the patterns of stigma reported in social distance studies? Have recent advances in our understanding of mental illness altered the stereotypes of persons with SMI? A number of studies have investigated these questions.

Correlations with Social Distance Measures

Two recent studies investigated the relationship between perceptions that persons with schizophrenia are unpredictable, and preferences for social distance from such persons. In one study involving two hundred undergraduate students at a London university, the researchers found strong and significant correlations between the perception that persons with schizophrenia were often socially inappropriate (i.e., rude, upsetting, or embarrassing when interacting with others), and the desire for social distance.[23] Another research team found the same result with data from a representative survey of more than five thousand German citizens.[24]

A number of studies have directly addressed the question, "What drives the *intensity* of the stigma toward mental illness?" using sophisticated statistical models to parse out the main effects. One such study involved two hundred undergraduate students at a Canadian university. The results showed that mental illnesses which were perceived to be dangerous or unpredictable elicited the strongest stigma.[25] In the study of German citizens, stereotypes of dangerousness, unpredictability, and stability (of a negative outcome) were found to be significant predictors of social distance.[26] Other studies produce slightly different lists of the most stigmatizing characteristics attributed to persons with mental illness, but the characteristics that appear on *every* list are unpredictability and dangerousness.[27]

Thus, the stigma directed toward mental illness in general, appears to be driven by a number of negative stereotypes, with perceptions of danger, unpredictability, and a stable and bleak prognosis being particularly important. The more intense stigma directed toward schizophrenia appears to be driven primarily by perceptions that persons with schizophrenia are more unpredictable, and more dangerous, than persons with other types of mental illness.

Changing Perceptions over Time

In general, the public is more likely to impute responsibility for an illness to persons with mental versus physical disorders.[28] Accordingly, strategies to reduce stigma toward persons with mental illness have often focused on educating the public about the biological origins of the disease, in an effort to combat the tendency to blame individuals for SMI. The campaigns emphasize that, "mental illness is a disease, just like any other."[29]

The efforts to educate the public about SMI appear to be having an effect. Recent research, using data from large population-based surveys, shows that people increasingly endorse genetic and biological factors as the source of mental illness. One U.S. study, for example, reported that the proportion of respondents endorsing a "chemical imbalance in the brain" as a potential cause of schizophrenia increased from 78 to 87 percent between 1996 and 2006. Over the same period, the proportion endorsing chemical imbalance as a potential cause of major depression increased from 67 to 80 percent. Less than one-third of respondents endorsed "his or her own bad character" as a source of mental illness.[30]

Another study, from the United Kingdom, investigated how attributions of responsibility for various mental disorders changed between 1998 and 2008. The results indicated that, by 2008, only a small minority of the public endorsed the responsibility attribution with respect to mental illness. When asked about depression or anxiety disorders, fewer than 15 percent of respondents agreed with the statement, "people with [this disorder] have only themselves to blame for their condition."[31] When asked about schizophrenia, only 9 percent ascribed blame.

Today, the vast majority of people do not hold persons with mental illness responsible for their conditions. However, the increased understanding that serious mental illness has biological origins has done little to change public perceptions that the outlook for patients is anything but stable and grim. While the proportion of the public endorsing medical treatment for persons with mental illness has increased with the increased acceptance of biological origins, the proportion who believe that medical treatment *will be effective* has not.[32] A stable 15–18 percent of respondents in the U.K. study believe that persons with mental illness "will not improve even if given treatment." One-fourth of respondents believe that persons with anxiety or depression "will never recover fully"; more than 40 percent believe that persons with schizophrenia "will never recover fully."[33]

Psychologist John Read at the University of Auckland argues that efforts to educate the public about the biological origins of mental illness have actually *increased* the stigma against schizophrenia. He posits that biological and genetic explanations of SMI reinforce the perception that persons with SMI are *fundamentally and irrevocably* different from "normal" people. According to Read, mental illness is perceived to be even more immutable than it was before, and the result is even greater stigma.[34] A study using population-based data from France supports Read's hypothesis. Researchers found that endorsing brain disease or chemical imbalance as causes of schizophrenia was associated with greater fear (but also greater sympathy).[35]

Other negative stereotypes of persons with SMI continue to be widely endorsed. Results from the U.K. study indicate that perceptions of unpredictability have declined only slightly over time.[36] Other research indicates that perceptions of dangerousness, associated with schizophrenia in particular, have *increased* in recent years.[37] Participants in one U.S. study, for example, were asked how likely it is that a person with mental illness will "do something violent toward other people." In 2006, 60 percent of respondents believed a person with schizophrenia was "somewhat" or "very" likely to be dangerous (up from 54 percent in 1996).[38]

Media Stereotypes

Some experts contend that news reports reinforce the negative stereotypes of mental illness that generate stigma. Patrick Corrigan and others have conducted surveys to document the way persons with mental illness are portrayed in the news. Corrigan is a psychology professor at the Illinois Institute of Technology, and an internationally recognized expert on mental illness stigma. He and his colleagues collected an exhaustive sample of stories on mental illness, from seventy U.S. newspapers with the largest daily circulations, over six one-week periods in 2002.[39] The study team searched for stories using the key words, "mental," "psych," or "schizo." More than 3,300 stories were retrieved.

The study team coded the content of each story into four broad themes (blame, dangerousness, treatment/recovery, advocacy actions/concerns) and a number of more specific sub-themes. Overall, stories related to dangerousness were most common, representing 39 percent of the sample. That proportion represents a favorable trend over time, down from 50 to 75 percent of stories related to dangerousness in studies from the late 1980s. However, within the dangerousness theme, two-thirds of stories dealt with violent crimes in which a person with mental illness was the perpetrator; these stories, together with stories dealing with suicide or self-injury, dominated front-page news coverage of mental illness. The authors concluded that, "the public is still being influenced with messages about mental illness and dangerousness" out of proportion to the number of violent crimes actually perpetrated by persons with SMI.[40]

Several recent episodes of horrific violence (e.g., the attack on Representative Gabrielle Giffords in Tucson, the theater shootings in Colorado, and the murders of children and teachers at Sandy Hook Elementary School) have been committed by persons whose behavior suggests untreated mental illness. News coverage of these events has reinforced the negative stereotype that persons with SMI are dangerous, even though far more acts of violence are committed by persons who do not have a diagnosis or symptoms of SMI (e.g., the Oklahoma City bombing, 9/11 attacks on the World Trade Center, bombings at the 2013 Boston Marathon, and recent attacks on police officers). The facts are:

- The risk of violence is increased by *acute* psychosis, but the vast majority of violent crimes (95–99 percent) are *not* committed by persons with psychotic disorders.[41]
- Males between ages fifteen and twenty-four are *more likely* to commit acts of violence than are persons with psychotic disorders (17 percent versus 12 percent).[42]
- Persons with mental illness are more likely to be the *victims* of violent crime than the perpetrators. Victimization rates among persons with schizophrenia are twelve times higher than among the general population.[43]

In short, public perceptions far overestimate the actual probability of danger associated with an individual who has schizophrenia.

The entertainment media also contribute to the distorted image that persons with SMI are prone to violence. Consider how often persons with mental illness are portrayed as the perpetrators of violent crimes in movies or on television. From my many years as a devoted fan of *Law and Order*, I remember only one episode in which a person with schizophrenia was depicted as a sympathetic character suffering from a serious illness. Before David became ill, I hardly noticed the one-sided portrayal of the mentally ill. Now the word "schizo" has a bite.

Workplace Stigma

One of the most damaging effects of stigma is that it restricts the opportunities of the stigmatized group across multiple facets of their everyday life. Stigma infects schools, communities, social groups, and the workplace, which is the particular focus of this book. Gary Becker, a Nobel prize-winning economist from the University of Chicago, was a pioneer in applying the concepts of social distance (which he called "tastes for discrimination") to study the impact of stigma in the workplace. In so doing, he created an entirely new field of study, the economics of discrimination.

According to Becker, there are three potential sources of discrimination in the labor market, all motivated by tastes for discrimination.[44] These include: (1) Discriminatory *employers*, who prefer not to hire members of a stigmatized group and will do so only at less than the usual wage; (2) discriminatory *coworkers*, who prefer not to work with members of a stigmatized group and will accept a lower wage to avoid them; (3) discriminatory *customers*, who prefer not to interact with members of a stigmatized group and will pay a higher price to avoid them. In all three cases, the desire for social distance devalues the labor of the stigmatized. In turn, discrimination *lowers the probability that members of a stigmatized group will be hired, and reduces their wages if they are.*

One of Becker's most useful insights is that the size of the wage (employment) differential between stigmatized and nonstigmatized groups can be interpreted as a measure of the intensity of stigma. In other words, *given that two groups are equally productive, on average,* the difference in their wages (or employment rates) will vary directly with the strength of preferences for social distance from the disadvantaged group. Becker's insight suggests that:

1. Discriminatory wage (employment) differentials will be larger for workers with mental disorders than for workers with physical disorders (because mental disorders elicit more intense stigma).
2. Discriminatory wage (employment) differentials will be larger for workers with psychotic disorders than for workers with other mental disorders (because psychotic disorders elicit more intense stigma).

In fact, we observe large wage and employment differentials between workers with and without disabilities, between workers with mental versus physical disorders, and between workers with psychotic disorders versus other types of mental disorders. Economists have developed statistical methods to identify what part of an observed differential is *explained* by differences in average productivity (Becker's theory applies to groups of equally productive workers) and what part is *unexplained*, and potentially attributable to discrimination. When the methods are applied to data for workers with disabilities, the estimates of discrimination effects are strongly consistent with the stigma rankings in the social distance studies.[45] Estimates of the potential effects of discrimination are larger for workers with mental versus physical disorders, and larger for workers with psychotic disorders versus other mental disorders.[46]

In one study, we used data from the 1999 Medical Expenditure Panel Survey to estimate the impact of stigma on employment rates for persons with mental disorders, relative to a no-disorder comparison group. We considered four types of mental disorders, namely: mood, anxiety, adjustment, and psychotic disorders. Here, I describe results for psychotic versus mood disorders, the two most disadvantaged groups.

The difference in estimated employment rates between persons with psychotic disorders versus the "no-disorder" control group was thirty-eight percentage points (51 percent versus 89 percent employed), compared to a six-teen percentage point differential (73 percent versus 89 percent) for mood disorders.[47] The majority of the employment differentials could be explained by differences in productivity measures (e.g., the groups with mental illness had less education, on average, than the nondisabled group). However, the unexplained differential (potentially attributed to discrimination) was larger for the group with psychotic disorders in both absolute (11 percentage points versus 3.5 for mood disorders) and relative (28 percent of the total differential versus 21 percent) terms. Hence, the results are consistent with results of the social distance studies suggesting that persons with psychotic disorders are subject to greater stigma and discrimination than persons with other types of mental disorders.

In another study, using data from the National Health Interview Survey, we compared workers' self-reports of work-related discrimination to our econometric measures.[48] Nearly one-third (29 percent) of workers with psychotic disorders reported experiences of discrimination at work, compared to only 21 percent of workers with mood or anxiety disorders. The experiences ranged from being refused employment or promotion, to being fired, laid off, or told to resign. Workers' self-reports of stigma and discrimination corresponded to our econometric measures, suggesting that the workers knew when they were being discriminated against.

Other evidence of workplace stigma directed toward persons with mental illness comes from interview studies with individual workers. Two researchers, an anthropologist and a psychiatrist, conducted one-on-one interviews with ninety persons who had diagnoses of schizophrenia or schizoaffective disorder. They aimed to learn about the participants' experiences of stigma in various social settings. The sample was relatively high-functioning and asymptomatic: all participants were clinically stable and being treated with atypical antipsychotics in the community. Nevertheless, 96 percent of participants reported experiences of stigma across a variety of social settings.[49]

More than half of participants who were currently working reported experiences of stigma in the workplace. They mentioned hostile, fearful, and insensitive attitudes on the part of coworkers or supervisors. They also reported experiences involving teasing, negative stereotyping, unfair treatment, and violations of confidentiality. Often, participants responded to stigma with feelings of shame, and efforts to conceal their illness. For example:

> When I was working in the hospital, I stopped taking the medication a couple of weeks or so after I got hired because I felt bad about having to take medication and having an illness and being diagnosed as schizophrenic. Instead of educating myself or educating other people about it, I chose to just stop taking it. That was bad.[50]

The comments of this individual describe one of the most insidious effects of stigma directed toward mental illness, namely, its power to invade the minds of victims, who then direct stigma toward themselves.

Self-Stigma

It is quite common for members of a stigmatized group to adopt the negative stereotypes associated with that group into their own self-image. I grew up, for example, in an era when male and female roles were sharply delineated. While my brother learned to work with tools and repair automobiles, I learned to cook and clean and sew. Until I was divorced, it never occurred to me that I was capable of a simple home repair, and to this day the automobile engine is a thing of mystery to me. How much more damaging is the self-stigma of persons with schizophrenia, who adopt the negative stereotypes of themselves as incompetent, volatile, and hopelessly ill!

Among persons with schizophrenia, self-stigma is associated with loss of self-esteem and self-efficacy, and with feelings of incompetence, inferiority, and guilt.[51] Such feelings cause shame and embarrassment, often inducing efforts to conceal the illness from others.[52] One woman likens her efforts to conceal her mental illness to putting on a mask:

> The mask is what we wear to conceal who we really are because of stigma. We can't be the real patient that we are like the person with cancer or diabetes or a broken leg can be. We have to be something other than who we are.[53]

The end result of self-stigma is loss of personhood. One either hides behind a mask of concealment or loses all other aspects of their personality to the stereotype of mental illness.

Certainly, there are many persons with SMI who do not become victims of self-stigma. Some react to the negative stereotypes of mental illness with anger, and become energized to advocate against stigma directed toward the mentally ill. Others react with indifference, as if the stigma were irrelevant or unimportant to them. In another of his many studies on mental illness stigma, Corrigan (working with coauthor, Amy Watson) proposed a situational model to explain the different individual reactions to stigma, where the key mediating factors are: (1) the extent to which an individual views negative stereotypes as a *legitimate description of themselves*, and (2) the extent to which an individual *identifies with the stigmatized group*.[54]

According to the model, when an individual with SMI encounters the negative stereotypes associated with the "mark" of mental illness, they must decide if the stereotypes apply to them. Those who accept the stereotypes as legitimate tend to assimilate the negative attitudes (stigma) into their self-image. Goffman describes the self-stigmatizing process as follows: Individuals who experience stigma eventually realize they are not being accorded the respect that other persons in their social position receive, and that the stigmatized person would normally expect. The object of stigma comes to understand that they are viewed as "tainted," as undeserving of the attention, friendship, employment, or other rewards reserved for "normal" people. They may reconcile the stigma directed toward them by identifying attributes *within themselves* that justify such treatment. In this way, the individual begins to adopt the negative stereotypes of mental illness as a legitimate description of themselves.[55]

The inclination to view a stereotype as legitimate or illegitimate depends partly on whether the realization (of membership in a stigmatized group) is gradual or abrupt. Persons who are born into a "marked" group (such as African Americans or Jews) learn about their stigma gradually, knowing they are a member of the group. As part of the group, they realize that the stereotypes do not apply to all members of the group, perhaps not even to a majority of the group, and need not apply to them.

In contrast, persons who develop a serious mental illness, typically as a teenager or young adult, find themselves abruptly included in a stigmatized group they have been taught to shun. All the negative stereotypes they have learned to associate with mental illness suddenly apply to *them*. Self-stigma would seem to be almost inevitable. Indeed, in a study of Chicago high school students, researchers found evidence of self-stigma related to a diagnosis of mental illness, as early as adolescence.[56] Students with and without mental illness were equally likely to perceive persons with mental illness as "threatening" or "out of control."

If a person with mental illness does not accept the negative stereotypes of the disease as a legitimate description of themselves, their response to stigma is likely to depend upon how they identify with others who have a mental illness. Strong group identification helps an individual maintain their self-esteem, even in the face of stigma. With a strong sense of group identity and intact self-esteem, individuals who reject the stereotypes of mental illness "may become righteously indignant about the negative social identity and discrimination bestowed on them."[57] One angry young man, for example, likens mental illness stigma to an "invisible cage":

> What bothers me is that my ambition is being restrained. They are trying to force me into some sort of a cliché and they don't leave me any possibility for development. The doctors said that I shouldn't bother studying, I mean, continuing my studies. I would really like to work as a programmer, but they tell me that isn't possible, because with that illness [schizophrenia], I wouldn't be capable for that. That's what bothers me, you know![58]

Anger is empowering, so it is not surprising that many of these individuals become vocal advocates against stigma toward mental illness.

On the other hand, there are persons with SMI who reject the negative stereotypes associated with mental illness, but do not identify strongly with others who are mentally ill. These individuals appear to be relatively unaffected by stigma, either oblivious or indifferent to it. Their self-esteem is not injured by stigma, and they do not seek the protection of others like them.[59] It is unclear what factors protect this group from self-stigma: intrinsic personality traits, support and encouragement from significant others, quality of mental health care, nature of illness? I suspect one of the most important factors is their determination not to be defined by their illness—that is, to break out of the invisible cage:

> What is schizophrenia? It's an eighteen year old whose time is spent as if she only lives in the present. She begins to see that one doctor is right. "No expectations," he told her, "just pay attention." Time passes and the anxiety and anger and noise persist, but she begins to see that she has a chance to break the spell of the master oppressor. She sees where she failed before and forges ahead of where the counselors ever thought she would be able to go. She can look down and see that they were just border markers of her domain.[60]

Postscript

Unlike his mother, David has always been one of those individuals who appear to be indifferent to the stigma associated with mental illness. The two of us responded quite differently to that first experience of stigma at the wedding reception. David, only recently discharged from the hospital, was unaware of, and untouched by, the stigma that we experienced. I, on the other hand, was very much aware. I was mortified when I realized that family members were avoiding us, and I responded with anger to the perceived insult to my son. At the first opportunity, I told my husband, "We are leaving."

I am not sure what has protected David from stigma and kept his self-esteem intact. He tells me he held on to five words that his psychiatrist said to him as he was about to be discharged from that first hospital stay: "You can recover from this."

I do know that David is determined not to be defined by his illness. When he first came home from the hospital, schizophrenia was my chief concern and my constant preoccupation. I watched for any change of mood, outburst of anger, or unusual behavior that might signal a relapse. My response is not unusual. Mental illness can alter the way an individual is perceived such that in some sense the patient *becomes* the illness.[61] One day, David said to me, "Mom, when I look at you all I see is the worry in your eyes." I could not see past the illness to find my son.

The extent to which persons with schizophrenia (and their relatives and friends) succumb to self-stigma has a direct impact on a patient's capacity to achieve a fulfilling life. Accepting the stigma of schizophrenia as applicable to oneself is an impediment to recovery, because self-stigma is demoralizing and fosters feelings of shame, unworthiness, and incompetency.[62] Accepting the stigma as applied to one's child (or brother, or spouse) is also an impediment to recovery, because it is an implicit agreement to conform to the limitations society places on those who suffer from the disease. Accepting the diagnosis of schizophrenia, but rejecting its negative stereotypes, is the first important step to escaping the invisible cage.

Chapter Three

Life Interrupted

HELL NO!

They say there's something special in the air at Chapel Hill such that every freshman who inhales it never wants to leave. In fact, there is something almost mystical about the campus, the oldest public university in the United States, with its centerpiece an old well dating back to 1897. To anyone standing there in springtime, when the azaleas and dogwoods are in bloom, there truly seems to be a "little bit of heaven in North Carolina."

Graduates of UNC are Tarheel fans for life. The school has a proud history of championship athletic teams, and the basketball team, in particular, is legendary. David attended school when Antawn Jamison, Vince Carter, and Brendan Haywood were stars of the team. He lived in the same building as the basketball players and knew many of them on a first-name basis. He was an avid fan of both the football and basketball teams, but still managed to attend classes often enough to make the dean's list. In short, David reveled in college life until, in the spring semester of his junior year, he got sick.

When I arrived at the emergency room, the first person to meet me was a university staff member with papers to be signed to officially withdraw David from classes. She reassured me that her office would take care of all the paperwork necessary to withdraw David from school without penalty. At the time I was grateful for her help; I did not know how much more difficult it would be for David to be *readmitted* to school in the fall.

Summer 1999

During those first months at home David was lethargic, quiet, and withdrawn. He rarely went outside and no friends came to visit. I struggled to entertain him as best I could: We played Scrabble in the evenings; we took

33

his dog for long walks; and I bought furniture for him to refinish, in anticipation of his return to school. Overall, an aura of sadness surrounded him. One afternoon I found him lying on his bed, staring at the ceiling, with tears running down his face. When I asked what was wrong he said, "My mind's playing tricks on me again, Mom." I suppose it was a good sign—he knew the delusions were not real—but his despair broke my heart.

One day I made a suggestion that roused him briefly from his lethargy. With fall semester approaching, I was apprehensive about David returning to school. I wanted to keep him close by, so I could monitor his meds and know that he was safe. I suggested that he stay home for a semester, take some classes at the local university, and then return to UNC in the spring. David simply stared at me as I talked. When I finished, he responded with more emotion than I had heard in months, *"Hell, no!"* And with that response, his determination to return to UNC became mine as well.

David's physician approved his return to school on a part-time basis, so we began the process of getting him reinstated for the fall semester. The Student Disability Services Office seemed to be a logical place to begin. The staff person there asked why David was only returning as a part-time student. I explained that we were complying with his physician's orders. "If he's not ready to return full-time, he shouldn't come back at all," I was told. I explained that David's physician believed it would help his recovery for him to return to school, but taking a full-time load would be too stressful. The staff person said, "Well, when your son got in trouble . . ." I stopped him in midsentence. "My son did *not* get in trouble," I said, "My son *got sick.*"

In anger and frustration, I appealed to the social worker assigned to David's research study. She connected us with the Student Services Offices at UNC, helped us complete the paperwork required for readmission, and obtained a statement from David's psychiatrist certifying that David was asymptomatic and capable of returning to school. Nevertheless, the dean decided that the Emergency Action and Evaluation Committee must approve David's readmission.

The committee, composed of UNC faculty and administrators, is convened whenever someone in authority believes that a student's behavior poses a threat to campus safety. In particular, the committee has jurisdiction over admission and readmission decisions involving students with a history of violence or criminal behavior, or of violating university drug policies. It exists to protect the campus community from anyone whose behavior makes them a potential threat to themselves or others. David had no history of violence or criminal behavior, or of violating university policies; and his psychiatrist said he was not a danger to himself or others. Why was it necessary to convene the committee at all? Would there have been a hearing if the diagnosis had been "adjustment disorder," instead of schizophrenia? I was offended by such a thinly veiled attempt at discrimination.

The committee hearing lasted for several hours. David testified, as well as his doctor, his social worker, and his father and me. When it was my turn, I walked into the hearing room where the dean, the board members, and my son were seated. I said:

> I am an economist who studies disability-related discrimination. If you would like to discuss my son's rights to an education under the Americans with Disabilities Act, I would be happy to do so. In fact, I have brought a sample of my published research on the topic. [I arrayed an assortment of reprints of journal articles on the table.] However, I would rather not talk about the ADA. I would prefer to talk about why my son deserves to be reinstated as a student in good standing at this university.

I continued on with my reasons: David had no record of any disciplinary action at the university. He had consistently maintained an academic record as a "student in good standing." His physician believed his return to school was important to his recovery. Finally, *it is illegal for an academic institution to discriminate against an otherwise-qualified student solely on the basis of disability.* The board was silent.

Within thirty minutes we received word from the dean that David could return to school. I like to think my legal arguments were the persuasive factor, but that is probably taking too much credit. More likely it was David's demeanor, as he sat there for three hours, calmly making his case and answering questions, which convinced the committee it was safe to allow him to come back to school.

David enrolled in three classes for fall semester and we settled him, and the newly refinished furniture, into an apartment near the UNC campus. I made excuses to travel to the Triangle area (Raleigh–Durham–Chapel Hill) on a frequent basis, so I could visit David without saying I was "checking up" on him. I frequently stayed overnight, cleaned the apartment, and stocked the refrigerator with food. That fall he successfully completed the two classes. After he completed four more in the spring, we began to think that he might graduate only one semester behind schedule. We did not realize that he had stopped taking his medication.

In July 2000, sixteen months after his first episode of psychosis, David suffered a serious relapse and was hospitalized again. This time his symptoms receded quickly once he was back on the medication, and he was released within a few days. The timing was good. Fall semester was scheduled to begin in only a few weeks; David was in and out of the hospital without ever having to withdraw from school.

Spring 2001

David graduated from UNC–Chapel Hill in May 2001, with a bachelor's degree in management and society. We had a small party with a few close friends and relatives. It was a joyful celebration—one I thought I might never see—and a huge credit to the strength and willpower of my son. I will never forget what he said to me as we were leaving, "Mom, no matter what happens, they can never take this away from me."

INVESTMENTS IN HUMAN CAPITAL

The fact that David developed schizophrenia while he was in college is not unusual. Measles, mumps, and chicken pox are, or used to be, diseases of childhood. Arthritis, heart disease, Alzheimer's disease, and other forms of dementia are diseases of the aged. Schizophrenia is a disease of young adulthood. It typically strikes around the time that a young person completes their formal education and is about to enter the labor force. The disease has no known cure and can be severely disabling, sometimes resulting in a lifetime of lost productivity. Economists call this a loss of *human capital.*

The term "human capital" refers to the productive potential embedded in human beings. Like investment capital, or capital equipment, human capital is an input into the production process. At any given age, each individual has a stock of human capital. That stock is determined, in part, by an initial endowment of health, intelligence, and basic personality characteristics acquired in early childhood; and, in part, by investments in human capital the individual makes over their lifetime. These investments can take the form of education, vocational training, work experience, or efforts to preserve or enhance one's health status.

For healthy persons, human capital accumulation typically peaks somewhere in middle age. The stock of human capital rises rapidly at younger ages, when an individual is making full-time investments in education or vocational training. Human capital continues to accumulate into middle age, as the individual gains work experience and on-the-job training. At some point, however, the stock of human capital begins to diminish with the effects of aging. The point at which the decline begins varies considerably, in part reflecting one's occupation and lifestyle choices. My brother-in-law worked in heavy construction all his life and retired at age fifty. Although he was the youngest of six siblings, he looked much older. He always said, "I may be younger than the others, but I have more mileage on me."

A typical profile of human capital accumulation and deterioration over the life cycle slopes steeply upward until approximately age twenty-five, rises more slowly until around age fifty, and then begins a slow decline that continues with age. Accordingly, a diagnosis of schizophrenia at age twenty can have a tremendous impact on productive potential. In Canistrus's time, and until the middle of the twentieth century, the onset of schizophrenia was typically accompanied by an almost total loss of human capital. Persons with the disease spent their lives writing treatises on interpretive geography, or living in an institution, or cared for by family and friends. If the symptoms of the disease were acute and unremitting, the entire productive capacity of a lifetime could be lost.

Modern pharmacology has miraculously produced effective treatments for schizophrenia. The drugs have the potential for restoring many persons with the disease to a more normal trajectory of human capital. Yet the second-generation antipsychotics have been on the market for more than twenty years and have scarcely made a dent in the expected earnings of persons with SMI. Why have these discoveries not had a greater impact on employment outcomes for this population? Part of the explanation may be the tremendous stigma that still surrounds mental illness; but the poor outcomes also reflect the disruptive impact a mental illness has on the process of accumulating human capital.

The Nature of Human Capital

Two broad types of human capital are valued in the labor market. *General human capital* encompasses the knowledge, skills, and abilities that increase a worker's productivity at many different firms or worksites. *Job-specific human capital* encompasses the sort of "insider information" that is valuable with only one employer, or at only one worksite.

General human capital may be acquired either before or after a worker is hired, because it is applicable in many different jobs. Health is an example of general human capital. Other examples are the knowledge that one acquires through formal education, and the technical skills (e.g., carpentry, drafting, electrical repair) derived from vocational training programs. Investments in general human capital are typically financed by workers, because employers have no incentive to pay for human capital that a worker may transfer elsewhere.

Job-specific human capital, on the other hand, is only valuable at a specific firm and must, therefore, be acquired after a worker is hired. The relationship between a worker and their supervisor is a form of job-specific human capital—so is understanding things like the layout of the workplace, where to find supplies, whom to call for help, and how to access the computer systems. None of these skills are transferable to another job. Employers typically pay for investments in job-specific human capital, because workers have no incentive to pay for skills that they cannot transfer elsewhere.

Which type of human capital is most valuable to workers with SMI? *General human capital* is most important for any worker, because general skills are transferable if a worker should need to change jobs. General human capital is even more important to workers with SMI, because of the cyclic nature of mental illness. If a worker with SMI is forced to leave their job because acute symptoms recur, the *transferable skills* associated with general human capital will facilitate a return to work once their symptoms are in remission.

One aspect of human capital that transcends the general/job-specific dichotomy is *social capital.* Social capital encompasses the person-to-person connections and interpersonal relationship skills that both enhance the quality of life and increase the likelihood of success in the labor market. Specifically, social capital refers to "the social characteristics . . . which enable [a person] to reap market and non-market returns from interactions with others."[1] Not surprisingly, research shows that the quality, strength, and diversity of an individual's social networks is a significant predictor of positive employment outcomes.[2]

Social capital may be job-specific (e.g., relationships with supervisors, clients, and coworkers) or general (e.g., relationships with friends, mentors, and others outside the workplace). Many top MBA programs require students to work in teams, attend training sessions in job interviewing, and even practice formal dining, to build the general social capital essential for a leadership position. After graduates are hired, they begin to accumulate the job-specific social capital that will be essential to their success with a particular employer.

SMI is often associated with deficits in social capital. The negative symptoms of schizophrenia, for example, make it difficult to communicate and to establish interpersonal relationships. The lack of social skills may impact both the ability to obtain a job (how is the individual perceived in a job interview?) and workplace relationships if they are hired (how is the individual perceived by coworkers and supervisors?).[3]

The destruction of social capital associated with schizophrenia is perhaps greater than with any other disease. This fact may help to explain why schizophrenia is perceived to be a "disease unlike any other" in terms of its negative impact on health.

Health Capital

Epidemiologists use the concept of *disease burden* to measure the overall loss of health capital associated with an illness or injury. The most current information on the disease burden associated with serious mental illness comes from the 2010 Global Burden of Diseases, Injuries, and Risk Factors (GBD) project. The project recently published estimates of the disease burden associated with 220 illness/injury categories for 2010, with comparison data for 1990 and 2005. The first results fill almost the entire December 2012 issue of *Lancet*.

Measures of Disease Burden

The summary unit of disease burden for the 2010 GBD is disability-adjusted life-years (DALYs), which incorporates both mortality losses (a measure of *years of life lost*) and morbidity losses (a measure of *years lived in a less than healthy state*) associated with a particular illness/injury.[4] Estimating the years of life lost to an illness/injury is a simple statistical exercise that accounts for the number of deaths associated with the illness/injury in a given year, the age at which those people died, and their life expectancy in good health. For example, when a forty-year-old with a life expectancy of seventy-five years dies of lung cancer, thirty-five years of life lost are attributed to lung cancer.

Estimating years lived in a less than healthy state is much trickier because it requires subjective assessments of the relative reduction in quality of life associated with an illness/injury. For example, a year spent in permanent confinement to a wheelchair is valued as less than a full year of healthy life, but exactly how much less? The GBD 2010 project assigns each of the 220 illness/injury categories a discount factor, or "disability weight," reflecting the reduction in quality of life associated with that illness/injury. In an effort to obtain disability weights that reflect a global consensus, investigators surveyed more than thirty thousand persons from five countries.[5] Respondents were presented with paired descriptions of illness/injury categories, written in lay language, and asked to select, for each pair, which category represents a higher level of health. Without dwelling on details, it is instructive to note that acute schizophrenia was assigned a discount factor of 0.756 (about 25 percent of perfect health), the highest disability weight of all 220 categories.[6]

Once the disability weights have been assigned, years lived with disability are computed by multiplying the number of persons living with a disabling illness/injury in a particular year by the disability weight assigned to that illness/injury category. Thus, if two hundred people in a given population suffer from migraine headaches, the years lost to disability associated with migraine headaches are 86.6 (200 times 0.433, the disability weight assigned to migraines).

Disease Burden of Mental Illness

It turns out that *mental disorders are not among the leading causes of disease burden* worldwide. The main reason is that mental disorders do not involve nearly as much loss of life as the leading causes. According to the GBD, cardiovascular/circulatory diseases, and infectious diseases (such as pneumonia and meningitis), were the leading causes of disease burden in 2010.

These killer diseases accounted for more than 30 percent of years of life lost; whereas mental and substance use disorders accounted for less than 1 percent. [7]

Schizophrenia is not a disease that kills. Although suicide rates are above average among persons with schizophrenia and other mental disorders, these deaths are attributed to self-harm, not to mental illness, in the GBD. Because schizophrenia is not an important cause of lives lost, it ranked only forty-third in importance as a cause of global disease burden in 2010. [8]

The story is different with regard to morbidity. When the focus shifts to nonfatal illnesses, *mental and substance use disorders are the number one cause of global disease burden.* Together, they accounted for 23 percent of the disease burden attributed to morbidity (years lived with disability) in 2010. Musculoskeletal disorders, the number two cause of morbidity losses, accounted for 21 percent. [9]

Across all 220 illness/injury categories, schizophrenia itself ranked sixteenth in importance as a global cause of years lived with disability. [10] Recall that schizophrenia has the highest disability weight of any illness/category, but it drops to sixteenth as a cause of years lived with disability, because its prevalence is far lower than the leading causes of morbidity (low back pain and major depression). Moreover, when a person with schizophrenia commits suicide, the years of life lost are attributed to self-harm, and the morbidity losses associated with schizophrenia are actually reduced!

Changes in Disease Burden over Time

The GBD study is an ongoing project, so it is possible to trace how the disease burden associated with various illnesses/injury categories has changed over time. Comparing results from GBD 1990 and 2010, we find the overall burden of disease declined over the twenty-year period. If we measure disease burden in terms of DALYs per one hundred thousand persons, to control for population growth, the decrease was an amazing 23 percent. This huge decrease in the population-adjusted burden of disease is explained foremost by a tremendous decrease in the burden associated with communicable diseases (-44 percent). [11]

Contrary to the overall trend, the population-adjusted disease burden associated with mental and behavioral disorders *increased by 6 percent* during this period. [12] Among the mental disorders, drug use and schizophrenia had the highest percentage increases in DALYs per 100,000 persons (17 percent and 11 percent, respectively). The 17 percent increase in disability burden associated with drug use disorders was primarily driven by a tremendous increase in the prevalence of opioid use over the twenty-year period. [13] In contrast, the prevalence of schizophrenia has remained stable over time. The 11 percent increase in disease burden associated with schizophrenia is primarily explained by differences in the disability weights assigned to the disease in GBD 1990 and 2010.

Perception versus Reality

Both GBD 1990 and GBD 2010 estimate morbidity losses for two categories of schizophrenia, but the titles and lay descriptions of the two schizophrenia states are different in the two studies. In GBD 1990, the disability weight for "untreated schizophrenia" was 0.627, and for "treated schizophrenia" was 0.351.[14] In GBD 2010, the disability weight for "acute schizophrenia" was 0.756, and for "residual schizophrenia" was 0.576.[15] Notably, neither lay description of schizophrenia in 1990 mentioned violence or self-harm as characteristic of the disorder, whereas both descriptions did so in 2010. Hence, we cannot know if the changes in disability weights (and morbidity losses) associated with schizophrenia in the two surveys reflect changes in public attitudes toward the *disease*, or toward its *description*.

In 1988, when the world's attention was focused on the AIDS epidemic, the editor of the journal *Nature* wrote, "Schizophrenia is arguably the worst disease known to mankind, even AIDS not excepted."[16] Apparently the editor would agree with the harsh assessments of disability accorded to schizophrenia in GBD 2010. Nonetheless, it is hard to believe that having schizophrenia in 2010 was worse than having the disease in 1990. That said, poverty is still commonplace among the population with schizophrenia, and the prognosis for a productive work life remains poor.[17]

Education

Education is crucial to success in the modern labor market. The U.S. economy is increasingly reliant on industries that demand a highly educated, highly skilled labor force. Education provides the human capital necessary to meet those demands, and a signal to employers that a worker has acquired the necessary skills. Better-educated workers typically have higher employment rates, and more stable jobs, than less-educated workers. Better-educated workers can also expect jobs with higher wages and lifetime earnings, more generous benefit packages, and greater intrinsic rewards (autonomy, creativity, novelty, opportunity for advancement) than their less educated counterparts.

Among persons with serious mental illness, education is consistently shown to be one of the strongest and most significant predictors of positive employment outcomes.[18] A meta-analysis of sixty-two studies analyzing predictors of employment for persons with schizophrenia, for example, shows that education and cognitive skills are more consistently related to positive outcomes than diagnosis, current symptoms, or history of hospitalizations.[19] When mental illness strikes at an early age, therefore, an individual is disadvantaged not only by the loss of health capital associated with the illness, but also by the *loss of potential human capital* associated with a disrupted education.

A recent study shows that persons with early-onset disabilities also earn *lower returns to education* than persons with late-onset disabilities. The study uses data from the 1993 Survey of Income and Program Participation (SIPP) to estimate the impact of additional years of education on the wages of men with early versus late-onset disability (onset of disability before/after age twenty-five), relative to a control group of nondisabled men. Holding severity of disability constant, men with early-onset disability have *lower* returns to education than nondisabled men, whereas men with late-onset disability have *higher* returns. Estimated returns for an additional year of secondary education, for example, are less than 1 percent for men with early-onset disability, compared to 9.4 percent for nondisabled men and 23.4 percent for men with late-onset disability. [20]

The authors speculate that education acts as an "insurance policy" against the possibility of becoming disabled later in life. That is, the higher returns to education experienced by adults with late-onset disability "protect" these workers from some of the human capital losses associated with a health shock. How might such an insurance policy work? One possible explanation relates to the role of education as a *signal* of productivity; another explanation relates to the role education plays in *job matching*.

Education as a Signal

Education not only functions as a means to acquire human capital for the labor market, but also as a "signal" of worker quality. The most visible quality signal is a diploma, indicating that an individual has completed a required course of study at an acceptable level. Thus, a diploma is more valuable than the equivalent years of schooling as a signal of productivity to employers. Someone with a bachelor's degree has better prospects in the labor market, on average, than someone with four years of college but no degree.

In a classic article, Michael Spence (an economist at New York University and winner of the 2001 Nobel Prize in Economics) outlines a conceptual model of the role of signals in the labor market. [21] Spence views the hiring decision as an investment that involves risk, because employers cannot observe the productivity of job applicants at the time of hiring (and perhaps even for some time after). When an employer decides to hire, the wage they offer is no greater than the applicant's expected *marginal value product* (that is, the value of the additional output the worker is expected to contribute to the firm). Otherwise, it is not profitable to hire the worker at all. But how is expected value determined, if productivity cannot be observed in advance of hiring?

According to Spence, the employer observes a host of other characteristics that provide indications of the productivity to be expected from a job applicant. Employers evaluate expected productivity based on their experience with workers exhibiting similar characteristics, whose productivity has been observed. Suppose, for example, a financial firm hires an MBA from Anywhere University who turns out to be an outstanding performer. The firm is likely to look favorably on other applicants from Anywhere U, may even recruit graduates from Anywhere U, given the performance of the graduate they have observed.

Some observable characteristics are fixed by nature (e.g., age, gender) but others, like education, are alterable. Spence calls these alterable characteristics "signals," because individuals can acquire these characteristics in hopes of increasing their wage offers. So, why do we not observe everyone investing in a PhD? Clearly because there are costs associated with education, so individuals acquire education only to the point where the expected returns on the investment (higher wages) exceed the costs. A key assumption in the Spence model is that *the costs of investment in a productivity signal are inversely correlated with expected productivity.* More intelligent workers, for example, have lower costs of acquiring an advanced degree than less intelligent workers, who may have to study harder, pay for tutoring, and take longer to graduate. Hence, the education signal acquires value because workers with higher expected productivity (more intelligence) have lower investment costs and are more likely to invest in advanced degrees.

The education signal is potentially even more valuable for workers with mental disorders than for nondisabled persons. Why might this be so? Goffman provides a clue in his discussion of mechanisms for combating stigma: "The stigmatized individual can also attempt to correct his condition indirectly by devoting much private effort to the mastery of areas of activity ordinarily felt to be closed . . . to one with his shortcoming."[22]

One of the negative stereotypes attributed to persons with mental illness is incompetence; they are thought to be incapable of rational decision making. Persons who are incompetent are expected to be high school dropouts, not to earn advanced degrees. What better way to confound the stereotype of incompetence than to earn a diploma? Based on the signaling model, education is exceptionally valuable for persons with mental disorders because it suggests productivity *far beyond what is expected* of them.

Education and Job Matching

Another way that education may "insure" against the human capital losses associated with disability is by enabling better matches between a worker's functional capacities and the demands of their job. The match is important because the impact of functional limitations on a worker's productivity depends upon the nature of their job. A person confined to a wheelchair, for example, may be equally as productive as their nondisabled coworkers in a sedentary job. The same worker employed in a job that requires movement around the workplace would tend to be slower at accomplishing tasks (less productive) than their nondisabled counterparts.

A colleague and I have examined the importance of job matching for workers with physical disabilities (i.e., health impairments that affect mobility, strength, or endurance). Workers are said to be "mismatched" in a job, if their physical limitations affect their ability to perform important job functions. Using data from the SIPP (1996–2008), we find that workers who are mismatched in their jobs earn lower wages than their counterparts whose physical limitations do not impact important job functions. By itself, this result is not surprising. The more important finding is that *education is a highly significant determinant* of the probability of finding a good match.[23] In other words, better-educated workers are more likely than less-educated workers to be in jobs where their functional limitations have little impact on important job functions. Some persons with mental disorders, for example, are easily distracted by extraneous noises. Such a person is more likely to be successful working in their own office (with good soundproofing), than working in a cubicle or open space. Education increases the value of this person in the labor market, making it more likely they can find, or bargain for, a job that accommodates their functional limitations.

Supported Education

For all these reasons (acquisition of human capital, signaling to counteract stigma, opportunity to find a good job match), education is a valuable investment for persons with serious mental illness. There are a few programs, primarily in the United States, Canada, and Australia, which aim to support persons with SMI who want to pursue a college education. The supported education programs fall into three categories:

- The *self-contained classroom*, in which students with SMI take classes in segregated settings, with instructors and teaching methods that accommodate their needs.
- *Mobile support*, in which students are enrolled in regular classes at a postsecondary institution, but receive support from mental health professionals in the community (e.g., staff at community mental health centers or clubhouses).

- *On-site support*, in which students are enrolled in regular classes at a postsecondary institution, and receive support from specially trained staff at the institution. [24]

These programs are a good beginning, but they are not designed to meet the needs of students who aspire to a four-year university degree. One problem is that most current supported education programs do not focus on graduation as a specifically defined objective. The authors of an article describing one of the Australian programs, for example, say that the purpose of supported education is, "to increase the ability of people with psychiatric disabilities to access and participate in post-secondary education, by providing necessary supports."[25] Access and participation are good first steps, but graduation is the signal that creates opportunities in the labor market.

Another problem is that existing supported education programs are not, for the most part, located on college or university campuses. To be specific, there were about one hundred supported education programs operating in the United States and Canada in 2005.[26] The majority of these programs follow the mobile support model. Suppose that the total number of programs had doubled in the last ten years. Even so, given that there are more than 4,250 postsecondary degree granting institutions in the United States, the likelihood that a student with SMI finds a supported education program *on their campus* is almost nil.

Training

Most jobs in a developed economy require a combination of general and job-specific human capital. The formal educational system focuses on developing general human capital, but vocational training can be either general or job-specific. Automobile mechanics, bartenders, electricians, hair stylists, home health aides, plumbers, all have *general training* for their jobs, that increases their value in many firms. By way of contrast, within a large hospital: Admissions clerks are trained to use the computer software that processes a patient into the hospital. Cleaning staff are trained to know where supplies are kept and how to dispose of different types of waste. Nurses are trained to know the color-coding scheme for medical supplies, and how to use the computer software that tracks patient medications. None of these job-specific skills can be readily transferred to another hospital system.

The litany of examples of general and job-specific skills may be getting tedious, but the distinction is probably the most important in all of human capital theory. It should be clear by now that general human capital (and therefore general training) is more valuable to workers than job-specific human capital (and job-specific training), because general human capital is *transferable*. It is unfortunate, therefore, that mainstream models of vocational training for persons with SMI have evolved in a way that places far greater (almost exclusive) emphasis on job-specific skills.

Mainstream Models

Historically, vocational training for persons with mental illness has been provided by free-standing psychiatric rehabilitation centers.[27] Perhaps the best-known model is the clubhouse, which provides a place where persons with mental illness can work and socialize in a supportive environment. The original clubhouse, Fountain House, was founded in Manhattan in 1948 by a group of former patients of a nearby mental hospital.[28] As the name indicates, the program operates as a club. Participants are called "members," and are expected to operate the clubhouse themselves, with support from paid staff. The model clubhouse program offers vocational training in three modes: the work-ordered day (volunteer work at the clubhouse), transitional employment (jobs at local firms set aside for clubhouse members), and supported employment (mainstream jobs with appropriate employment supports, such as on-site job training).[29]

Beginning in the 1990s, other approaches to vocational training for persons with mental illness began to emerge. One model, the Diversified Placement Approach (DPA), was initiated at Thresholds, a psychiatric rehabilitation agency in Chicago. Founded in 1959, Thresholds originally followed the clubhouse model of vocational training, until studies in the 1970s raised questions about its effectiveness. Thresholds eventually phased out the transitional employment program in favor of diversified placement, which offers "members" an array of job options, ranging from employment in businesses that are run by the agency, to independent employment in competitive jobs. Upon entry into the DPA program, clients are assigned to unpaid jobs in the agency's day program, where their "work readiness" is assessed. Members receive prevocational job training, and are eventually placed in jobs consistent with their readiness. DPA is characterized by a gradual entry to employment, in a paid job that may or may not be competitive, often with placement in local businesses that have established partnerships with the agency.[30]

Today, the gold standard in vocational training for persons with mental illness is the Individual Placement and Support (IPS) model. Unlike DPA, the focus of IPS is competitive employment, defined as "regular community jobs, alongside nondisabled coworkers, that pay at least minimum wage."[31] The core philosophy of IPS is to achieve rapid job placement consistent with consumer preferences, accompanied by benefits counseling and personalized job supports.[32] Vocational services are integrated with other services provided to patients, so most IPS programs are operated by agencies within, or aligned with, the mental health system. The distinguishing feature of the program is its emphasis on immediate placement in a competitive job ("place, then train") as opposed to the pre-vocational training emphasized in the DPA ("train, then place").

Studies comparing IPS to other models of vocational training consistently show that IPS achieves superior employment outcomes.[33] A recent meta-analysis pooled results from four such studies. All the studies were randomized trials comparing outcomes of IPS to outcomes of another model of vocational training (DPA, group skills training, psychosocial rehabilitation, and training in a sheltered workshop), among persons with mental illness who expressed a desire to work. The results indicate that IPS produces better competitive employment outcomes—that is, higher rates of job placement and longer job tenure, than other models, regardless of patients' demographic or clinical characteristics.[34]

Nevertheless, research shows that the IPS model does not achieve high rates of stable competitive employment for its target population.[35] One study, for example, evaluated employment outcomes among participants in an IPS training program funded by the Massachusetts Department of Mental Health. The program maintained high fidelity with the core principles of IPS, and produced employment outcomes as good as, or better than, other IPS programs described in the literature. Still, the average participant earned less than $200 per month over the four-and-one-half-year observation period.[36] Two-thirds of job placements were in low-paid service or sales jobs. More than 80 percent of jobs involved working less than twenty hours per week, and less than 5 percent of jobs paid benefits. More than 90 percent of participants continued to receive federal disability benefits and, in fact, were counseled on how to maximize earnings while maintaining benefit eligibility.

Another study, involving clients of a mental health agency serving inner-city Baltimore, compared employment outcomes of patients randomly assigned to IPS or to a psychosocial rehabilitation program. Clients participating in IPS were more likely to obtain jobs, worked more hours, and had higher earnings over the study period than the comparison group. However, the jobs obtained by IPS patients were "short-term, entry-level, part-time jobs."[37] Job retention was also a problem. The average job duration among clients assigned to either program was less than four months.

The sad fact is that most participants in vocational training programs for persons with SMI do not attain regular earnings above the poverty level. A fundamental problem is that mainstream supported employment programs do not help participants acquire the general human capital that enhances their value in the labor market. The "place, then train" principle underlying IPS implies that the program is almost exclusively focused on job-specific training. To achieve rapid employment, participants must be placed in unskilled jobs that require no general training or certification. To be sure, some of the clientele participating in supported employment programs may have residual symptoms or functional limitations that make sustained competitive employment impossible. For those who are capable, however, the focus on job-specific as opposed to general training is counterproductive to long-term, stable employment outcomes.

Alternative Models

Some experimental programs are underway which augment supported employment with general skills training. One model combines a supported employment program with neurocognitive enhancement therapy (NET). NET is a remediation program specifically designed to address the cognitive and social limitations associated with schizophrenia. In one trial of a NET intervention, seventy-two patients with schizophrenia were randomized to receive either vocational services plus NET, or vocational services only.[38] The vocational services program was a hybrid transitional/supported employment model, consistent with the core philosophy of IPS. The NET intervention included computer-based cognitive training and twice-weekly participation in small-group meetings. At the meetings, one participant presented a talk on an issue encountered in their job, following which other participants offered feedback and constructive criticism. Participation in group meetings required good oral communication skills, as well as the ability to recognize and relate to another person's feelings, all of which are essential aspects of social capital.

The employment experiences of study participants were followed over a two-year period. Compared to the control group (vocational services only), persons in the experimental group achieved higher rates of employment, worked more hours, and were more likely to sustain employment in the second year of follow-up, after NET training had ceased.[39] One particularly important finding was that persons with the poorest social functioning at intake benefitted most from the NET intervention, reinforcing the idea that investments in training can compensate, somewhat, for the losses of social capital associated with schizophrenia.

Other pilot projects combining supported employment with supported education (SE/SE) are underway in Ra'anana, Israel, and Ontario, Canada.[40] The training program in Israel consists of three stages: Stage I (three months or less) provides general training in cognitive, computer, and social skills. Stage II (up to one year) is a supported education program that prepares participants for a skilled occupation, such as accounting, computer programming, electrical repair, graphics design, etc. Stage III is on-the-job training in the individual's chosen field, with employment supports if necessary.

The number of participants in the pilot project was small (ninety-six), and only preliminary data have been published to date, but early results were promising. Two years into the project, 40 percent of participants had completed Stage I; four-fifths of those were in Stage II training. Sixteen percent of participants had completed Stages I and II. Among the graduates of stage II: 40 percent were competitively employed in their vocation of choice, 47 percent were in transitional/supported employment or further training, and the remainder (two persons) were looking for work.[41]

The alternative models of vocational training for persons with serious mental illness represent a clear departure from mainstream supported employment services. The new models place a strong emphasis on acquisition of general human capital. An implicit assumption underlying the models is that many persons with SMI are capable of working independently in competitive jobs that demand higher-level cognitive and social skills. These types of jobs are seldom an outcome of mainstream vocational training for this population. The preliminary evidence on SE/SE and NET is promising, but it remains to be seen if the newer models can demonstrate significantly better outcomes than IPS when applied to larger and more diverse populations.

Postscript

The first episode of acute positive symptoms of schizophrenia usually occurs in the late teens or early twenties, exactly the time when a young person is making the investments in human capital that will determine their future earnings potential. One of the great tragedies of the disease is the loss of self-reliance and self-esteem associated with being denied a productive work life. Although medical science has made tremendous progress in restoring the health capital of persons afflicted with schizophrenia, this progress has not been translated into significant gains in employment.

I have argued that investments in human capital can significantly improve employment outcomes for persons with schizophrenia, and other serious mental illness. Completing a two- or four-year college degree increases their value in the labor market, acts as a signal of achievement to employers, and facilitates a good job match. Vocational training programs that match patients' aptitudes and interests with transferable skills that are valued in the labor market can have a similar impact. A premise of this book, to which I shall return in later chapters, is that employment outcomes for persons with SMI can improve if: (1) educational supports are in place to ensure that young adults can return to school, after onset of SMI, and complete their formal education; and (2) vocational training programs focus on general human capital, as opposed to job-specific skills that are valuable to only one employer.

Over the last twenty-five years we have learned that advances in pharmacology are not sufficient, by themselves, to restore persons with serious mental illness to productive and fulfilling lives. Investments in human capital are important. So is the mental health services system, but that system has not evolved in ways that encourage stable competitive employment and financial independence for persons with SMI. The next chapter tells that story.

Chapter Four

The Supply of Mental Health Services

WE CAN'T DO ANYTHING

A diagnosis of schizophrenia thrusts you abruptly into a strange new world—the U.S. mental health services system. With all its varied parts: medical professionals (psychiatrists, psychologists, psychiatric nurses, etc.), community care centers, state social service systems, general and specialty hospitals, case managers, vocational counselors, and nonprofit support organizations, one would expect a plethora of services available for patients and their families. In fact, the refrain I heard repeatedly was, *"I can't do anything for you."* Overall, my experiences with the mental health system remind me of the nursery rhyme about the little girl who had a curl right in the middle of her forehead: "When it was good, it was very, very good; but when it was bad, it was horrid."

Spring 1999

The very best was the care David received at the University Hospital in Chapel Hill, after he was first diagnosed with schizophrenia. The hospital was a study site for clinical trials comparing two antipsychotic medications: halopenidol, a first-generation drug, and olanzapine, one of the new atypical antipsychotics. David agreed to participate in the study and was randomly assigned to one of the drugs. In theory, the study was double-blind: *Neither* patients nor providers were told which drug a particular patient was receiving. In reality, the side-effect profiles of the two drugs are distinctly different, so the nurses knew within days that David had been assigned to olanzapine.

At Chapel Hill, the study was directed by Diana Perkins, a psychiatrist with a national reputation for her research on the treatment of psychiatric illness. The study staff included a social worker, who served as case manager for patients and liaison to their families. In exchange for regular neurological and psychiatric testing, David received his medical care at no charge. After he was discharged from the hospital and living at home, the study provided a private car and driver to transport him back to Chapel Hill for weekly follow-up visits and testing.

The study sought to compare how the two drugs performed under nearly ideal conditions, so the protocols included education and support for family members, who were the patients' informal caregivers. The social worker was our contact to answer questions, resolve problems, or simply listen to our frustrations. She also conducted a monthly support group for families. Each spring, the research team held a one-day conference on treatment options for schizophrenia, to which patients' families were invited. In short, we were surrounded by a community of experts who were committed to helping us provide the best possible care for our sons, daughters, or spouses.

I met with Dr. Perkins several times in those first months, but I particularly remember one meeting between the three of us immediately before David was discharged. The point she emphasized repeatedly was, "Stay on your medication." We were lucky, she said, that David was so responsive to the drug, but if he stopped taking the meds his psychotic symptoms would recur. He could function normally for a while because the drug levels recede gradually from the brain, but eventually he would relapse. Dr. Perkins told David that, after each successive relapse, it would become more difficult to bring him back, and his recovery level of functioning would be lower. By the end of the meeting I was sufficiently frightened, David not so much. One year later and back at school, David stopped taking his meds; within a few months, he experienced a second psychotic break.

Summer 2000

Police found David wandering the streets of Durham in the middle of the night and immediately took him to the state psychiatric hospital. I was out of state when I received a phone call from my husband telling me what had happened. I immediately called the hospital, in a panic to know about David's condition. "Have you contacted his psychiatrist? Have you given him any medication?" I asked. The response was maddening; beyond confirming that my son was a patient, the nurses could not provide any information. "*I can't tell you anything.* Your son refused to give permission for us to release any information." I was furious: at the nurse who wouldn't talk to me; at my son who refused permission to release information to me; at a system designed to protect a patient's privacy before his well-being. "But can you just tell me if you know what medication he's supposed to be on?" I pressed the nurse. "*I can't say anything,*" she said, "but I can listen to whatever information you'd like to give me." I was beyond furious. I told the woman, "If you won't talk to me, I'm certainly not going to talk to you."

I took the redeye home and met with David the following morning. He said "Mom, they gave me a bunch of papers to sign, but I didn't think I was in any shape to sign anything." I had to agree. That day we transferred David back to the UNC Hospital. In less than a week he had responded to the meds, the positive symptoms of illness disappeared, and he returned to school. I thought he had learned his lesson, but I was wrong. Twice more David stopped taking the meds.

Spring 2005

By 2005, David was living in Charlotte and had landed a job as sales representative for a commercial security systems company. We had moved to Arizona three years earlier. David seemed stable on his meds, although a Christmas visit in December 2004 should have been an early warning sign. He was more than usually talkative—but the talk made sense. He was somewhat irritable—but irritations often arise when families gather for the holidays. Such are the rationalizations of parents who do not want to see what they are seeing. In January, back in Charlotte, David suffered another psychotic break.

This time the phone call came from David's uncle in Wake Forest. David's roommates had contacted him because they had not seen or heard from David for several days. They told my brother that David's employer was also looking for him. I made plans to fly to Charlotte; my older son offered to drive to North Carolina and accompany me. We agreed to meet at my brother's home. When I arrived, my sister-in-law was at the doorway with a stricken face. "Aaron's been in an accident—a head-on collision a few miles from here. His car is totaled." It was the worst day of my life.

Thankfully, no one was hurt in the crash. Aaron insisted on traveling to Charlotte with me as planned. When we arrived, we found David's life in a shambles. He had thrown most of his belongings in the trash; he had parked his car on the street, locked it, and thrown away the keys; he had "quit" his job without notifying his employer; he was staying in a hotel, running up credit card bills. But he was bright and cheerful. He thought he had met his future wife. He was not troubled about quitting his job, because he had a great idea for a career as the "date doctor." (Are you having trouble meeting women? I can cure your problem.) He had even printed and passed out advertising flyers. Life was great and he was sure glad to see us!

We took David to the psychiatrist who was treating him in Charlotte. He gave David his meds and watched him swallow them in his office. Then he gave David an ultimatum—stay with your mother for the following week and take your meds as prescribed, or I will put you in the hospital. So we spent the following week together: David angry and sullen as he came down from his mania; I frightened and uncomfortable in my role as Nurse Ratched. When we returned to the psychiatrist the following week, I was certain there would be another ultimatum—go to Arizona with your parents or go into the hospital.

But no. David had been on his meds for a full week. He was no longer psychotic. There was no need for him to be hospitalized. I pleaded with the doctor, "You know he won't take his meds after I leave. He'll just get sick all over again. He can't stay here." The psychiatrist agreed David should return home with us but said, *"There's nothing I can do."* And so I left my son there, with no job and no money, and returned to Arizona to await the inevitable disaster.

Back home, I called Adult Protective Services in Charlotte and told them about David's situation. They picked him up and took him to the Mental Health Center, where he was evaluated. The psychiatrist on call determined that David was not a danger to himself or others, and he was released. Adult Services called back to tell me, *"There's nothing we can do."* I called the local police, warned them that my son had schizophrenia, was not taking his meds, and I was worried about what might happen. Until someone gets hurt, they told me, *"There's nothing we can do."* A former girlfriend called to say she had convinced David to admit himself voluntarily to the psychiatric hospital, but the hospital had refused to admit him. "He's not sick enough," they said. *"There's nothing we can do."*

There was nothing left for me to do but wait, and take care of myself. My physician recommended two psychologists to help me deal with the stress. I called the first, told him that my son had schizophrenia and I needed help dealing with it. "Schizophrenia," he said, *"I don't handle anything as serious as that."* "I wish I didn't have to either," I replied.

And when it was bad, it was horrid.

PLANNERS VERSUS SEARCHERS

The history of mental health services in the United States is a chronicle of unfulfilled promises. Repeated efforts to reform the system have been accompanied by promises that serious mental illness can be cured and prevented. Each reform movement has failed. To the present day, we have been unable to construct a mental health system that consistently provides compassionate and effective treatment to persons with the most serious mental illnesses. The evidence is on the streets (an estimated 216,000 persons with SMI were homeless in 2010);[1] and in the jails (2.1 million persons with SMI were booked into jail in 2007).[2] Part of the problem is money, although billions of dollars are spent on state and federal programs that provide health care and other assistance to persons with mental illness. Part of the problem is an ill-placed faith in the plans of "experts" (bureaucrats, social scientists, public health officials) to solve a problem from which they are far removed.

We can draw parallels between failed attempts to solve the problem of mental illness, and failed attempts of Western nations to solve the problem of poverty in developing countries. Economist William Easterly makes the case that too much foreign aid is allocated to the grandiose ideas of "Planners," and not enough to grass-roots efforts of "Searchers." According to Easterly, Searchers succeed where Planners fail because:

> Planners announce good intentions but don't motivate anyone to carry them out; Searchers find things that work and get some reward. Planners determine what to supply; Searchers find out what is in demand. Planners never hear whether the planned got what it needed; Searchers find out if the customer is satisfied.[3]

Free markets abound with Searchers hunting for solutions that generate profits. Consider John Freund, Frederic Moll, and Rob Younge, who developed the da Vinci robotic surgical system;[4] Paul Janssen, who discovered Haloperidol;[5] and Wilson Greatbatch, who invented the implantable cardiac pacemaker and manufactured fifty prototypes in a backyard workshop.[6] Profit-making in health care is sometimes branded as immoral, but to economists the search for profits is a sign of a healthy marketplace. Profits give Searchers the incentive to solve problems and deliver solutions to consumers; losses hold Searchers accountable when they fail.

Alas, we cannot leave either foreign aid or mental health care entirely up to free markets! In theory, government planners can intervene in these markets in ways that will enhance social welfare; but in practice, public officials often respond to economic incentives, social attitudes, and political ideologies in ways that undermine their lofty goals. As we trace the evolution of the U.S. mental health system from its colonial beginnings until today, we observe the collective effect of these forces. The system that has emerged has the *capability* to deliver high-quality, compassionate care, but usually *fails* to meet the needs of patients and their families in crisis. That situation will not change until we pay more attention to the Searchers who deal with the reality of mental illness every day.

The Case for Government Intervention

In many ways, mental health services are analogous to ordinary goods and services like food, shelter, clothing, automobiles, and computers. As with other goods, mental health services must be produced with scarce resources, and distributed to those who want or need the services. The production of mental health services, or other goods, involves an opportunity cost; in other words, resources used to produce mental health services are not available for other purposes, such as caring for cancer patients, educating children, or supporting the local symphony.

As with other goods, consumers are willing to pay for mental health services to obtain benefits (improved health and well-being); and providers are willing to supply those services to obtain profits. Unlike other goods, the connection between demand and supply of health services is disrupted in unusual, or even unique, ways. One source of disruption occurs because the benefits of mental health services are not limited to those who consume the services. When a person with SMI receives treatment, they are less likely to burden their family, annoy their neighbors, or disturb their community. Economists call these benefits to others *positive externalities.* Because of the positive externalities, free markets for mental health services will provide less than the optimal quantity of services. Patients are typically unaware of the way their consumption of services benefits others, and even if aware, they are generally unwilling to pay for benefits that accrue to others. Under these conditions, the government can use tax dollars to pay for services that yield *social benefits above and beyond private willingness to pay.*

A second source of disruption in the market for mental health services is the belief that (at least within reason) everyone should have access to necessary health care, regardless of their insurance status or ability to pay. In other words, we are unwilling to deprive persons with serious mental illness of the health services that they need, even if they do not have the resources to pay for those services themselves. Economists call these kinds of commodities *merit goods.* Free markets tend not to supply the socially optimal quantity of a merit good because, obviously, providing a good without payment is not profitable. Hence, there is a role for government (and charitable organizations) in the provision of mental health services and other merit goods.

Finally, the market for mental health services is disrupted in a way that is virtually unique, namely, that those who need diagnosis and treatment do not necessarily want it. Persons afflicted with SMI often do not believe they are sick.[7] (In the midst of his relapse in Charlotte, David thought his life was just great. He was paranoid and psychotic, but that was clear to everyone except David.) If a person with mental illness lacks insight into their condition and will not seek treatment on their own, and society deems treatment is necessary and appropriate, only government has the coercive power to make an individual consume services involuntarily.

Despite a wide range of opinion on the acceptability of involuntary treatment for persons with SMI, there are good arguments for a government role in the mental health system, solely on efficiency and equity grounds. Free markets will not produce the socially optimal quantity of services that takes account of positive externalities, and free markets will not provide services to persons who are unable to pay. It is, therefore, left to the government to resolve the fundamental questions of resource allocation that are normally decided in a free market:

- What part of society's resources should be allocated to the mental health system?
- What types of services should the system provide?
- How should those services be distributed among the mentally ill?

As the U.S. mental health system has evolved, decisions about services for the mentally ill have been transferred from local to state to federal governments, and finally to a system where decision making is shared. The way government Planners have responded to questions about resource allocation has been heavily influenced by economic circumstances as well as by prevailing social attitudes, legal mandates, advances in medical practice, and politics.

Evolution of the U.S. Mental Health System: 1750–1950

Prior to the late eighteenth century, mental illness was not a major social concern. The U.S. population was small and dispersed, and the number of persons with mental illness was correspondingly small. Virtually every American colony adopted some version of the English Poor Law system, in which local communities assumed fiscal and supervisory responsibility for persons who were unable to care for themselves, including the mentally ill. [8] Persons with mental illness were cared for in their communities, usually by family members. Those without families or private resources became the responsibility of local officials, who boarded them with other families or cared for them in public almshouses.

Local Financing

As the U.S. population expanded and consolidated, and the locus of work moved outside the home, mental illness became a greater problem for communities. Large urban areas like Philadelphia (1752) and New York (1792) established wards in local hospitals for collective care of the mentally ill. [9] In 1773, the first state hospital devoted exclusively to the mentally ill was built in Williamsburg, Virginia. [10] Conditions in these establishments reflected prevailing beliefs that associated mental illness with evil or amoral behavior. Patients were often shackled or isolated in locked cells; treatments were often punitive and abusive. [11]

Toward the end of the eighteenth century, a *moral treatment* movement arose in Europe, in opposition to the harsh institutional treatment of persons with mental illness. Moral treatment reformers believed the mentally ill were sick, not evil, and could be cured if treated with humanity and dignity.

Mental illness was thought to result from living in an adverse environment, hence the "cure" was to treat patients in more desirable surroundings. Reformers advocated for care in small asylums with a family atmosphere. Treatments involved occupational therapy and recreation as well as medical care; there was limited use of restraints, and absolutely no physical violence.[12]

After 1800, the moral treatment movement spread to private and public institutions in the United States. The first private asylums devoted to moral treatment were the Friends Asylum, founded by Pennsylvania Quakers (1817) and the Hartford Retreat (1824). By 1850, thirty private asylums practicing principles of moral treatment for persons with mental illness were operating in the United States.[13]

Simultaneously, Dorothea Dix and other outspoken advocates convinced state legislatures to allocate funds for the construction of public hospitals devoted to more humane care for persons with mental illness. Fifty years after the Williamsburg hospital was built, public mental hospitals were opened in Lexington, Kentucky (1822), Worcester, Massachusetts (1833), and Utica, New York (1833).[14] By the Civil War, almost every state had constructed at least one public mental hospital.[15]

State hospital administrators assumed *supervisory* responsibility for persons referred to them by local authorities, but local authorities retained *fiscal* responsibility for treatment and upkeep. The divided authority eventually created tensions between state and local officials. State officials, who were responsible for the design and administration of patient care, believed the care in local almshouses was "substandard, and fostered chronicity and dependency."[16] Local officials, who paid the bills but had no control over spending, had strong economic incentives to provide custodial care within the community whenever possible. Costs were lower in the local almshouse than in the state hospital, so local officials often exerted pressure on state hospital superintendents to release patients to community care, regardless of the patient's condition.[17]

Around the end of the nineteenth century, states began to pass laws that ended the system of divided responsibility. New York passed the first of these State Care Acts in 1890, transferring full responsibility for the indigent mentally ill to the state, and relieving local authorities of any fiscal obligation to the state hospital.[18] Other states followed New York's lead, and for the next fifty years U.S. mental health policy was centralized at the state level.

State Financing

The State Care Acts had unforeseen consequences for the state hospitals and their capacity to care for the mentally ill. Once the states assumed financial responsibility for patients, local governments had strong incentives to send *all* long-term cases of mental illness, including elderly persons suffering from dementia, to the state hospital. The influx of these patients, together with increasing demand for services from an expanding population, led to overcrowded conditions and a higher proportion of chronic cases in the hospitals.[19] Larger facilities had to be constructed. The moral treatment model, which involved high staff-to-patient ratios and high per-patient costs (and had never demonstrated success in treating long-term and severe cases of mental illness), was impractical in the large custodial institutions which the state hospitals had become. As the hospitals filled to capacity and beyond, living conditions and quality of care deteriorated.

In 1908, Clifford Beers, a former mental patient, published an autobiography recounting his tenure in a state mental hospital. The book describes the harsh treatment he endured, the cruelty exhibited by some of the attendants, and his eventual recovery and release. Motivated by a "consuming desire to effect reforms" of the institution he had observed so intimately,[20] Beers enlisted the help of Adolf Meyer, a prominent psychiatrist, and William James, a Harvard professor of psychology. While Beers's purpose was "to improve the dreadful conditions and eliminate the physical abuse that was so prevalent" in the hospitals, [21] Dr. Meyer had broader goals. Meyer sought to prevent mental illness and preserve mental health, by creating healthy and stable community environments.[22] Hence, when Beers organized a committee to promote his reform objectives,[23] Meyers named the movement[24] the National Committee for Mental Hygiene.

Mental hygiene reformers believed that: (1) mental illness was caused by exposure to unhealthy, unstable environments, and (2) SMI could be effectively treated using the latest scientific advances in psychiatry, including Freudian psychoanalysis. State hospitals were deemed unsuitable environments for treatment, so reformers favored the construction of psychopathic hospitals, connected with large research universities or general hospitals, where patients could be evaluated and receive high-quality care. The nation's first psychopathic hospitals were affiliated with Albany Medical College (1902), the University of Michigan (1906), Harvard University (1912), and Johns Hopkins University (1913).[25]

If, as mental hygiene reformers believed, the root cause of mental illness was exposure to unhealthy environments, it followed that mental illness could be prevented by creating stable and supportive communities that produced mentally healthy children and adults. Dr. Meyer acknowledged that "the art of building a community is an intricate one," but believed that psychiatrists and social workers could play a vital role in helping people achieve well-balanced lives within communities that he called "mental hygiene districts."[26] In 1922, the Committee for Mental Hygiene launched an initiative to develop child guidance clinics in eight major cities. Teams of psychiatric social workers, under the direction of psychiatrists, were assigned to clinics to treat emotionally disturbed children. By the mid-twentieth century, more than six hundred child guidance clinics were operating across the country. [27]

Despite their intimate knowledge of the reality of mental illness (Beers as an ex-mental patient and Meyer as director of the Phipps Psychiatric Clinic at Johns Hopkins University), founders of the mental hygiene movement acted more like Planners than Searchers. Planners are inclined to focus on large and complex problems, for which they develop comprehensive solutions:

> The fondness for the Big Goal and the Big Plan is strikingly widespread. . . .
> The setting of utopian goals means [that Planners] focus efforts on infeasible
> tasks, instead of the feasible tasks that will do some good. . . . Searchers look
> for any opportunity to relieve suffering . . . and don't get stuck on infeasible
> objectives. [28]

Mental hygiene reformers had utopian visions that: new cases of SMI could be prevented by creating mentally healthy communities; existing cases could be cured by applying the latest advances in psychiatry; and the state hospitals would become obsolete once the mental hygiene reforms were implemented. Predictably, the movement failed to achieve its grandiose ambitions. The community clinics, founded with an incomplete understanding of the complexity of the causes of mental illness, and faced with the herculean task of creating mentally healthy communities, could not possibly prevent new cases of severe mental disorders. The psychopathic hospitals, designed as acute care facilities, had insufficient resources to manage patients with SMI who did not respond to "the latest advances in psychiatry." These chronic cases were transferred to the state hospitals for custodial care. [29] Far from becoming obsolete, the census of patients in state and county mental hospitals peaked at 558,922 in 1955. [30]

Evolution of the U.S. Mental Health System: 1950–2015

Between 1930 and 1955, state mental hospitals experienced not only an influx of chronically ill patients, but also a period of financial retrenchment brought about by the Great Depression, and a significant loss of resources diverted to World War II. The combined effects of an expanding patient population and fewer resources, led to further deterioration of conditions in the hospitals. [31]

During the war, more than three thousand conscientious objectors, mostly Quakers and Mennonites, worked in state mental hospitals in lieu of military service. Appalled at the conditions they observed, many of these young men published their stories. [32] As the public became aware of the tragic conditions in the hospitals, the perception grew that the states had failed miserably in caring for the mentally ill. When President Kennedy appointed an interagency task force to make recommendations for a national mental health plan, in December 1961, the time seemed right for a new approach that would move primary responsibility for care of mental patients away from the again-discredited state hospitals.

The approach that emerged was largely the brainchild of Robert Felix, the aggressive and visionary director of the National Institute of Mental Health (NIMH) from 1949 to 1964.[33] In 1941, as part of his master's thesis for Johns Hopkins University, Felix set forth a plan to repair the mental health system by moving the primary locus of care for mental patients from state hospitals to a network of federally supported outpatient clinics.[34]

Felix's plan became the centerpiece of the recommendations the task force forwarded to the president. The idea of federally funded outpatient clinics as substitutes for state mental hospitals was consistent with Kennedy's vision of a larger federal role in mental health policy. At Kennedy's urging, Congress passed the Community Mental Health Centers (CMHC) Act of 1963, which allocated an initial $150 million to construct the centers.[35] Between 1967 and 1980, 789 CMHCs were constructed at a cost of $2.7 billion ($13.3 billion in 2010 dollars).[36] Deliberately bypassing state authorities, none of the federal funds appropriated under the CMHC Act were allocated to state hospitals.

First-Generation Antipsychotic Drugs

Meanwhile, in the decade preceding passage of the CMHC Act, a revolution had taken place in the state hospitals. The change began in 1954, when the Food and Drug Administration approved the first antipsychotic drug, chlorpromazine (trade name, Thorazine) for U.S. markets. By 1956, chlorpromazine and a second antipsychotic, resperine, were being administered to hospital patients in thirty-seven states.[37] The drugs addressed one of the most persistent problems facing hospital administrators, namely, maintaining order among patients whose behavior was so disruptive that they had been "expelled" from their homes and communities. The new drugs were life changing:

> Robert W was admitted to the state hospital in a highly excited homicidal state. . . . This patient was loud, screamed that he would kill someone, and communicated his sincerity in this purpose to attendants and other personnel. [Thorazine] administration was begun soon after admission. . . . In the course of two more weeks of hospitalization, this patient had quieted down, had lost his anxiety almost altogether, and was able to discuss his illness and his future plans in an objective and rational manner. Within two months, Robert W. was discharged.[38]

Entire hospital wards were transformed:

> Prior to this study, these wards presented the usual picture . . . namely, 10 to 12 patients in seclusion, some also in camisoles or other types of restraint. In addition, heavy sedation and electroconvulsive therapy, as well as hydrotherapy and wet packs, were necessary and being utilized daily. Owing to the raucous, hyperactive, combative, sarcastic, resistive, uncooperative patients, the ward was in a continual turmoil. . . . Since the advent of therapy with resperine. . . . Patients have undergone a metamorphosis from raging, combative, unsociable persons to cooperative, cheerful, sociable, relatively quiet persons who are amenable to psychotherapy and other rehabilitative measures.[39]

The attitudes of attendants changed dramatically:

> They are overjoyed at the prospect of being converted from custodians to rehabilitation therapists. . . . [They] would be alarmed if such therapy were discontinued because they know that their duties would again involve restraining combative patients.[40]

In the years following the introduction of the first-generation antipsychotics, hundreds of thousands of patients were discharged from state and county mental hospitals. From 1956 to 1965, the inpatient population in public mental hospitals decreased by almost 14 percent, reversing a trend of steady increases since passage of the State Care Acts.[41] It is safe to say that this sharp turnabout was the direct result of more effective treatment through antipsychotic drugs. However, the inpatient population decreased by *another 57 percent* in the following decade, primarily for reasons unrelated to the improved treatments for SMI.[42]

Federal Financing

The primary explanation for the exodus from state mental hospitals after 1965 was the introduction of a number of federal social welfare programs. These programs dramatically altered the locus of care for the mentally ill by providing incentives for states to shift fiscal responsibility for mental health services to the federal government.[43] Three federal programs were particularly influential:

- Medicaid, established as part of the Social Security Act Amendments of 1965 to provide health insurance for eligible persons with low income;
- Social Security Disability Insurance (SSDI), established in 1956 to provide income for working-age persons who are unable to support themselves because of a disabling health condition;
- Supplemental Security Income (SSI), established in 1972 to provide subsidies for elderly or disabled persons who have limited income and resources.

Medicaid is funded jointly by state and federal governments. Participation is voluntary (all states have opted to participate), but states must operate their programs within federal guidelines in order to receive federal matching funds. One of those guidelines, known as the IMD exclusion rule, is that Medicaid funds may not be used to pay for care in an Institution for Mental Disease.[44] Funds may be used, however, to pay for long-term nursing home care for elderly patients with dementia. The economic incentives are unambiguous: A state could either pay all the costs of care for elderly dementia patients in the state hospital, or use federal dollars to subsidize 50 to 75 percent of costs in a nursing home. In 1963 (two years before Medicaid), nursing homes cared for 188,000 persons age sixty-five or older with mental disorders. By 1969 (four years after) that number had doubled.[45]

SSDI and SSI are financed entirely by the federal government. Like Medicaid, SSI is unavailable to residents of state mental hospitals. SSI funds may be used, however, to subsidize living expenses of former mental patients who are placed in group homes or boarding facilities. Thus, states could either pay the full costs for patients in the state hospital, or discharge patients to another facility and allow the federal government to subsidize living expenses. In New York, for example, the mental health system could save more than $9,000 per patient transferred out of the state hospital.[46] States responded to the new economic incentives, and the pace of discharge from mental hospitals accelerated after SSI was established.[47]

In addition to deliberate revision of the economic incentives surrounding inpatient psychiatric care, social attitudes changed during the 1960s and 1970s to challenge the concept of involuntary hospitalization. During the 1970s, a series of legislative changes and court decisions established that a person with mental illness has the right to: (1) treatment in the *least restrictive* setting; (2) *due process of law* before being confined to a hospital; (3) *adequate treatment*, if confined; and (4) to *refuse treatment* if they choose. The courts also established that a person with mental illness cannot be committed to a mental hospital involuntarily, unless the person poses "a danger to themselves or others."[48] Each of these changes to the legal structure rendered involuntary commitment more costly and more difficult. It is therefore not surprising that *admission rates* to state hospitals, which had risen steadily since 1955, began a downward trend in 1970.[49]

Community Mental Health Centers

As enrollments in state hospitals declined, community mental health centers were (theoretically) poised to assume primary responsibility for care of the mentally ill. According to the vision of Robert Felix and his followers, Community Mental Health Centers (CMHCs) would both *treat* acute cases of mental illness, without long-term hospital stays, and *prevent* future cases of serious mental illness, through early detection and treatment of less serious cases. If the vision of the CMHC reformers sounds remarkably similar to the vision of the mental hygiene reformers—it was. And if the plan to use community clinics as the mechanism for treatment and prevention of mental illness sounds similar to the plan that failed fifty years earlier—it was. Focused on the Big Goal, Planners of the CMHC movement were not daunted by the failures of others:

> One of the key predictions about Planners . . . is that they keep pouring resources into a fixed objective, despite many previous failures at reaching that objective, despite a track record that suggests the objective is infeasible or the plan unworkable. . . . Planners even escalate the scope of intervention when the previous intervention fails. [50]

Needless to say, the CMHCs failed to achieve the Big Goal of preventing SMI. The centers also failed to achieve the attainable goal of successful treatment for persons with SMI within the community. Part of the problem was that Planners banked their hopes and expectations on *unsupported assumptions*, namely, that: (1) discharged mental patients had homes in the community, (2) a sympathetic family would assume responsibility for their care, (3) the organization of the household would not impede rehabilitation, and (4) the patient's presence would not cause undue hardships for other family members. [51] In 1960, however, more than 60 percent of the patients in mental hospitals were either unmarried, widowed, divorced, or separated. Many discharged patients simply had no home to which to return. Others, who did have a home, had to rely on a family support system that was often ill-prepared to deal with serious mental illness.

Another part of the problem was *bypassing the state authorities* who had responsibility for mental health policy. The legislation establishing CMHCs deliberately eschewed a role for state mental hospitals in its reforms. Robert Felix, and others who were instrumental in the community mental health movement, viewed the state mental hospital as an "inherently repressive institution, on par with the prison."[52] Hence, CMHCs were structured as local/federal partnerships, wholly disconnected from state hospitals and state regulatory authorities, with no formal paths of communication between hospital superintendents and center directors. [53] How could the mental health system possibly provide a continuum of care, when essential components of the system were controlled by different levels of government, operating independently?

A final part of the problem was the *misdirected mission* of the CMHCs. Rather than focusing on treatment of persons with SMI in the community, framers of the 1963 act viewed "prevention of mental illness and promotion of positive mental health" as the primary mission of the CMHCs. [54] In 1968,

Congress expanded the mission to embrace an entirely new set of populations that included substance abusers, at-risk children, and the elderly. Directors of the CMHCs, faced with limited operating budgets and an expanding mission, chose to allocate their resources to treating mild adjustment and behavioral disorders, rather than to providing costly after-care for the severely mentally ill.[55]

Accordingly, most centers treated very few patients with SMI. Between 1968 and 1978, less than 7 percent of patients seen by the CMHCs were discharged mental patients receiving follow-up care. A 1979 report on service utilization in the CMHCs found that only 10 percent of clinic patients were diagnosed with schizophrenia.[56] By 1980, even the strongest advocates of the reforms were forced to admit that the program had not provided coordinated follow-up care for former mental patients. In 1984, Robert Felix publicly expressed doubts about his legacy:

> Many of those patients who left the state hospitals never should have done so. We psychiatrists saw too much of the old snake pit, saw too many people who shouldn't have been there and we overreacted. The result is not what we intended, and perhaps we didn't ask the questions that should have been asked when developing a new concept.[57]

One "unasked question" is simply, where would the patients go? As it turned out, they went to a diverse collection of destinations. A substantial percentage of patients, like Clifford Beers, recovered and were discharged even before the discovery of effective drug treatments.[58] Others found their way to "planned" outcomes, making a successful transition to living in the community or in other institutional settings, supported in part by Medicaid, SSDI, or SSI. Far too many ex-patients ended up in jail or back in a mental hospital after being charged with criminal behavior. (Notably, the rate of involuntary criminal commitments to mental hospitals increased by 81 percent between 1972 and 1980.[59]) Another sizable cohort ended up on the streets. As the problem of the homeless mentally ill became increasingly visible, the failure of the CMHCs to treat or prevent SMI became increasingly obvious.

In 1976, President Carter established a commission on mental health to assess the CMHC program and make recommendations regarding the future of federal mental health policy. Despite the obvious failures of the CMHCs, the commission recommended *continued funding* for the program, and appropriation of *additional* funds for "the prevention of mental illness and the promotion of positive mental health"![60] Here is a spectacular example of Planners responding to failure by proposing more of the same!

Toward the Present-Day Mental Health System

The recommendations of the Carter Commission became the substance of the Mental Health Systems Act, signed into law in October 1980 by President Carter. But the act became moot after Ronald Reagan won the presidential election in November. Reagan favored policies of lower federal taxes and limited federal involvement in social welfare programs. The 1981 Omnibus Budget Reconciliation Act ended federal funding for the CMHC program, and instead appropriated smaller block grants to the states for mental health services.[61] The era of nominal federal "responsibility" for the mentally ill had ended.

The next two decades were a period of rising health care costs and increasing dissatisfaction with the performance of the mental health system. The costs of mental health services did not rise as rapidly as other health care costs in the 1980s and 1990s, but by 1997, the United States spent "almost $71 billion on treating mental illnesses."[62] In terms of inputs, the mental health service system was fragmented and disorganized, and more than half of all persons with SMI were not receiving treatment.[63] In terms of outputs, a disproportionate share of persons with mental illness were either homeless, in prison, or unemployed.

In February 2001, President Bush announced a New Freedom Initiative to improve the lives of persons with disabilities. As part of the initiative, he created a New Freedom Commission on Mental Health "to study the problems and gaps in the mental health system and make concrete recommendations for immediate improvements."[64] The commission released its final report in July 2003. In a cover letter to President Bush, Michael Hogan, president of the commission, wrote that the nation's mental health services were:

> [F]ragmented, disconnected and often inadequate, frustrating the opportunity for recovery. Today's mental health care system is a patchwork relic—the result of disjointed reforms and policies. Instead of ready access to quality care, the system presents barriers that all too often add to the burden of mental illnesses for individuals, their families, and our communities.[65]

The commission's report sets out six broad goals for "fundamentally transforming how mental health care is delivered in America." Accompanying the goals are a set of nineteen recommendations designed to "aid in transforming the mental health system."[66] One has only to peruse the recommendations to know that the commission members were Planners, not Searchers.

Goal 4 states that "Early mental health screening, assessment, and referral to services are common practice." To attain this goal the commission recommends that the government "Promote the health of young children," and "Improve and expand school mental health services."[67] Laudable ideas to be sure, but how are they to be achieved? (*Planners identify a Big Goal, but typically have no concrete ideas how to attain the goal.*)

Where the commission's recommendations are more concrete, the proposed solutions are often costly, naïve, or untested. Goal 2 states that "Mental health care is consumer- and family-driven." One recommendation under this goal is to, "Develop an individualized plan of care for every adult with a serious mental illness and [every] child with a serious emotional disturbance."[68] How can this plan possibly be accomplished when over half of adults with SMI are not receiving treatment? (*Because Planners are disconnected from the problems they are attempting to solve, the ideas that Planners present are often impossible to implement.*)

The report recommends, also under Goal 2, that each state "Create a comprehensive State Mental Health Plan."[69] The plans are intended to hold state authorities accountable for mental health services, and to overcome the problems of fragmentation and lack of coordination in the mental health system. (*One favorite tactic of planners is to recommend more planning.*)

Once it was clear that the CMHCs had failed to achieve the Big Goal, Planners shifted responsibility for results elsewhere, unwilling to hold the federal government accountable for its part in creating the fragmented, uncoordinated system the commission bemoans. Given the kind of roadmap the commission set forth, it is not surprising that their recommendations have had little impact. The fragmented, disconnected, inadequate, and disjointed system described in the report, is what I encountered in Charlotte in 2005, and what we have today.

The Mindset of a Searcher

In 1986, Paul Janssen gave an interview in which he described the steps leading to his discovery of Haloperidol. The following are excerpts from the interview, revealing the mindset and motivations of a Searcher:

Interviewer: What led to the discovery of haloperidol?

Janssen: By varying the structure of some anesthetic drugs, we stumbled upon compounds that antagonized the effects of amphetamines on rat behavior. Since amphetamine poisoning in man produces symptoms which are also observed in paranoid schizophrenics, we did not overlook the idea of trying amphetamine antagonists in psychiatric patients. The lesson is to pay attention to unexpected findings, and to . . . link them to known facts.[70]

Interviewer: What are the responsibilities of an explorer [i.e., Searcher]?

Janssen: The specific responsibility of an explorer is to keep his eyes open and his mind prepared. . . . Somebody once told me that *a human mind is like a parachute. It works better when it's open!* [71]

Interviewer: Who should be involved, financially, in developing new drugs?

Janssen: I don't really care who [is] involved as long as they find a solution. . . . But, there must be a willingness to take needed, calculated risks. . . . Bureaucrats in general hate to take a risk. There is nothing to gain and everything to lose. It's deplorable but it seems to be a fact. . . . Then what is also needed, of course, is the motivation to reach a certain goal. Now for us as a company . . . to succeed in research is a matter of life and death. If we don't succeed we will disappear. It's very simple. The motivation to find something, to do something useful, is very, very, very, great. [72]

Interviewer: What factors are most likely to facilitate the exploratory process for a researcher [i.e., Searcher]?

Janssen: I would say the most important factor there is, is freedom. Freedom of thinking. Freedom of action. Freedom, in a general sense of the word, being the opposite of slavery and bureaucracy. . . . [But] what is most important, I think, is to learn from the past, and try to do better in the future. [73]

As Janssen's comments make clear, Searchers differ from Planners in all phases of the problem-solving process: [74]

- *Approach*—Planners come to a problem with ideology in place and corresponding solutions on the shelf. Searchers come without a preconceived idea of what the solution will be. Searchers find solutions first, ideology later.
- *Implementation*—Planners implement policy at the macro level to achieve the Big Goal. They attempt global, top-down solutions with little understanding of the complexities at the bottom. Searchers look for small opportunities to do something useful, and do not get stuck on unrealistic objectives.
- *Follow-up*—In the aftermath of a policy change, Planners have little interest in objective evaluations of the results. Far-removed from the people who are implementing their ideas, or the people who are supposed to benefit, Planners have little accountability for their actions, and no incentive to obtain feedback from those on the front lines. When Searchers implement a solution, they are accountable for results. Searchers have

incentive to evaluate outcomes because success or failure matters *to them*. In Janssen's words, success "is a matter of life or death."[75]

The NIMH emphasis on prevention activities in the community mental health centers provides a good example of disconnect between Planners at the top and those responsible for implementing plans at the bottom. Administrators of the CMHCs were cognizant of the futility of their efforts to prevent SMI, even as the directors at NIMH continued to press prevention as their primary mission. One clinic administrator declared, "When we in psychiatry wave our preventive banners we must look ridiculous to even the gods on Mount Olympus who once held the keys to all the mysteries of the universe."[76]

In sharp contrast to the glorious visions of Planners, Charles Lindblom calls policy implementation (i.e., problem solving) "the science of muddling through."[77] When I sought Dr. Perkins's advice as David was about to be discharged from his first hospitalization, she told me "trust your instincts." There was no other advice she could give; we had to "muddle through."

Postscript

In a popular educational toy for children, the "problem" is to fit geometric blocks of different shapes into a box with cutouts of corresponding shapes. Solving the puzzle is a metaphor for the cure and prevention of schizophrenia, where the interior of the box represents "mental health" and the blocks represent "persons with mental illness."

The one-year-old (Planner) has a preconceived idea of what *should* work. He finds a cutout and starts pushing blocks into it—one block fits but the rest will not. In frustration, he tries *more of the same*, and continually fails. The two-year-old (Searcher) discovers a solution that *does* work. If a block doesn't fit in one cutout he tries another place, until all the blocks are neatly in the box. The five-year-old (Wise Man) achieves the Big Goal. Just by looking, he knows which block fits which cutout, and he quickly puts the blocks away.

When it comes to treating SMI, we are not Wise Men. Scientists are beginning to unravel the complex causes of schizophrenia, but we do not yet know enough to prevent the disease. Pharmacologists have discovered drug therapies that control the symptoms of illness for many patients, but we do not yet have a cure. In our knowledge of schizophrenia we are at about the two-year-old stage: We've stumbled upon some treatments that work, we're not sure why, and what works for one case won't necessarily work for another. We have to keep trying until we get it right. Until scientists achieve the Big Goal (effective prevention and a cure for schizophrenia), policy makers must do what they can to meet the needs of persons with SMI and the families who are their primary caregivers.

The fact that the CMHCs failed to provide adequate care does not mean that a community care model cannot succeed. Even before the introduction of first-generation antipsychotics, Karl Menninger successfully implemented a model of community care in Kansas, with Topeka State Hospital as the center of an entire mental health system. Large numbers of inpatients, who had improved as much as possible with available treatments, were discharged to their communities with follow-up from hospital staff. Staff members coordinated with local agencies to ensure a successful transition. The state hospital was available if a crisis occurred.[78] Unfortunately, the lessons of Topeka were ignored by Planners of the CMHC movement.

As Menninger demonstrated, a community care model can succeed if it is driven by Searchers who are held accountable for outcomes, and staffed by people who are empowered and motivated to solve the problems that walk through their doors every day. Patients and families in crisis deserve a mental health system that says, "What do you need?" instead of, "*We can't do anything for you.*"

There are thousands of Searchers working in today's mental health system. Diana Perkins and her team at UNC Hospital are some of them. But it was Planners who created the dysfunctional mental health system I encountered in Charlotte, where no one had the freedom, or the responsibility, or the motivation, to act. In the end, it took the authority of a judge, and the persistence of a lawyer, to find a solution that worked.

Chapter Five

Default Caregivers

WHAT AM I DOING HERE?

As they were growing up, my two boys had an uncanny ability to alternate periods of problem behavior so as not to overtax their mother's resilience. When Aaron was in fifth grade, David was a well-adjusted kindergartener. Aaron disliked schoolwork and did as little of it as possible. On parents' night, his teacher asked us to sit at our child's desk. All the desks were arranged in neat little groups around the room except one; my desk was next to the teacher's. "I was always a good little girl in school," I thought, "*What am I doing here?*" Fifteen years later, Aaron had a master's degree in computer science from Boston University and a good job working for the Center for Naval Analyses in Virginia. David was having a psychotic breakdown in Charlotte.

Spring 2005

The crisis came on a Saturday morning in April, when David had a fight with his housemate. The young man filed charges for assault, and a warrant was issued for David's arrest. We tried to contact him by cell phone throughout that day and evening, and finally reached him Sunday morning. We advised him to turn himself in to the police, which he did, whereupon he was arrested and incarcerated in the county jail. Through contacts in North Carolina, we found a lawyer who specialized in criminal cases involving persons with disabilities. The lawyer was somewhat reassuring: David had no prior criminal record; his housemate was not seriously injured; David would likely be released on his own recognizance the following day.

My experience with the justice system went no further than jury duty and settling a few traffic tickets. To me, the fact that my son was in jail, and charged with assault, was appalling. To David's lawyer, it was a minor felony. Still, at the arraignment the next day the judge refused to release David without bond, because of his diagnosis of schizophrenia. David, who had been denied admission to the psychiatric hospital because he was "not sick enough," was apparently "too sick" to be released from jail. Once again, we flew to Charlotte.

My first priority was to see my son. We talked by intercom, seated on opposite sides of a glass barricade, David dressed in an orange prison jumpsuit. He looked so pathetic that my eyes filled with tears. He was clearly relieved to see us and agreed to admit himself to the hospital immediately after he was released from jail. He had one pressing concern. "Mom, I parked my car in front of the jail when I turned myself in. Is it still there?" On that awful day, we had one piece of good luck: His car was still there.

Our next task was to post bond. How does one go about bailing someone out of jail? Although the bond office is conveniently located in the same building as the jail, that is the *only* convenient part. Contrary to the advertising slogan ("For everything else there's . . ."), you cannot post bail with MasterCard. We secured a certified check and took our place in line to pay. The scene was surrealistic. The bond office was open; everyone stood obediently in line; but there was no one at the counter. I thought, "*What am I doing here?*"

Eventually, I asked the people ahead of us what was wrong. They obviously had some experience with the system, because they merely sighed and said, "Nothing. It's always like this." I decided it was not prudent to make a fuss about poor service in such close proximity to the jail, so we waited, and waited. Finally, the bond was posted and David was released. He gave me a huge hug.

We proceeded to the hospital, where I was certain David would be admitted now that he was "a danger to himself or others." But no. David had been taking his medications while he was in jail. He was lucid, he was rational, and the physician on call refused to admit him. Instead, she asked me what I wanted to do:

"I want David to come home with us, on certain conditions."

"What conditions?"

"He has to see a psychiatrist regularly and take his medications as prescribed. No drinking. No recreational drugs."

"What about smoking?"

"It's OK—outside the house. I can't take everything away from him."

"That all sounds quite reasonable. What do you say, David?"

David agreed. Our Charlotte nightmare had almost ended—except that David had been living there for nearly three years and we had only two days to pack and store his belongings before flying home. We cleaned and scrubbed the house, assured his roommates we would continue to pay David's share of the rent, loaded a rental truck with his furniture, and left everything with my brother in Wake Forest.

Before departing from Charlotte, we met with David's lawyer. He assured us that David could leave the state, so long as he returned to Charlotte when his case went to court. There was just one glitch in this plan. North Carolina has a jail diversion program designed to redirect persons with SMI out of the criminal justice system and into treatment in the community mental health system. The lawyer wanted David in the program, because once completed, the felony charges against him would be dropped and his criminal record expunged. The glitch was that David would not be living in North Carolina. So the lawyer charged us with finding a similar program in Arizona which the court might be persuaded to allow as a substitute.

With this charge, and our son, we left Charlotte behind. On the flight home to Phoenix, I was physically and emotionally exhausted. I wondered how I could summon the energy to help David put his life back together— one more time.

Summer 2005

Here is the situation we faced when we arrived home: David had nowhere to live, except with his parents. He owned a car, on which he owed monthly payments, and little else. The car was in North Carolina, along with all his other belongings. David had not worked in four months. He had exhausted his savings and charged his credit card to the limits. He was facing assault charges in North Carolina. He had schizophrenia and needed medication and psychiatric care. *If only the system had helped us get him home in February, before the legal problems and the huge debts! Now, where did we begin?*

The first priority was medical care. With the help of friends, I found a wonderful psychiatrist in Phoenix who agreed to treat David until we could enroll him in the state behavioral health system. The state would provide medications and mental health services at no charge. The covered services included physician visits, case management, vocational counseling, even a crisis hotline. Had we found another model system of mental health care such as we had known in Chapel Hill? Not exactly.

The public behavioral health system in Arizona did not have sufficient resources, nor was it structured, to provide the kind of comprehensive, supportive care we received when David was first diagnosed. Staff turnover in the behavioral health offices was so common that I never had regular contact with David's physicians, and even David could not predict who he would see on any given visit. I discovered that the "crisis team," which responded to emergency situations involving a patient with mental illness, could not be activated by family members. The team only responded to calls from a patient, or with a patient's consent. The vocational services were useless. On the plus side, every physician and case manager I encountered while David was a patient in the system was a caring and competent professional, and the system provided psychiatric services and medications for David at no out-of-pocket cost to us.

The second issue was David's finances. We decided that he should declare bankruptcy to eliminate his credit card debt. We salvaged his one valuable possession, his car, by transferring the title to his father's name and assuming the payments. Perhaps I should feel guilty about cheating the system this way, but I don't. I feel the system cheated David, by not allowing anyone to help him until he was penniless and in jail.

The legal issues were some of the most difficult to resolve. I searched in vain for a jail diversion program in Arizona that was comparable to the one in North Carolina. I contacted Arizona Department of Health Services, Division of Behavioral Health Services, Adult Probation Offices, even the Superior Court, with no success. In July, with David's court date approaching, I told his lawyer there was no such program in Arizona, please just settle the case. The lawyer resisted. He requested an extension from the court and told me to keep looking.

Finally, I found the website for the Treatment Assessment Screening Center (TASC). TASC is a private, nonprofit corporation that works collaboratively with the Arizona Department of Corrections to facilitate drug testing and behavioral health programs in the state. In Maricopa County, TASC manages an adult deferred prosecution program for individuals facing felony drug charges, and a misdemeanor deferred prosecution program for first-time offenders whose offense does not involve physical injury to another person. Neither program exactly fit David's situation, but with another court date looming, I was desperate. I called the director of TASC and found—a Searcher. He volunteered to contact David's lawyer and to personally monitor a diversion plan for David. He was confident they could work out a plan the court would accept. He was right.

Fall 2005

David's diversion plan consisted of community service (janitorial work at the local YMCA), regular visits to his psychiatrist, and adherence to his medication. In addition, he had to submit to regular drug and alcohol testing at TASC. Whenever TASC announced a "red" day, David had twelve hours to report for testing. The diversion plan resolved David's legal problems and gave me a few months respite from policing his medications.

We had addressed David's immediate problems, but we were years away from putting his life back together. He was twenty-eight years old, with no job, no money, and no friends. He was living at home, dependent on his parents for everything from food to entertainment. *What was he doing here?*

Most days he amused himself by playing poker online, but as the months wore on, he became more and more depressed.

FAMILY CAREGIVERS

In the wake of massive discharges from state mental hospitals, family members became the default caregivers for persons with serious mental illness. Planners of the community care movement assumed the vast majority of ex-mental patients would return home to live with a sympathetic and supportive family.[1] Quite the contrary, many patients had no home to which to return and nowhere to go. Today, approximately 40 percent of persons with schizophrenia are either homeless (4.5 percent), institutionalized (6 percent in jail; 12 percent in hospitals or nursing homes), or living in other supervised settings (18 percent).[2]

Even so, families shoulder a tremendous share of the caretaking responsibilities for persons with SMI. Approximately 55 percent of persons with schizophrenia either live with their families, or have daily contact with family members.[3] Yet there are few institutional structures in place to educate family caregivers. There is no one to facilitate communication between family members and formal caregivers; no one to provide support in dealing with the challenges of caregiving; and no one to call in a crisis, except the police. In fact, the legal system has erected barriers that often prevent family caregivers from having any input into medical decisions that affect their relatives. Sometimes, as in the case of William Bruce, the results are tragic.

At age twenty-one, William Bruce had a first psychotic episode, but he refused to seek medical care. Two years later, after threatening two men with an assault rifle, William was committed to a psychiatric facility. He was successfully treated with antipsychotic drugs and released, whereupon he stopped taking his medications.

Within one year, William physically attacked both parents. He was committed to an extended care psychiatric facility, but he refused all medical treatment. His psychiatrist described his condition as "hostile, paranoid, and dangerous to others." Nevertheless, patient advocates employed by Disability Rights Maine began working with William to obtain his release. His psychiatrist opposed their efforts, stating that William's paranoid psychosis was unlikely to improve without treatment.

The case became so contentious that a new psychiatrist was assigned. He requested permission to speak with William's parents, but William and his advocates refused. The advocates claimed William's parents were "a negative influence in his life." Given the advocates' position that William was not dangerous, the psychiatrist had no authority to keep him hospitalized beyond his court-ordered confinement. Against his doctors' recommendations,

William was released on April 20, 2006. He returned home to live with his parents. On June 20 of the same year, William killed his mother with an axe to the skull.[4]

Burden of Care

The term *burden of care* (or *family burden*) is used to describe the myriad ways caring for a relative with mental illness affects a family. Fortunately, the story of William Bruce is a rare and extreme example of the price a family pays. It is much more common for the story to end in jail, suicide, or alienation of family members.

Caregiving imposes a combination of physical work, emotional stress, social alienation, and economic pressures, all of which can have a tremendous impact on family members.[5] In the family support group we joined when David first became sick, I was struck by the high proportion of single parents, mostly mothers, in attendance. Many of these families had broken apart under the burden of caring for a son or daughter with SMI.

When caregivers are asked to describe the negative impact of schizophrenia on their family, they talk about *economic* pressures, their own *health* problems, difficulties participating in *social* activities and maintaining social relationships.[6] They also identify *emotions* ranging from depression, embarrassment, and hopelessness to a profound sense of loss. Thus, it is not only the magnitude of the crisis of mental illness that affects family members so deeply, but the sheer breadth of the impact on almost every aspect of their lives.

Economic Burden

The economic burden of caring for a relative with schizophrenia can be a significant drain on family resources. Direct costs borne by family members may include: out-of-pocket expenditures for the *patient's medical care* (psychiatric hospitalizations, outpatient visits, medications, rehabilitation services, etc.); costs associated with the *criminal justice system* (lawyers' fees, damages, fines, etc.); and *travel costs* (if the patient is in a hospital, jail, or living at a distance from their family). Indirect costs include *losses of income* associated with family members' lost work time; and out-of-pocket expenditures for *medical care for family members* whose health is compromised by caregiving responsibilities.

In many cases, the family also provides support for living expenses for the patient (housing, board, clothing, social activities, insurance payments, unpaid bills, etc.). Strictly speaking, these costs represent a transfer of income within the family unit, rather than a net loss of resources. Nonetheless, the costs are a greater burden at the margin to the family than to the patient, if they were well.

There are no current and comprehensive estimates, specific to the United States, of the economic burden on families caring for a relative with schizophrenia. Some studies attempt to parse out the portion of the overall burden of the disease that is borne by family members, but these estimates do not provide micro-measures of the resources expended by individual families.[7] One of the first studies to provide such micro-estimates was conducted by Deborah Franks in the late 1980s. Franks collected data on illness-related expenditures from a sample of 408 Massachusetts families caring for a relative with SMI. Thirty percent of families were caring for their relative at home. Among these families, average annual expenditures associated with the relative's mental illness were $4,458, or 10 percent of median family income in Massachusetts in 1987.[8]

Around the time of the survey, one Massachusetts region was under a consent decree to escalate deinstitutionalization of mental patients and expand community residential facilities for patients who were released. Because of the increased public funding in this region, a smaller proportion of persons with SMI were living with their families, and average family expenditures on SMI were lower than in other regions of the state. Franks exploited this natural experiment to estimate the degree to which family expenditures on mental illness substitute for expenditures by the state. The results showed that for every $1 decrease in state spending, family spending increased by $4.[9] Thus, what is viewed as an economic burden by the family is a major contribution of private resources to the care of the mentally ill. Moreover, shifting the costs onto families increases the total costs of care.

A more recent study of the economic burden of care reports estimates of illness-related expenditures for 150 Belgian families who were primary caregivers for a patient with schizophrenia. The authors conducted face-to-face interviews with family members, asking about various aspects of caregiver burden, including illness-related expenditures. On average, families reported spending 2,623€ (or about US $4,070 in 2013) on patients in the year preceding the interview. Median annual income of respondents was between 14,868€ and 20,820€, so the economic burden represented a significant (13 percent to 18 percent) share of an average family's resources.[10]

Studies such as these suggest that families bear a considerable economic burden when a relative is diagnosed with SMI. We do not have comprehensive, current estimates of the costs to family caregivers in the United States, but the available evidence suggests total annual costs may be 10 to 20 percent of median family income, a nonnegligible sum.

Social Burden

The social burden of care reflects the impact of caregiving on interpersonal relationships and social activities, both within and beyond the immediate family. Within the family, the social impact ranges from small frustrations, such as having difficulty getting away for family outings, to major upheavals, such as alienation of family members, separation, or divorce. Outside the family, the social burden is perceived through experiences of stigma, losses of friendships, and feelings of isolation.

The Belgian survey of families caring for patients with schizophrenia included a number of questions to assess the social burden of care. In response to these questions:

- 46 percent of participants said that their household atmosphere was tense
- 31 percent said that contact with certain friends had diminished or broken off entirely
- 19 percent said that a family member had left home or threatened to leave home[11]

A recent study examined how the social burden of caring for a family member with mental illness changes with duration of illness.[12] The study compared family functioning among 150 Greek families who were either caring for a relative with *first-episode psychosis*, or caring for a relative with *chronic psychotic illness*, or part of a control group that reported no history of psychiatric illness in the family. Family functioning was assessed on measures of cohesion (emotional bonding), flexibility (with respect to leadership and family roles), and communications.

The results showed that *families dealing with chronic illness had significantly higher levels of dysfunction* than families caring for a relative with first-episode psychosis. In other words, family cohesion and flexibility appeared to deteriorate with chronicity.[13] As the woman in my support group (chapter 2) said, "You're new to this dear, wait until you've been dealing with it for years."

In 2002, two nursing professors conducted in-depth interviews with twenty-six families, who were primary caregivers for a relative with schizophrenia, to assess how the family was functioning. The themes that emerged provide poignant evidence of the social upheaval SMI can create within a family:

> It is easier for [other] family members to ignore the problem and offer advice—kick our son out of the house if he wouldn't get help. A parent can't do this to a child. [Our other children] wouldn't visit because of our son's behavior. So we lost all our children and grandchildren.[14]

The social isolation extends beyond the boundaries of the family:

> People are unfriendly. I have not felt that people disliked me, but I do know that mental illness has a strange effect on those not familiar with the illness.[15]

Health Burden

In light of the economic and social stressors associated with caring for a relative with schizophrenia, it is not surprising that caregiving often has a negative impact on the health of family members. Research shows that the health-related burden of care manifests itself in lower self-reported health status, increased utilization of health services, and poorer physical/mental functioning among caregivers, relative to the general population.[16] One study, for example, used 1998 administrative data from Blue Cross/Blue Shield, to compare health care costs for family members living with a relative with SMI, versus control families not dealing with mental illness. Living with a family member who has schizophrenia increased annual expenditures on health care for *others* in the family by $161 (in 2013 dollars) per family member. Surprisingly, health costs were significantly higher for those dealing with bipolar disorder ($312 per family member), despite the fact that patients with schizophrenia were more seriously ill (as measured by the annual health care costs of *patients* in the study).[17]

A more recent study focused on the elevated risk of depression in a sample of eighty-five Latino caregivers of relatives with schizophrenia. Forty percent of participants reported psychiatric symptoms that met or exceeded the criterion for elevated risk of depression, far higher than the norm in general population studies of Latinos (13 percent to 18 percent).[18]

Emotional Burden

The emotional strain of caring for a relative with schizophrenia is intense and, at times, overwhelming. Caregivers express fears about the future, concerns about disruptions in the lives of other family members, feelings of embarrassment or shame, and even a haunting guilt that they somehow caused the illness.[19] The emotional burden is almost universal among family caregivers. In the study of Belgian families caring for relatives with schizophrenia, for example, 98 percent of respondents indicated that they felt emotionally burdened by their role, at least some of the time.[20]

A small Canadian study of parents' reactions to their child's first psychiatric hospitalization reveals some of the emotional turmoil that accompanies a diagnosis of mental illness. Most parents initially responded as I did: with relief, that the problem had been identified; and hope, that the problem could be cured.[21] Once the family realized there was no cure, relief and hope changed to disbelief and shock, "it's like, this is not happening. This is *not* happening."[22]

In the interview study conducted by the nursing professors, participants had, on average, seventeen years of experience caring for their relative. Yet they still reported overwhelming emotions associated with caregiving, ranging from anger and bewilderment, to hopelessness and chronic sorrow.

Watching their relative struggle with schizophrenia, family members said that they felt confused, frightened, and frustrated, because they did not know what to expect, or how to help. One caregiver said, "I felt hopeless. There was nowhere to turn."[23]

Researchers in Italy compared family burden among caregivers dealing with several different types of chronic illnesses, including schizophrenia. Data were collected from more than 1,350 key relatives. The results indicate that the emotional burden of care is significantly more prevalent among families dealing with schizophrenia or brain disease, than among families dealing with other chronic illnesses.[24] Among the families dealing with schizophrenia:

- Eight percent reported that they felt embarrassed by their relative in public places, compared to almost none of the relatives dealing with other diseases.
- Eleven percent said that they "were not able to handle the situation much longer," compared to less than 6 percent of relatives dealing with other diseases.
- Fifty percent reported constant feelings of loss, compared to only 25 percent to 40 percent of relatives dealing with other diseases.[25]

I empathize with these family members. To me, the heaviest burden of having a son with schizophrenia was the grief I felt over the loss of a beloved child. In a very real sense, the person that I watched grow from infant to young adult was gone, along with my hopes for his future. Other parents express similar feelings:

> You've lost the person, the expectations, the athletic guy, the pretty good marks. . . . You're losing your dreams of where he will be, of having a normal life and having a family and of grandchildren . . . and you're grieving for yourself but also grieving for them because you know . . . that their lives will be different.[26]

Determinants of the Burden of Care

As suggested from the various comments here, the nature and intensity of family burden depends on characteristics of both patient and caregiver, and the ways they respond to the near-complete disruption of their lives.

Patient Characteristics

The severity of a patient's symptoms is one of the most important determinants, if not the most important determinant, of family burden. Both positive (e.g., delusions, hallucinations) and negative (e.g., apathy, poverty of speech) symptoms are disruptive to family members. Neither cluster has been established as more troublesome than the other.[27] Simply put, the more severe the symptoms, the greater the burden of care.

Similarly, the greater the functional limitations, the greater the burden of care.[28] If a patient has limited functional capacities (e.g., ability to manage housework, prepare meals, handle money), family caregivers must assume the functions on the patient's behalf, making caregiving more time-consuming and disruptive. On the other hand, if a patient has the capacity to work, the family burden is significantly eased.

A German study of 102 primary caregivers of patients with chronic mental illness evaluated the relative impact of various patient/caregiver characteristics, including the capacity to work, on the family's burden of care. Among the patient characteristics the authors considered (severity of symptoms, duration of illness, problems with everyday living, regular employment), they concluded that a "patients' regular employment appears most important in reducing caregivers' psychological distress and enhancing their well-being."[29] The result makes sense. Regular employment provides income and social connections for the patient, thereby easing some of the family's concerns about the future.

Other research suggests that the younger the patient at onset of illness, the greater the burden of care.[30] Age at onset primarily affects the emotional burden of caregiving. Caregivers express greater emotional concerns about the patient's physical safety, everyday life, financial resources, and prospects for the future, when onset occurs at a young age.[31]

Family burden also increases with patient substance abuse, nonadherence to medications, and suicidal ideation, with the latter being by far the most distressing to caregivers.[32] A study led by a clinical psychologist at Washington State University tested a model of family burden using data from ninety patients with schizophrenia, and their family caregivers.[33] The model included a number of patient behaviors (substance abuse, depression, suicidal ideation) along with other patient characteristics. Caregiver awareness of a patient's suicidal thoughts was found to be a strong and significant predictor of family burden, while substance abuse was only marginally significant.[34]

Unfortunately, thoughts of suicide are common among patients with schizophrenia. Over the course of the study cited previously, 49 percent of patients reported suicidal thoughts, and 13 percent attempted suicide (none were successful). A meta-analysis of more than five dozen studies estimates that the lifetime risk of suicide is 4.9 percent among persons with schizophrenia.[35] The risk of suicide is even higher in the early phases of psychosis, and may be as high as 10 percent in the year following an initial psychiatric hospitalization.[36] The emotional impact on caregivers is unimaginable.

Caregiver Characteristics

On the caregiver side, the burden of care depends largely on an individual's ability to cope with demands that far exceed the demands of everyday life.[37] The capacity to identify and adopt successful coping strategies depends on resources both internal (an individual's innate approach to problem solving) and external (a support network of friends, counselors, spiritual advisors etc.).

With respect to internal resources: A *passive* approach to coping is characterized by strategies such as avoidance, resignation, assigning blame, or wishful thinking. An *active* approach is characterized by problem solving, reaching out to others for support, and thinking positively ("count your blessings").[38] In general, active coping strategies lead to better outcomes for both patient and caregiver. Active and supportive family relationships help patients adapt to their illness, improve their adherence to treatment, and increase their likelihood of recovery.[39] Caregivers with a broad range of active coping skills also experience less burden of care, all else equal, than caregivers who cope in passive ways.[40]

With respect to *external* resources: Support networks ease the burden of care by providing assistance with the practical problems of caregiving (e.g., information, periods of respite) and by helping the caregiver adopt more effective coping strategies. High levels of support are associated with active, problem-solving coping strategies that reduce the burden of care. Low levels of support are associated with passive coping strategies, in part because avoidance and resignation are natural responses to the kind of desperation that external support might alleviate.[41]

Given the many ways that support networks ease the burden of caring for a relative with schizophrenia, it is telling that many family members identify "inadequate economic and social support," and "lack of access to information and support networks" as among the greatest problems they face.[42] In the Italian study of caregivers dealing with various chronic illnesses, schizophrenia differed from all other illnesses in the low levels of professional and social support reported by family members.[43] Similarly, lack of support was frequently mentioned by participants in the study of parents dealing with a child's first psychiatric hospitalization:

> Most of our friends didn't understand it. Lord knows we didn't, so it was hard for them. They stayed away because they didn't know what to say. [So] here we are on this little island and we're all floating and we're going to drown real soon.[44]

I was lucky. When David became ill, I had strong support from family, friends, colleagues at work, and the study team at Chapel Hill.

One encounter in particular stands out. In the first summer after David was diagnosed, I went through a low period of anger and self-pity, wondering "Why did this happen to *my* son?" I sought help from my pastor, who told me the following story:

> My grandchildren and I like to go down to the bay to watch the ducks swimming. They make it look so easy, gliding across the top of the water. But if you look underneath, you'll see their feet are paddling just as hard as they can go. That's how it is with other people. They look like they're gliding easily through life, but underneath they're all paddling just as hard as they can.

After that conversation, instead of wondering, "Why me?" I tried to think, "Why not me?" The story of the ducks pulled me out of many emotional troughs.

The Mental Health System and Family Burden

The American Psychiatric Association (APA) recognizes that the "social circumstances of the patient can have profound effects on adherence and response to treatment."[45] Because the "social circumstances" of so many patients with schizophrenia are confined to their immediate family, the APA practice guideline for schizophrenia includes specific recommendations to involve families in treatment plans. For example:

- *Engagement of family and other significant support persons*, with the patient's permission, is recommended to further strengthen the therapeutic effort.
- *Efforts to engage and collaborate with family members and other natural caregivers* are often successful during the crisis of an acute psychotic episode . . . and are strongly recommended.[46]

The APA guideline recognizes that a family's ability to cope with the demands of caregiving has a significant impact on patient outcomes, and that professional and social support are key determinants of the family's ability to cope. Therefore, the guideline for schizophrenia also recommends,

- *Interventions that educate family members* about schizophrenia . . . to provide support and offer training in effective problem solving and communication,
- It is equally critical to maintain a level of momentum aimed at improving community functioning in order to *instill a sense of hope and progress for the patient and family*.[47]

The support we received from the team in Chapel Hill conformed to every aspect of the guideline. However, this kind of all-encompassing care is not the norm in the U.S. mental health system. Family psychosocial interventions, which have demonstrated efficacy in reducing family burden and improving patient outcomes, are not widely used in practice.[48] Mental health professionals often ignore (and are sometimes even hostile toward) family members.[49] All too often, as we discovered in Charlotte, there is simply no help available when a crisis occurs.

So, why does the mental health system put so much responsibility on family members, yet provide so little support? There are likely many factors involved, but here I will focus on two: the misallocation of resources in the public mental health system, and the still widely held belief that families cause more harm than good.

Resources: An Embarrassment of Riches

In a recent book recounting the evolution of U.S. mental health policy since 1950, economists Richard Frank and Sherry Glied document the tremendous increase in spending for mental health services that occurred over the last half of the twentieth century. "Spending [in current dollars] grew more than seventyfold, from $1.14 billion in 1956 to $85.4 billion in 2001."[50] State spending increased more than 440 percent over the period, federal spending increased almost 840 percent.[51]

The tremendous infusion of funds for mental health care, coincident with the movement of patients out of state hospitals, dramatically changed the landscape of mental health services in the United States. The number of inpatient psychiatric beds declined from more than twenty-four per ten thousand persons in 1970, to fewer than seven per ten thousand persons in 2000. The staff-to-patient ratio in state and county mental hospitals increased, and length of stay declined. There was tremendous growth in the size and diversity of the mental health workforce including increases in the number of clinical psychologists, psychiatric nurses, and others providing direct patient care. New institutional arrangements emerged to expand options for community care, including partial hospitalization programs, and specialty managed care programs for behavioral health services.[52] In summing up the expanded supply of mental health services that emerged over this period, the authors say, "The consumer in 2000 had, by historical standards, a vast array of well-trained professionals and institutions from which to receive treatment."[53]

The new psychiatric specialties and institutions that emerged, however, were best equipped to deal with mental illnesses of moderate severity. For persons with serious mental illness, the outlook was not so rosy. The one mental health specialty qualified to prescribe antipsychotic drugs, the psychiatrist, declined in supply relative to other medical specialties between 1965 and 2000. Likewise, the one institution equipped to deal with acute psychosis, the psychiatric hospital, contracted sharply over this period. In many states, the decentralization of mental health services left no one, except families, responsible for persons with SMI. Thus, in describing the overall transformation of mental health services in the last fifty years of the twentieth century, Frank and Glied conclude (emphasis added):

> The consequence has been to exchange a set of bureaucratic failures and tight budgets that took care of all services for a circumscribed population for a vastly richer, decentralized system of care that suffers from market failure, and *allows some people with significant impairments to fall through the cracks.*[54]

The redirection of mental health funds to providers and service organizations best suited to care for the moderately ill is one reason why there are insufficient resources in the public mental health system to provide appropriate care (as outlined in the APA Practice Guideline) for patients with SMI and their family caregivers. Resource constraints help to explain why we could not get David admitted to a psychiatric facility in Charlotte, even when he agreed to voluntary hospitalization.

Between 2001 and 2012, the number of inpatient beds in state psychiatric hospitals in North Carolina declined by nearly 50 percent, from 1,755 to 850.[55] The state hospitals serve a small and well-defined population, namely, persons with chronic and severe mental illness, who are nonresponsive to antipsychotic drugs and lack family or social support. David responded well to antipsychotic medication and had family support, so he clearly did not belong in a state hospital.

Without health insurance, David's only realistic option for inpatient care was Randolph Community Mental Health Center. The center, which serves the city of Charlotte and surrounding Mecklenberg County, maintained forty-four adult inpatient beds in 2005. Between 1998 and 2005, average daily adult occupancy rates at the center increased from 82 to 95 percent of capacity.[56] On the day we tried to admit David in 2005, forty-two inpatient beds were likely occupied. What I understand now, but did not know then, is that David had little chance of being admitted unless he arrived in custody of the police. In fact, among those persons brought to North Carolina hospital emergency rooms with behavioral health crises in 2012, only 28 percent were admitted to a community psychiatric facility. The majority (53 percent) were released to their families or self-care.[57]

Attitudes: Families Are Part of the Problem

Resource constraints can explain, at least in part, why family support services are not common practice in the mental health system, but not why patient advocates for William Bruce expressed such negative attitudes toward his family. Without ever having met Joe and Amy Bruce, the advocates concluded that William's parents were "a negative force" in his life. The attitude is reminiscent of the early twentieth century, when Freudian theories dominated psychiatry, and environmental theorists viewed families as the root cause of mental illness. Today, genetic research has made tremendous strides in identifying the physiological bases for mental illness, but medical models of SMI have not entirely dispelled the view that families are, at least in part, to blame.[58]

A 2003 study reported data from a survey of forty-eight mental health providers and thirty-nine family members that was designed to assess their beliefs about the causes of mental illness. The vast majority of respondents (90 percent of providers and 92 percent of family members) agreed with the statement that "Severe mental illness is biologically based." However,

- Forty-four percent of providers and 23 percent of family members also agreed that, "Behavior of family members can cause the onset of mental illness."
- Twenty-seven percent of providers and 15 percent of family members agreed that "Poor family communication can cause severe mental illness."[59]

It is intriguing that survey respondents expressed beliefs supporting both biological and family causation theories of mental illness. The authors argue that simultaneous support for the two theories is consistent with the prevailing *diathesis-stress* model of mental illness.[60] In this model, the environment is viewed as a contributing risk factor to the onset of mental illness, although not the primary cause. Still, the link to the environment may explain why beliefs in family causation persist, and continue to be a barrier to provider/family interaction.

Providers who believe that a dysfunctional family is partly to blame for mental illness are unlikely to see any point in collaborating with family members.[61] For example, clinicians participating in a Veteran's Administration trial of a family intervention program for patients with psychosis generally perceived patients' families to be "dysfunctional, inconsistent, and usually the problem."[62] These same clinicians expressed skepticism about the benefits of family interventions *even before the study began.*

In the extreme, there are professionals, like the patient advocates for William Bruce, who contend that family engagement is not merely unhelpful, but also harmful for patients with SMI.[63] But where do the patients go, after the advocates obtain their release? To their "dysfunctional" families, *of course,* because there is nowhere else for them to go. And, the families willingly pick up the burden, *of course,* because that is how families become default caregivers in the first place. Amy Bruce paid the ultimate price for the failure of the mental health system to collaborate with family members, but Joe Bruce has not given up on his son.

William Bruce was charged with murder following his mother's death. In March 2007, he was found "not criminally responsible by reason of insanity," and was confined to a psychiatric facility for an indefinite period. Facing the alternatives of taking antipsychotic medication willingly, or being physically restrained and forcibly medicated, William agreed to take the drug as prescribed. Within weeks, his mental status improved.

Joe Bruce is William's court-appointed guardian and talks with his son nearly every day. In May 2013, Joe testified before a Congressional Committee examining the performance of the Substance Abuse and Mental Health Services Administration, the federal agency that supports the patient advocacy program. Mr. Bruce testified that neither he nor his wife had ever met any of the advocates who claimed that William's family was "a negative force in his life." Mr. Bruce further testified that neither the patient advocates, nor Disability Rights Maine, ever admitted any wrongdoing in facilitating William's discharge, or any intention of changing their procedures in the future.[64]

Today, William is doing well. He takes criminal justice classes online and hopes to attend law school someday. Of his mother's death, he says, "I blame the illness and I blame myself. The guilt is—tough." Of his father, "He stood by me the whole time, despite . . . what I did. I am the man I am today because of my dad." Of the patient advocates and the mental health system, "There are times when people should be committed. Institutions can really help. Medications can help. None of this would have happened if I had been medicated."[65]

The U.S. mental health system imposes an enormous burden on families to care for persons with even the most serious mental illnesses. Mental health providers and policy makers must recognize that everyone benefits when the system allocates a share of its resources to ensure that family members are not overwhelmed, or harmed, by the caregiver role. Beyond that, the system has a moral responsibility *to* the families on whom it places such a tremendous responsibility *for* care.

Postscript

The fact that we refer to caregiving as a *burden* gives the role an entirely negative connotation. The word burden derives from an Old English word related to birth, and means "that which is borne." The Oxford English Dictionary (OED) defines burden as "a load of labor, duty, responsibility, blame, sin, sorrow."[66] Caring for a relative with schizophrenia is all these things, and more.

Most of the research on caring for a relative with mental illness focuses on the negative aspects of caregiving, but a few studies investigate positive aspects of the role as well. Caregivers generally are able to identify at least one reward associated with their experience, and most can identify several rewarding aspects. The rewards they mention reflect the growth in character that comes from dealing with adversity: feelings of empowerment and inner strength, increases in self-esteem, and the maturity and life experience that comes with meeting a challenge. [67]

From my own experience I can add two more items to the list, namely, a clear understanding of priorities, and a unique bond with my son. During the summer David was recovering from his first psychotic episode, one of my colleagues told me that he was feeling pressured by the competing demands of teaching, research, and family, and did not know what was more important. I said, *"I always know what is most important."* He understood. Another wise colleague told me, around the same time, *"You will have a different relationship with your son."* He was right. David and I walked through hell together. It changes you.

Part II

Working with Schizophrenia

Chapter Six

Work First

HAPPY UN-BIRTHDAY

Fall 2007

David's thirtieth birthday was one of the saddest days of my life. By then, he had been living with us for more than two years and still had no job. We did the usual birthday things: dinner at a nice restaurant, cake and candles, presents. David went through the celebration halfheartedly, but after opening all the presents, his eyes filled with tears. When I asked what was wrong, he said, "I'm thirty years old. I live with my parents. I have no money, no job, and no future. Don't ever celebrate my birthday again. It's just another day." I held my son in my arms and cried with him.

We had tried repeatedly over the previous two years to address David's employment situation. A few months after he arrived in Arizona, in summer 2005, David and I met with his case manager from the state behavioral health services office. I asked about vocational services. "Oh yes, we have a social worker who helps our clients find jobs." I was delighted, and frankly surprised, to have an offer of someone to help. Within a few weeks we met with the social worker, whereupon my delight quickly turned to disappointment. She was a meek little grandmotherly type, whose only suggestion for David was a job collecting coins from vending machines. Was this why he had struggled so hard to complete his degree?

Over the next few months, David made several attempts to find employment on his own. He saw an advertisement online and thought he might try being a model. Of course, I thought he was handsome enough. We paid for a portfolio of photos and David registered with a modeling agency. They called him for one job, a photo shoot for a billboard, but he never heard from the agency again. The possibility of a modeling career fizzled.

Then David interviewed for a job as a cost estimator for a local construction company. During college, he had worked weekends with my brother, Gordon, who was designing and building his own home. It was an enormous project that gave David experience in all aspects of construction, from framing to roofing. He seemed to have an intuitive understanding of the building process. Gordon told me one day, "I love working with David, I only tell him once, and he understands exactly what I want him to do." The experience paid off and David was offered the job with the construction company. I was elated—a real job at last! David completed three half-days of training, but when it came time to work a full day, it was too much. He called me and said, "I couldn't do it, Mom, I was on the highway driving to work, but I just turned around and came home." I was immensely disappointed, but I didn't want to make him feel worse. I simply said, "It's OK. You'll know when the right job comes along."

By fall 2006, David had stopped searching for work. Except for regular visits to his case manager and psychiatrist, he stayed home, where his father and I were his only social contacts. The three of us usually went out to dinner on Friday nights, but otherwise David refused to go to parties or social events. When a close friend invited the three of us to her annual St. Patrick's Day party, I urged him to come along, but he still said "no." "What would I talk about Mom? I don't do anything. I don't have anything to say." In fact, his only regular social interaction was watching *Fear Factor* with me. There's something about watching people leap onto speeding trucks, or eat scorpions, which makes conversation easier—even for someone with mental illness. We laughed together at the crazy stunts, and the *really* crazy people who did them.

During these days, David spent most of his spare time (and *all* of his time was spare) playing poker online. At first he played in no-stakes games, but as he improved he thought he might become good enough to be a professional poker player. Of course, I thought he was smart enough. Eventually, we gave him a $1,000 stake to see what he could win. When it was gone, his poker career fizzled.

By then, I was chair of a dysfunctional department at my university. (Most academic departments are dysfunctional, but ours had more than its share of histrionic personalities.) I was paid well, but working long hours, short on staff, and frustrated that my research was stalled. David had free time, no money, and good computer skills. One day I put the pieces together and told David I would personally pay him to work as my research assistant on an hourly basis. At first he balked; it was easier to simply ask us for what little money he needed. But I told him the free money had stopped. We settled into a work routine, and he was *earning* money again.

Fall 2008

As birthday thirty-one approached, I could not ignore it, but I did not want a repeat of thirty, and David had ordered, "No more birthdays." So I made a card for him saying, *"Happy Un-Birthday!"* I put candles on an *unfrosted* cake and gave him *unwrapped* presents for his *unspecial* day. David smiled. Perhaps there would be better birthdays to come.

It reminded me of an incident that occurred during the first summer he was sick. I had to travel to western North Carolina to visit the worksite of one of our research projects. I invited David to come along, as a break from sitting around home every day. He agreed. We began driving west late one afternoon. As we came over a ridge in the little town of Wilson, North Carolina, the setting sun unexpectedly appeared before us as an enormous, blazing ball of light. "It's a sign," I said, "of better days to come." David smiled.

MENTAL ILLNESS AND WORK

Why work? Work is, first and foremost, a source of income, security, and financial independence. But in modern economies work is much more than a means of support. Work is a source of pride and dignity in a job, any job, well done. Work is a way to connect with others, to make friends, to engage in social interaction. Work is a source of self-esteem, a validation that one is a productive member of society, that one's skills and talents are respected. In a very real sense, work is a source of identity. Meeting a stranger at a party, the first question is, "What is your name?" The second is, "What do you do?"

Work is all this and more to persons with SMI. Gainful employment (i.e., a job in which earnings exceed the threshold for disability benefits) gives workers with SMI both a sense of empowerment (having the resources to achieve one's goals) and inclusion (belonging to a workplace community). Work supports the process of recovery from mental illness by adding struc- ture and purpose to life.[1] Elyn Saks, a professor at the University of Southern California and a patient with schizophrenia, says work is her "best defense" against the symptoms of mental illness she continues to experience. Work "keeps me focused, it keeps the demons at bay."[2]

Work is also an important source of identity for persons recovering from SMI. Rather than assuming the primary identity of a mental health consumer, with all its negative stereotypes, a worker can redefine themselves, as we all do, in terms of a job. "I am a teacher," rather than "I am bipolar." Some workers with SMI say that working in a paid job where no one knows about their mental illness makes them feel, "normal . . . and being normal validates you."[3] Indeed, the ability to support oneself through work may be one of the clearest and most visible signs of recovery from mental illness. Today, it is a realistic goal for many persons with SMI, and ought to be a top priority of the mental health system.

An analogous situation occurs in housing policy. In dealing with the problems of chronic homelessness, many U.S. cities have made safe and permanent housing the top priority. The "Housing First" initiatives provide free and permanent housing (as opposed to temporary shelter) for homeless persons, regardless of income or substance abuse issues. The assumption is that a stable home provides an essential foundation from which other problems, such as substance abuse or psychiatric symptoms, can be addressed. [4] Gainful employment plays a comparable role for persons with SMI who are willing and able to work. A stable job provides a foundation from which other problems, such as damaged self-esteem, financial insecurity, and social isolation, can be addressed. Indeed, employment was one of the primary concerns of the coalition of disability groups that advocated for the civil rights protections embodied in the Americans with Disabilities Act (ADA).

Americans with Disabilities Act of 1990

Title I of the ADA establishes the rights of persons with disabilities with respect to employment. The act declares that persons with mental or physical disabilities have the right to equal treatment in the labor market, with respect to jobs for which they are qualified, and in which their disabilities can be accommodated with relative ease. Supporters of the ADA anticipated dramatic improvements in employment outcomes for the disabled population after the act took effect in 1992, but they were disappointed. Relative employment rates of persons with disabilities actually declined in the immediate post-ADA period. [5] In 2008, Congress passed the ADA Amendments Act of 2008 (ADAAA), in part to strengthen the law's provisions with respect to employment. The story of how the ADA was passed, why it was amended, and why it failed to achieve its employment goals, is instructive for those of us who believe that, with appropriate public policies, many more persons with SMI could be working.

Enacting the ADA

It took twenty-six years from the passage of the Civil Rights Act of 1964, which prohibits employment discrimination against individuals on the basis of "race, color, religion, sex, or national origin," [6] to extend the same protections to persons with disabilities. [7] One reason for the delay was that passage of the Americans with Disabilities Act presented a number of challenges that did not apply to groups covered under the original Civil Rights Act.

First, "persons with disabilities" is a heterogeneous group, and far more difficult to delineate than persons of a particular race, gender, or ethnic origin. The population with disabilities includes persons with a vast array of health conditions (e.g., blindness, deafness, partial paralysis) who require different aids to ensure their full inclusion in society (e.g., audio signals at crossways; text telephones, wheelchair ramps, and bus lifts). At times, the different subgroups are openly hostile in their competition for scarce resources.

I recall a research conference on disability issues that I attended several years ago, where many of the participants were persons with hearing, mobility, or visual impairments. The conference organizers were diligent in selecting formats and venues for the meetings that were accessible to everyone. The guidelines for presenters, sent in advance, specified that all audience handouts must be available in formats accessible to persons who are blind. Not having access to a Braille printer, I opted not to provide handouts at all. Some presenters, however, overlooked the guidelines and brought handouts in normal typeface. Many of the participants with visual impairments were offended by what they perceived to be exclusion and discrimination, so the conference organizers decided not to allow the handouts to be distributed to anyone. In all fairness, that is exactly what the preconference guidelines established, but participants without visual impairments were disgruntled by what they perceived as spitefulness.

Passage of the ADA occurred only after years of advocacy efforts by a coalition of these diverse disability groups. Organizations such as the American Foundation for the Blind, the Epilepsy Foundation of America, National Association of the Deaf, National Mental Health Association, and many others united to support a broad definition of disability in the act, and strongly opposed any attempts to exclude particular groups from coverage. In reflecting on the meeting I attended, it is amazing that disability groups with such competing needs and agendas were able to maintain unity over two decades to ensure passage of the ADA with a broad and inclusive definition of disability.

Another challenge to extending civil rights protections to persons with disabilities is that, unlike most groups protected by antidiscrimination laws, persons with disabilities may require special accommodations (e.g., ramps or special telecommunications devices) to access their rights. The employment provisions of the ADA require covered employers (all public and private employers with fifteen or more employees) to provide reasonable accommodations to workers with disabilities *at the employer's expense*. Previous antidiscrimination laws, prohibiting race-based discrimination, for example, impose no direct monetary costs on employers. An employer may be discomfited by having to interact with members of a stigmatized group, but these "psychic costs" are the essence of the discrimination that the laws aim to eliminate.

In sharp contrast, the ADA imposes an affirmative obligation to accommodate that may involve direct costs to employers in addition to any psychic distress. Legislators acknowledged the potential costs as they debated the act:

> Some persons may assert that costs should not be a factor in designing a disability civil rights law. In the context of a disability rights law, however, costs may have to be incurred in order to provide nondiscriminatory treatment; e.g., putting in a ramp, providing auxiliary aids and services, and other accommodations. Indeed, the failure to incur reasonable costs in order to provide access is regarded as discriminatory. At some point, however, the undertaking of an accommodation can be so costly or represent such a fundamental alteration in the covered entity's program that the failure to undertake the accommodation is simply not discriminatory. [8]

Some legislators expressed concerns about allocating the entire cost of accommodations to the private sector:

> How will the bill's mandates affect the owners of small businesses who must make reasonable accommodations to handicapped employees? . . . If we are going to ask Americans to bear the costs of this action, we should assure that the real costs are clearly identified and fairly allocated between the public and private sectors. Only then can we vote intelligently on this major civil rights proposal. [9]

Another challenge to enacting the ADA, as with any civil rights law, is the pervasive stigma against some of the persons the law is attempting to protect. Stigmatizing attitudes were quite apparent in the debates that preceded passage of the ADA, in which legislators attempted to restrict the definition of disability. Senator Armstrong, for example, introduced an amendment which explicitly excluded coverage for persons with "certain sexual disorders, impulse control disorders, and drug-related disorders." Even so, he did not think the amendment went far enough in excluding coverage of persons with mental illness:

> [I]f ADA is enacted the private sector will be swamped with mental disability litigation. My amendment excludes some of the mental disorders that would have created the more egregious lawsuits, but my amendment does no more than brush away a handful of the vast numbers of mental disorders and potential mental disorders. [10]

Senator Helms was unflinching in his questions regarding whether the ADA would, or should, cover persons with certain types of mental disorders:

> Does an employer's own moral standards enable him to make a judgment about any or all of the employees identified in our previous question [transvestites, kleptomaniacs, manic-depressives, schizophrenics]? . . . How far does

your covered list of individuals go in denying the small businessman the right
to run his company as he sees fit?[11]

Consistent with the theories of stigma (chapter 2), the legislators' objections to coverage under the ADA focused on health conditions for which the
individual was believed to be *morally responsible* and/or *unable to control
their behavior*. In all the lengthy debates over the definition of disability in
the act, the *only* conditions subject to direct attack on the floor of Congress
were AIDS, substance use disorders, and various types of mental illness.[12]
These conditions top the stigma rankings in almost every social distance
study. Nevertheless, the law passed with a broad, albeit ambiguous, definition of disability.

Employment Provisions of the ADA

Title I of the ADA prohibits discrimination against persons with disabilities
in: job application procedures and hiring decisions; job training programs;
promotion and discharge decisions; wages, and other employee benefits.[13]
The law states that (emphasis added):

> The term "disability" means, with respect to an individual—(A) a physical or
> mental impairment that *substantially limits one or more of the major life
> activities* of such individual; (B) a record of such an impairment; or (C) being
> regarded as having such an impairment.[14]

Congress did not specify a list of covered impairments, but the employer
guidelines issued by the Equal Employment Opportunity Commission
(EEOC) were somewhat more specific. With respect to mental impairments,
the guidelines say that persons with a "mental or psychological disorder,
such as an intellectual disability (formerly termed "mental retardation"), or-
ganic brain syndrome, emotional or mental illness, and specific learning
disabilities" are covered by the law.[15] The act itself states that the term
disability *shall not include* persons with certain "mental" conditions, namely,
current users of illegal drugs, persons with sexual behavior disorders, and
persons with certain compulsive disorders (e.g., compulsive gambling).[16]

Prior to extending a job offer, employers are prohibited from asking job
applicants about disabling health conditions. Once a job offer is extended,
employers are expected to provide *reasonable accommodations* to *otherwise
qualified* individuals with a disability, who can perform the *essential functions* of the job. Employers must provide accommodations at their own expense, unless the costs impose *undue hardship* on the firm. The key terms are
defined in the ADA, but the definitions are often ambiguous. For example,
instead of giving an explicit definition of reasonable accommodation, the act
lists a number of actions that may be considered as such:

(A) making existing facilities used by employees readily accessible to and usable by individuals with disabilities, and (B) job restructuring, part-time or modified work schedules, reassignment to a vacant position, acquisition or modification of equipment or devices, appropriate adjustment or modifications of examinations, training materials or policies, the provision of qualified readers or interpreters, and other similar accommodations for individuals with disabilities.[17]

Failure to provide reasonable accommodation is considered discriminatory, but the language of the act provides little guidance to employers regarding what is reasonable. If reassignment to a vacant position violates seniority rules, is that a reasonable accommodation?[18]

The ambiguities in the language of the ADA served a useful political purpose in maintaining the coalition of disability organizations that supported the law. By not identifying specific covered disabilities, or what it means to be substantially limited in a major life activity, supporters of the ADA enlisted the cooperation of the broadest possible spectrum of disability organizations. Nevertheless, once lawsuits were filed alleging disability-related discrimination, the judicial system was obliged to define specifics of the law.

Adjudicating Issues under the ADA

Judges struggled with the meaning of "reasonable" accommodation and other ambiguous terms in the law, but the most contested issue was the definition of a "qualified person with a disability." In deciding whether a claimant was sufficiently limited in major life activities to qualify for the act's protections, courts tended to make narrow rulings that severely restricted eligibility to file claims. As a result of these conservative interpretations of "disability," defendants (employers) won the vast majority of lawsuits filed under Title I in the decade and a half following implementation of the ADA.

In 2001, for example, employers prevailed in more than 95 percent of resolved cases.[19] Plaintiffs with mental disorders fared even worse than others. Employers prevailed in 98 percent of resolved cases involving mental disorders; all of which were summarily dismissed.[20] In other words, the allegations of discrimination were never addressed because a judge determined the plaintiff was not disabled according to the requirements of the ADA, and therefore not entitled to its protections. Similar ambiguities precluded plaintiffs from demonstrating the requirements of an "otherwise qualified person with a disability" that would trigger an employer's duty to provide reasonable accommodation. The following hypothetical scenarios illustrate some of the ways actual cases were lost.

Scenario 1   "Sam" had a first psychotic episode at age nineteen, while he was training to be an auto mechanic. He was admitted to a psychiatric hospital and diagnosed with schizophrenia. Sam's symptoms receded once he started taking antipsychotic medications. He was discharged after three weeks and returned to the training program, which he successfully completed. Sam worked as a mechanic with a large automotive service center for five years. Three years into the job, he weaned himself off medications, with his physician's approval, and has experienced no symptoms since that time. Recently, his employer learned about Sam's diagnosis and psychiatric hospitalization from another employee. When Sam confirmed his medical history, his employer told him, "I don't need any psychos working here." Sam was fired. He filed a lawsuit charging discrimination under the ADA.

In this scenario, the employee neither needed nor requested job accommodations. He was fully capable of performing the tasks required in his job, as evidenced by five years of successful employment. The employer's remark confirms that the worker was fired solely because of his disability. Can we assume that the discrimination claim will be upheld in court?

Not necessarily. In determining whether individuals are entitled to protection under the ADA, judges must determine if the plaintiff has a health impairment that *substantially limits* their activities. In this scenario, the plaintiff is able to function with no apparent limitations, so the lawsuit could be summarily dismissed because the worker does not have a disability within the ADA's definition. There have been cases filed under the ADA in which a worker was fired, demoted, or involuntarily transferred explicitly because of their disability, yet the case was dismissed because the individual was judged not to be "substantially limited."[21]

Scenario 2 "Olivia" had been employed as a registered nurse at a large metropolitan hospital for two years when she suffered an episode of major depression. She attempted to continue working, but was frequently late, forgot important tasks, and had little energy to care for patients. She applied for, and was granted, a medical leave. Olivia's physician prescribed medications, which effectively treated the episode of depression. Olivia also began seeing a therapist regularly. She returned to work, but requested a scheduling accommodation so she could continue her therapist visits. The hospital refused the accommodation, saying it was unfair to other employees. Olivia feared that, without continued therapy, she would become depressed again. She took another medical leave and filed a lawsuit claiming the hospital had a duty to accommodate her under the ADA.

In this scenario, the issue under contention is an employee's request for a job accommodation. Her work performance was satisfactory until she developed a mental condition that limited her ability to function as a nurse. Upon returning from medical leave, her request for a schedule that would accommodate continued psychiatric treatment was denied. Can we expect adjudication of the case to focus on whether the requested accommodation is reasonable?

Not necessarily. Before courts hear arguments on the reasonableness of accommodations, judges must determine if the plaintiff is a "qualified person with a disability," entitled to protection under the ADA. In this case, the plaintiff's mental condition is being treated effectively with medication; thus, when she is on medication she is not substantially limited in her activities and not protected by the ADA. Without medication, her functioning is severely limited, but in this state she is unable to perform the essential functions of her job, and therefore not entitled to reasonable accommodation. Thus, the plaintiff faces an insurmountable burden—to prove that she is both severely limited in activities, *and* able to perform the essential functions of her job. Her case could be summarily dismissed without the issue of reasonable accommodation ever coming before the court.

The U.S. Supreme Court considered an analogous factual scenario in 1999. In *Sutton v. United Airlines*, two sisters sued United Airlines because they were disqualified from employment as commercial airline pilots due to poor but correctible vision. The sisters argued that disqualification on this basis constituted unlawful employment discrimination in violation of Title I of the ADA, because their vision was fully corrected with glasses.[22] The court affirmed dismissal of the sisters' discrimination claim, concluding that the sisters were "not disabled" because their vision could be corrected with glasses. The court's ruling established a precedent that, in determining whether a plaintiff is a "qualified person with a disability," health conditions should be considered in their *ameliorated* state.

Many serious mental illnesses can be treated with medications that restore patients to a near normal level of functioning. According to the Supreme Court ruling, these persons are not "disabled" as defined by the ADA, and therefore are not protected by the ADA, because they are not severely limited when their condition is treated. Without medications, they are severely limited, but then they are excluded from the ADA's protection on the grounds that they are unable to perform essential functions of the job.[23]

Scenario 3   "Alex," a day cashier in a large banking firm, had difficulties interacting with other people. He missed social cues, avoided making eye contact, and often misinterpreted what others said. He had never had a steady girlfriend for longer than a few months. Alex's social problems carried over to the workplace, where he had difficulties getting along with coworkers. He had been reprimanded by his supervisors for making unwanted social advances to a female coworker, and for verbally abusing a male coworker (whom Alex perceived had taken unfair advantage of him). After seeing a psychologist about his problems interacting with others, Alex was diagnosed with an autism-spectrum disorder. He told his supervisors about the diagnosis, assuming that they would be sympathetic. Instead, they demoted him to the position of night clerk, a lower-paying job. Alex filed a lawsuit alleging disability-related discrimination.

In this scenario, the employee performs his cashier responsibilities satisfactorily, but his disability affects the tenor of the workplace. The ADA prohibits discrimination against an "otherwise qualified person with a disability, who can perform the essential functions of the job." Can we expect the court's decision to depend on whether or not interacting with coworkers is an essential function of a cashier's job?

Not necessarily. Before Alex's case can get to trial, the judge must determine whether he has "a physical or mental impairment that substantially limits the performance of one or more *major life activities*." Alex is clearly limited in his ability to get along with others. Is interacting with others a major life activity, like walking, hearing, and seeing? Courts have wrestled with this question, not only with respect to interacting with others, but also regarding other common everyday activities, such as driving.[24] The federal circuit courts are in agreement that driving is *not* a major life activity, but decisions with respect to interacting with others have been mixed.[25]

In a 1995 Compliance Manual issued for employers subject to the ADA, the EEOC included "interacting with others" in a list of examples of major life activities.[26] However, the Court of Appeals for the First Circuit rejected the manual's guidance as "hardly binding," stating that the concept of getting along with others is "remarkably elastic, perhaps so much so as to make it unworkable as a definition," and quite different from the major life activities included in the original EEOC regulations for implementing the act.[27] Paradoxically, the Second and Ninth Circuit Courts have ruled that interacting with others "easily falls within the definition of major life activity."[28] The question of whether or not interacting with others is a major life activity was never fully resolved under the original terms of the ADA.

ADA Amendments Act of 2008

Given the rate at which lawsuits filed under Title I of the ADA were being summarily dismissed, by 2005 it was clear that the law was not working as Congress had intended. In 2008, Congress amended the ADA to resolve some of the ambiguities that were causing plaintiffs to lose their lawsuits even before the cases were argued in court. The clear intent of the ADAAA of 2008 was to reestablish broad coverage of persons with disabilities.

The ADAAA made several key modifications to the original law that were specifically designed to overrule court decisions which had narrowed the ADA's scope of protection. First, Congress clarified its intent that the definition of disability in the ADA should be interpreted broadly:

> The definition of disability in this Act shall be construed in favor of broad
> coverage of individuals under this Act, to the maximum extent permitted by
> the terms of this Act.[29]

Second, Congress clarified its intent that "major life activities" should be
interpreted to include a broad range of normal activities. The ADAAA provides a nonexhaustive list of qualifying activities that includes communicat-
ing, concentrating, and thinking; and adds a new category of "major bodily
functions," that includes functions of the brain.[30]

Third, Congress clarified ambiguities in the interpretation of "substantial
limitations." The ADAAA specifies that, in determining whether a plaintiff is
substantially limited, episodic impairments and impairments in remission
should be evaluated according to their active states. Further, the ADAAA
expressly overrules the Supreme Court's ruling in *Sutton v. United Airlines*
by providing that,

> The determination of whether an impairment substantially limits a major life
> activity shall be made without regard to the ameliorative effects of mitigating
> measures.[31]

The ADAAA also includes a nonexhaustive list of possible mitigating measures, with "medications" first on the list.

Overall, the ADAAA will almost certainly ensure that a larger proportion
of discrimination cases involving persons with mental disorders are heard in
court.[32] The ADAAA makes clear that the main inquiry in a case of disability-related discrimination should not be whether the plaintiff is covered by
the ADA, but whether the covered employer has fulfilled their obligations
under the law.[33] Indeed, in determining who is an "otherwise qualified person with a disability," the ADAAA dramatically expands the reach of "disability."

Some legal analysts, however, argue that the ADAAA may still fail to
protect persons with mental disorders because the ADAAA does not change
the threshold for interpreting what it means to be "qualified." Prior to 2008,
two-thirds of plaintiffs with physical disorders failed to have their cases
heard in court because they were deemed not to be disabled (an issue which
the amendments address), whereas two-thirds of plaintiffs with mental disorders failed because they were deemed not to be qualified individuals with
disabilities (an issue which the amendments do not address).[34]

It is still too soon to draw definitive conclusions regarding the impact of
the ADAAA in the courtroom. The act is not retroactive, so the new standards do not apply to cases in which the alleged discriminatory actions occurred prior to the effective date (July 1, 2009). Between 2009 and 2013, a
substantial proportion of Title I court cases were still decided according to

preamendment standards. That said, there is a small sample of postamendment decisions from which some preliminary findings are available.

In one study, the author examined all summary judgments in cases decided under Title I of the ADA between January 2010 and April 2013, and compared outcomes for cases decided under preamendment and postamendment standards. As expected, the proportion of summary judgments in favor of the employer was significantly lower for cases in which ADAAA standards applied, than for cases in which ADA standards applied (46 percent versus 74 percent).[35] When the standards of the ADAAA applied, there were significantly fewer summary dismissals on the grounds the plaintiff was "not disabled," but significantly more summary dismissals on the grounds the plaintiff was "not qualified." The results suggest that the ADAAA is having an effect on the number of Title I cases that proceed to trial, albeit not to the extent Congress may have expected.

The foregoing describes the current legal landscape under which persons with SMI seek competitive employment: It is clearly unlawful for employers to discriminate against qualified persons with mental disabilities. Any person with a diagnosis of schizophrenia, bipolar disorder, or other psychotic disorder should have little trouble satisfying the disability criterion under the amended ADA. It may be more difficult to convince judges they are qualified for the job, particularly given the negative stereotypes of persons with mental disorders as incompetent, unpredictable, and dangerous. In summarizing the likely impact of the ADAAA, one author states that:

> Although Congress has expressed its disapproval of how "disability" was defined under the pre-Amendments Act ADA and how so few plaintiffs were successful, it is unclear whether such congressional expression will be effective in convincing judges to grant protected class status to the most highly stigmatized sub-group of persons with impairments—those alleging mental disabilities.[36]

The clear intent of the ADAAA is to establish the rights of all persons with disabilities to work in jobs for which they are qualified. Just as persons with mental disorders have the right to live in the least restrictive environment possible, they also have the right to equal employment opportunities in the competitive workplace, wherever they are qualified. Just as a safe and permanent home can be the first step toward normal life for a homeless person, productive work can be the first step toward normalcy for a person with SMI.

The Value of Work

According to the Oxford English Dictionary, the word *work* is derived from an Old English word and has been part of the English vocabulary since at least the tenth century.[37] One of the many meanings of the word is "to accomplish, achieve; to cause, produce." No wonder so many persons with SMI say *work* is their number one recovery goal; those who accomplish, achieve, and produce are valued members of society.[38] In fact, my interest in the *Oxford Dictionary* was piqued by the involvement of one man, Dr. William Chester Minor, whose great achievement in life was his contribution to the making of the dictionary during nearly forty years of confinement in an asylum for the insane.

In April 1872, Dr. Minor was admitted to Broadmoor Asylum for the Criminally Insane in Berkshire, England. Three months earlier, around 2 a.m. on a cold Saturday morning, he had shot and killed George Merrett, a workingman on his way to the morning shift at a local brewery. When the constables arrived, Dr. Minor told them the shooting was a terrible mistake. He was chasing an intruder who had broken into his room and he had accidentally shot the wrong man.[39]

The doctor was charged with murder, but during the trial it became quite clear that he was seriously mentally ill. Dr. Minor told the constables that strangers often came to his room at night, to abuse and violate him in unspeakable ways, so he slept with a loaded revolver to protect himself. The doctor's landlady assured the court his story was unfounded—there were no intruders. Dr. Minor's brother testified that the doctor had a history of persecutory delusions. The jury returned a verdict of not guilty by reason of insanity, and the judge ordered that the doctor be confined to Broadmoor, "until her Majesty's pleasure be known."[40]

Dr. Minor's accommodations at Broadmoor were not uncomfortable. As a well-born, well-educated man with a regular income, he was given two adjoining "cells" in the least secure part of the asylum. The doctor furnished one cell comfortably as a study—with floor to ceiling bookshelves holding a small library of rare volumes. The other cell was for sleeping and painting. These two rooms would likely be the doctor's home for a long time, because the delusions of night visitations and persecution continued. Still, by day, he lacked for nothing except a useful way to employ his mind and energy.

The solution came in the form of an advertisement from the editor of the *Oxford English Dictionary* (OED). The idea for the dictionary was conceived in 1857, almost two decades before George Merrett's murder. The goals were ambitious—to create a dictionary that contained a complete etymology of every word in the English language. The origin and meanings of each word would be illustrated with literary quotations, demonstrating when and how the word was introduced into the English vocabulary. But by the time Dr. Minor was settled in Broadmoor, the project had languished for almost twenty years.

In 1878, James Murray, a schoolmaster and member of the British Philological Society, was hired to edit the dictionary. Murray sent out the advertisement for "a vast fresh corps of volunteers," to read important literary works from the sixteenth through nineteenth centuries and extract quotations for the massive dictionary.[41] Dr. Minor answered the advertisement, offering his services as a volunteer, listing his address only as "Broadmoor, Crawthorne, Berkshire." Murray responded promptly. He sent the doctor an agreement welcoming him as a volunteer reader, along with explicit instructions for reading and citing quotations. From the moment the doctor received the letter, his mental condition seemed to improve.

> The invitation seemed a long-sought badge of renewed membership in a society from which [he] had been so long estranged. By being sent these sheets of rules he was, he felt, being received back into the real world. . . . And with what he saw as this reenlistment in the ranks, so Minor's self-worth began, at least marginally, to reemerge, to begin seeping back. . . . He appears to have started recovering his confidence and even his contentment, both with every moment he spent reading Murray's acceptance letter, and then when he prepared to embark on his self-set task.[42]

Dr. Minor worked on the dictionary project for the next two decades, sending a prodigious number of quotations to Murray and his assistants, as many as one hundred a week. Yet he remained, unquestionably, seriously mentally ill. In letters to the Broadmoor superintendent, he complained that intruders entered his rooms at night and defaced his books, that the attendants were abusing him, that the hospital must install solid wooden floors to prevent fiends from creeping between the floors and ceilings, that the villagers were allowed into his room to abuse him. And yet, his work for the great dictionary continued.

In the preface to the first volume (A–B), completed in 1888, Murray generously acknowledged the "services of Dr. W. C. Minor, which have week by week supplied additional quotations for the words actually preparing for press."[43] The first complete edition of the OED, in twelve volumes, was published in 1928. Dr. Minor's work on the project was his only source of joy, purpose, and accomplishment during the years of his confinement at Broadmoor.

Postscript

Dr. William Minor was fortunate. He had an intelligent mind, well-organized thought processes, and a roomful of rare and old editions. He found a job that required intelligence, organization, and access to old books. As with Elyn Saks, his work "kept the demons away."

The amended ADA guarantees people with mental disorders equal rights in employment, but the legislation cannot guarantee that individuals are able to take advantage of their rights. Have they acquired skills and abilities that are valuable in the competitive labor market; and can they find a job that is a good match for those skills and abilities, considering any residual functional limitations? Are they willing to disclose their diagnosis to an employer, in order to access the job accommodations to which they are entitled; or are they too fearful of the stigma and negative stereotyping that may result? Most important, have they been encouraged to believe it is possible to do valuable work, even after a diagnosis of SMI?

Recall (chapter 2) the young man with schizophrenia who wanted to work as a computer programmer, but was told by his physicians that he "would not be capable of that." In this respect, David was more fortunate. Before he was discharged from his first hospital stay, Dr. Perkins told him, "You *can* recover from this disease." He says, "I held onto those words for my life."

Chapter Seven

The Disclosure Predicament

DON'T ASK. DON'T TELL.

Wilkie Collins, nineteenth-century author and playwright, is best known for his sensation novels in which apparently random forces, outside the control of the characters, propel the plots forward. Often, one or more characters narrates the story, and we discover that a secret from their past threatens to destroy them. Their efforts to evade detection place them in predicaments in which they face no good alternatives and, inevitably, their secret is revealed.

> Nothing in this world is hidden forever. . . . Look where we will, the inevitable law of revelation is one of the laws of nature: the lasting preservation of a secret is a miracle which the world has never yet seen.[1]

Persons with schizophrenia also have a secret that threatens them, and places them in a predicament: to tell, and face the stigma of mental illness; or to conceal, and cope with the stress of keeping a secret.

Summer 2002

The year after David's graduation from Chapel Hill, I accepted a faculty position at Arizona State University, and prepared to move to Phoenix. At the same time, David was preparing to move to Charlotte, where he had accepted a job as a leasing agent for an apartment complex. As his first real job postgraduation (and postschizophrenia), the leasing position had many advantages: David could live onsite for a reduced rent. His commute was trivial—a short walk from his apartment to the front office. If he became tired in the middle of the day (his medications caused fatigue), he could rest at home during his lunch hour. We helped him furnish his apartment, stocked up the cupboards and refrigerator, and, with much trepidation, prepared to leave him on his own.

David's employers knew nothing about his psychiatric history, although their job application asks about chronic physical or mental conditions. When he came to that question, David called to consult with me. "How shall I answer this, Mom?" I had no idea what to say. The question is illegal under the ADA, but if David said "you have no right to ask me this," it was certain that there would be no job offer. If he answered "yes," it was equally certain that there would be no job offer.

My brother Gordon resolved the predicament for us. He argued that the owners of the company *must* know that it is illegal to ask job applicants about their medical history because, by that time, the ADA had been in effect more than ten years. It *is* legal, however, to ask a job applicant if they have a health condition that *prevents them from performing the essential functions of the job.* Therefore, Gordon argued, that must be the intent of the question, and David should answer "no." And that is what he did.

"Say nothing to anyone. Because silence is safe."[2]

David worked in the leasing agent position for two years. None of his supervisors or coworkers ever knew about his history of psychiatric hospitalization. As he gained experience, he helped design marketing materials for the firm and was invited to regional conferences to give training seminars. But he did not particularly like the job or the schedule, which required him to work every Saturday. In 2004, he found a new job with a company that leased commercial security systems.

Fall 2004

At first, David was excited about the new position. It was a small and growing firm, and the earnings potential was good. David would be responsible for managing security contracts, negotiating contract renewals on an annual basis, and developing a long-term marketing plan for the firm. He liked the owner; and the owner liked David's energy and enthusiasm. It appeared that David had made a good career move, but the appearance was short-lived. The energy (restlessness) and enthusiasm (verbosity) that his employer admired were, in reality, the first signs of an acute psychotic episode. Unknown to me, David had been taking a reduced dose of medications ever since his relapse in 2000, and one weekend in December he had forgotten to take any at all.

Within six weeks, David was experiencing delusions and disorganized thinking. With visions of a brilliant new career, he stopped going to work. By February, his condition had deteriorated so badly that his roommates called Gordon, and Aaron and I made the trip to Charlotte to try to get David stabilized and back on his meds.

While in Charlotte, I made an appointment to meet with the owner of the security company. I believed that he deserved an explanation for David's abrupt departure. The meeting was a revelation for both of us: *He* had no idea that he was dealing with SMI. *I* had no idea how David's irrational behavior had upset the workplace.

The owner told me that David's demeanor had changed from outgoing to offensive. He was loud and overbearing in meetings and often had to be told to be quiet. He was reprimanded for making sexually inappropriate remarks to the office receptionist. And then, he just disappeared.

David's employer and coworkers were not aware of his psychiatric history, but once he stopped taking his meds, the symptoms revealed themselves. No one at work could identify the symptoms as *schizophrenia*, but they knew that something was terribly wrong.

> It is the nature of truth to struggle to the light . . . to pierce the overlying darkness, and to reveal itself to view. [3]

Fall 2007

Two years after we brought David home from Charlotte, my marriage was crumbling. It was not that schizophrenia had placed an unbearable strain on our relationship. Rather, the marriage was already stressed, and when schizophrenia came along, it was as if a glacier turned the fissures into chasms. My husband and I separated in December 2007. David chose to live with his father, because, "A guy in his thirties does *not* live with his mother." The two of them moved closer to central Phoenix, near a church that David remembered from an encounter at his psychiatric clinic months before.

On that day, David had gone to a regular appointment with his case manager. In the waiting room, he met a woman with five young children. "You have a beautiful family," he told her. "Thank you, but they're not all mine." After his appointment, David was surprised to find the woman waiting for him outside the clinic door.

"You don't need this," she told him.

"Need what?" he asked.

"The medicine."

"What do you mean?"

"You are a tortured soul."

"Huh?"

"You need to go to a church where they believe in demons."

"Where should I go?"

Pondering for a moment, she finally said, "Right across the street."

"But I can't go there. I live on 114th Street; it's too far away." After he and his father moved, the church was only a few miles from David's new home.

Phoenix First Assembly is a mega-church with a mission: "to reveal Christ to the world by loving people, cultivating community and inspiring hope."[4] The existing church was established in 1980 by Tommy Barnett, author, senior pastor, and chancellor of Southeastern University. By 2011 it was the second-largest Assembly of God church in the United States. Every day, the church aims to carry out Pastor Barnett's vision of compassionate evangelism. "Lost people matter to God, therefore they matter to us. We believe that acts of compassion express the love of God to our community."[5]

Phoenix First welcomes lost people, and I had a son who was lost. David began attending church services there regularly, and soon became involved in the Men's Ministries. One of the projects in which his group participated was the "Great Toy Giveaway." Each December, the church gives away thousands of bicycles and toys to local children who are living in foster homes or in families struggling with poverty. The bicycles are assembled, organized by size and gender, and amassed on the church grounds the day before the Giveaway. David invited me to observe the process. No matter what your religious beliefs, the sight of three thousand new bicycles gleaming in the sunshine, ready to be given away to underprivileged children, is not something you will quickly forget.

I visited Phoenix First Assembly with David in spring 2008. After the service, he introduced me to Pastor Barnett, the man whose vision created the church. The pastor held my hand, looked me in the eye, and said, "We just love your son."

I felt as if someone had pulled me out of a dark place.

"At last," I thought, "there is someone who is willing to help." Tommy Barnett did not know the nature of David's illness at the time. When David eventually told him, *it did not make any difference.*

DISCLOSING MENTAL ILLNESS IN THE WORKPLACE

The decision to disclose a mental illness at work is not simply a question of *whether* or not to disclose, but also a question of *how much* to disclose, *to whom* to disclose, and *when* and *why*. The decision is risky. Sometimes, disclosure is an empowering act that results in necessary job accommodations, as well as greater support from supervisors and coworkers. Then again, disclosure can lead to discrimination, harassment, isolation, negative stereotyping, and even job loss.[6]

Persons with mental illness generally have control over the decision to disclose their diagnosis because, unlike many physical disorders (e.g., vision or hearing impairments, paralysis or disfigurement), mental illness can often be concealed. As with the characters in Collins's novels, however, the "secret" may reveal itself, if the symptoms of mental illness become acute. Alternatively, if a worker participates in a supported employment program, disclosure happens implicitly, if not explicitly. Either a vocational staff member informs the employer about the worker's condition, or the employer knows because particular jobs are set aside for persons with disabilities.[7]

My focus is on workers with SMI in *competitive jobs*. By this I mean, jobs that pay at least the minimum wage, are not restricted to persons with disabilities, and do not involve placement by a vocational or supported employment program. In these jobs, the worker controls the disclosure decision, so long as their symptoms are concealable.

We have very little quantitative evidence pertaining to disclosure of SMI in the competitive workplace. We do not know, for example, what proportion of workers choose to disclose, what their motivations are, or whether the outcome of disclosure is likely to be positive. Most of the evidence that is available comes from descriptive studies with small sample sizes, so it is impossible to draw conclusions that are representative of the population. But the descriptive studies provide a framework from which to model the disclosure decision, by identifying the factors that determine a worker's optimal choice of privacy versus revelation.

Pros and Cons of Disclosure

The word *disclose* has roots in Middle English and Old French, where it originally meant "to unclose, open, free."[8] In modern English, disclose can mean, "to open up to the knowledge of others; to make openly known, reveal, declare," or "to reveal itself, to come to light." A *disclosure* is "a revelation, discovery, or exposure." The nuances of meaning in the words make clear the predicament that one faces in deciding whether or not to disclose a secret. On the one hand, disclosure is "freeing," on the other hand, it is "exposure." Disclosure may be a deliberate act of "revelation," or the secret may "reveal itself."

In the context of telling an employer or coworkers about SMI, disclosure may be *proactive*, a revelation designed to obtain an objective (such as job accommodations), or *reactive*, an explanation of symptoms that have made the illness difficult to conceal.[9] Either way, disclosing a condition like mental illness is a gamble that *might* result in sympathy and support, but could just as easily generate suspicion and rejection. As in the world of fiction, disclosure of private information in the real world fundamentally changes the relationship between the one who tells and the one who hears.[10]

Chapter 7

Pros: Disclosure as Revelation

In the best-case scenario, a worker discloses their history of SMI to an enlightened employer and coworkers, who respond with sympathy and support. The worker gains the legal protections of the amended ADA and the right to reasonable accommodations for their disability. The employer is forewarned in case the worker experiences a recurrence of symptoms that affects their job performance. Informed coworkers are in a position to provide practical and emotional support in ways that increase the likelihood of successful employment. As a bonus, the worker is relieved of the stress of trying to keep a secret:

> I feel I would be happier [to disclose] because I could really be myself and not have to work so hard to make sure nobody notices that maybe I'm a little bit stressed or tired. [11]

In the best-case scenario, disclosure can have societal benefits as well as private benefits. Disclosing a diagnosis of SMI provides an opportunity to educate others about the realities of mental illness, as opposed to the negative stereotypes that perpetuate stigma. In fact, research consistently shows that the most powerful antidote to stigma is *personal contact with a stigmatized individual who is occupying a valued role*. [12] Workers who disclose a history of mental illness have a unique opportunity to counteract stereotypes of persons with mental illness as helpless, incompetent, and unable to take care of themselves. For some, this opportunity provides an additional motive to disclose:

> I like to think I've changed people's attitudes. . . . I'd just explain to them what it was like. I said "this is what it was like for me" . . . "everyone's not the same" . . . I said "I'm not dangerous or anything.". . . The only things they hear about [mental illness] are the ones on the news. [13]

Cons: Disclosure as Exposure

In the worst-case scenario, a worker discloses their diagnosis of SMI to an employer and coworkers who respond with negative stereotyping, stigma, and discrimination. Employers with strong tastes for discrimination can react in ways that adversely affect a worker's employment status. Thus, the worker who discloses SMI risks being demoted to a lower-paying job, being passed over for promotion, or even being fired. Disclosure can also trigger changes in performance expectations, with consequences of being assigned to less important tasks, having closer supervision, or being given a heavier workload. [14]

To a certain extent, I've noticed that normal people, even though they might not work as well, they're tolerated more on a regular job than mentally ill people are. . . . I've also noticed that if you don't watch, the boss will put more on a mentally ill person to do, especially if that mentally ill person doesn't complain.[15]

Coworkers who believe the negative stereotypes may react to disclosure with avoidance, fear, hostility, or condescension (believing the worker with SMI is incompetent). As a result, a worker who discloses their history of mental illness risks becoming socially isolated from their peers. Apprehensions about being ostracized, and being perceived as "different," create powerful motives not to disclose:

Usually when you start talking about yourself on the job, that tends to make them treat you different. . . . I don't want to tell anybody, because people who aren't ill, they do have a tendency sometimes to treat you different. They'll start teasing you or they'll shy away from you. It's a strange thing about us, the mentally ill, we've got to disguise ourselves a lot, because people who aren't ill, when they know things about you, they tend to treat you different.[16]

Paradoxically, many workers who say they *would not disclose* their diagnosis of SMI at work still believe that *work would be easier for them* if their employer knew about their illness.[17]

Two psychologists have formulated a model of the disclosure decision in which disclosure represents a trade-off between approach and avoidance motivations.[18] In this framework, the decision not to disclose SMI to an employer is primarily an *avoidance* strategy—that is, a worker sacrifices the potential advantages of job accommodations, sympathy and support, in order to avoid potential stigma and discrimination. The decision to disclose SMI is primarily an *approach* strategy. A worker risks being ostracized, demoted, or even being fired, in order to gain the legal protections of the ADAAA, emotional support from supervisors and coworkers, and relief from the stress of keeping their mental illness hidden. Either strategy is a gamble that may turn out badly.[19]

Experiences of Disclosure

It is probably a bad strategy to walk into work one morning and tell a supervisor, "I am psychotic." The outcome of that gamble is almost certain to be negative. Workers with SMI do not, however, have to be so blunt. They typically have some freedom to manage the disclosure event, because mental illness is concealable so long as symptoms are well controlled. Thus, workers with SMI can hedge on the disclosure gamble by strategically controlling how much information they disclose, and when.

Strategies

Under the ADA, a worker may disclose a disability and request employer-provided job accommodations at any time: during the hiring process, after receiving a job offer, immediately after starting a job, or at any time thereafter.[20] However, among workers with SMI who have shared their experiences with disclosure, there is almost universal agreement that revealing a history of psychiatric illness *before* hiring, will likely preclude any job offer:

> I don't think you'd get a foot in through the door that way. You wouldn't get taken on in the first place if you told them you had a big mental history.[21]

After receiving a job offer, workers who need to request job accommodations are forced (by the ADA) to tell their employer something about their illness. Workers whose symptoms of SMI are observable may also be compelled to disclose some information, even if they do not need to request accommodations. In either case, the worker may choose how much detail to provide, and what words to use in describing their diagnosis. Many workers with SMI say they are careful to avoid stigma-laden terms like "schizophrenic" or "psychotic."

> Basically, what I told them at work was that I'd got severe depression and most of them are ok with that. . . . Well, I've only told them an edited version . . . if anybody at work or my professional body knew that I'd got schizo-anything I wouldn't be allowed to practice.[22]

Some workers make up fictional diagnoses, like "metabolic disturbance" or "exhaustion syndrome," to describe their illness.[23] The workers' careful choice of language reflects an awareness of the hierarchy of stigma against different types of mental illness, namely, that depression, anxiety disorders, and other mental illnesses elicit far less stigma than schizophrenia or psychotic disorders (see chapter 2).

> I mean, you can talk about well, perhaps a depression or something but if you say "psychosis"—God forbid! When I recovered from my first episode, I tried to explain [my diagnosis to my previous employer]. . . . They were sort of interested in that they asked whether my wife is still with me, but that was it. "We can't do anything for you anymore," they said, and then they interrupted the conversation. It would have been better not to mention a word.[24]

If a worker does not need to request job accommodations, or does not have obvious symptoms of SMI, their disclosure can be strategically timed. The worker may choose to postpone disclosure until they feel secure in their position, have established themselves with their work group, and are confident about the attitudes of their supervisor and coworkers. Given the intense stigma against mental illness, that may be a long time, or never.

> Believe it or not, I've been on the job for seven months, and they do not know I have schizophrenia. They do not know I have a mental illness. They do know I have diabetes. It's incredible, when you think about it, it being a professional type job, ten and a half hours a day, nine days every two weeks, working closely with these people. I'm doing so well on my new medication that I'm virtually indistinguishable from the normal.[25]

Quantitative Evidence

Most of the evidence we have on disclosure of SMI at work comes from interviews or focus group discussions with small samples of workers with SMI. These types of studies can provide insights into personal experiences of disclosing mental illness in the workplace, but cannot answer questions like,

- What proportion of workers with SMI discloses their illness at work?
- Are they more likely to disclose to their employer or coworkers?
- Is disclosure more often proactive, or reactive?
- Are employers and coworkers more likely to respond with help and support (the best-case scenario) or stigma and discrimination (the worst-case scenario)?

I am aware of only two published studies that have sufficiently large samples to provide this type of quantitative evidence on disclosure of SMI in competitive jobs.[26]

One study reports data on workplace disclosure from a sample of 209 professionals and managers with mental illness.[27] All the respondents were employed in health or social service occupations, or in business, educational, or technical services. About 45 percent of respondents had a diagnosis of bipolar disorder, 10 percent had a diagnosis of schizophrenia, and the remainder had diagnoses of less stigmatized types of mental illness.

Overall, 80 percent of respondents said they had disclosed something about their mental illness at work. On average, they waited six months after beginning the job to disclose. One-third of those who disclosed said the decision was proactive ("when they felt comfortable"); the remainder said that disclosure was a reaction to negative circumstances associated with their illness (e.g., recurrence or escalation of symptoms, psychiatric hospitalization). Respondents who were employed in health or human services were more likely to disclose voluntarily (46 percent) than respondents who were employed in business, educational, or technical services (30 percent).

The second study draws on survey data collected by the National Alliance on Mental Illness (NAMI).[28] It is particularly relevant because the sample was comprised entirely of persons with SMI (schizophrenia, schizoaffective disorder, or another schizophrenia spectrum disorder). The survey included questions about disclosure of mental illness within various relationships (e.g., friends, extended family, employers, coworkers). A total of 258 eligible participants completed the online survey, 178 of whom responded to questions on workplace relationships.

Participants were asked to rate, for each relationship, how open they were about disclosing their diagnosis of schizophrenia. Possible responses were "not at all open" (nondisclosure), "somewhat open" or "quite a bit open" (selective disclosure), and "completely open" (full disclosure). Respondents who indicated that they had disclosed something about their diagnosis within a particular relationship were asked to evaluate whether they were treated "better," "worse," or "about the same" after disclosure.

The average respondent was not particularly open about disclosing SMI at work. Only 40 percent said that they were even "somewhat open" with their employer or coworkers[29] (compared to 80 percent of participants in the study of professionals and managers where half had diagnoses of depression or other less stigmatized mental illness). Respondents to the NAMI survey were most open about their illness in relationships with medical professionals; they were least open with neighbors, telling the neighbors little or nothing about mental illness, on average. ("People have discovered that they can fool the Devil; but they can't fool the neighbors."[30])

Among the respondents who disclosed something about SMI at work, the majority said that they were at least as well accepted by their employer and coworkers after disclosure as before. However, 38 percent of respondents reported being treated "worse" by their employer, and 35 percent reported being treated "worse" by coworkers, after they disclosed something about SMI. Among all the relationships studied, only police and corrections officers were more likely (39 percent) to dole out "worse" treatment after disclosure than employers and coworkers. At the other end of the scale, fewer than 20 percent of respondents said that they were treated "better" at work after disclosure of SMI. Among all the relationships studied (even the neighbors), coworkers were least likely to react to disclosure of SMI with "better" treatment. Only 13 percent of those who disclosed to a coworker reported being treated "better" afterward, compared to 15 percent who disclosed to a neighbor!

For this sample, neither the best-case scenario (sympathy and support) nor the worst-case scenario (stigma, discrimination, and harassment) were the norm following disclosure of mental illness at work. Most respondents, however, said that they were only "somewhat open" about their diagnosis. We can only speculate that the results would have been far more negative if the workers had said "schizo-anything."

Neither the results of the NAMI survey, nor the survey of professionals and managers with psychiatric disorders, can be generalized to describe the experience of disclosing mental illness at work. Respondents to the NAMI survey were a convenience sample contacted through NAMI affiliates nationwide. The sample was not designed to be representative of the overall population of persons with schizophrenia, or those who are employed. Respondents to the professional/manager survey were recruited through advertisement, direct solicitation, and word-of-mouth, hence also not representative of the population with SMI.

In short, there is no published research that describes the experience of disclosing mental illness in the competitive workplace, using data from a representative sample of workers with SMI. In part, the lack of evidence reflects the almost exclusive focus of research in this area on supported employment programs, where disclosure is almost a nonissue. In part, the lack of evidence reflects the need for a model of disclosure, which yields testable hypotheses to guide the data collection. An economic model of *rational consumer choice* provides a useful starting point for such a model.

A Rational Choice Model of Disclosure

Those who are unfamiliar with modern applications of economics in the social sciences may find it strange to view a person with schizophrenia as a "rational economic agent." Economic theory does not, however, question or pass judgment upon the preferences of the individual. It accepts preferences as they are. Without a pretense of knowing an individual's preferences, economic analysis proceeds from the *fact* that all people (including those with SMI) have preferences, and the *assumption* that people are capable of making choices that they perceive to be in their best interests. This so-called rationality postulate has been fruitfully applied not only in the narrow context of consumer choice, but also to decisions that lie well outside the traditional marketplace, such as decisions regarding marriage, fertility, and drug addiction.

Objectives of the Worker

Following this path, I use consumer choice theory as a framework for analyzing the disclosure decision in the workplace. I will not attempt to justify this approach, but merely point out that persons with SMI who are capable of independent competitive employment are not experiencing flagrant symptoms of mental illness and are capable of thinking clearly. That said, their objectives in seeking employment may differ substantially from the objectives of a "representative employee." Whereas the latter is focused on some combination of desired wages, benefits, hours, and workplace amenities, these choice dimensions lie well outside this discussion. For both practical and analytical purposes, I shall ignore them entirely.

Above all, the worker with SMI seeks *acceptance*. Accordingly, acceptance in the workplace becomes a valuable commodity:

> I want to work, and I want to fit in, and I want to be normal. I don't want people staring at me like I'm a zombie or something from the zoo. I don't want to be stared at like I'm different just because I have bipolar.[31]

Like most economic commodities, greater acceptance is preferred to less, up to a level of full acceptance, where the worker with SMI is treated just like any other worker. There is nothing complicated about the objective of maximizing acceptance; the interesting part lies in the trade-offs and constraints that interact with it.

As noted earlier, *disclosure* is also a valuable commodity in the workplace, particularly for workers who need to request job accommodations, or want to be "the real person they are," or are burdened by the stress of keeping a secret. In contrast to preferences for workplace acceptance, however, it is not always true that more disclosure is preferred to less. Workers with SMI generally prefer to keep some details of their history of mental illness to themselves. A simple reason is privacy:

> [If I feel forced to disclose] I'll be angry that I had to reveal the most intimate part of myself to people I would not want to do that with.[32]

Another reason is that some memories are painful:

> There are very, very few people that I talk about the [electroconvulsive therapy] to. . . . I don't really want to talk about it because I hate it and it's horrible.[33]

A more complex reason not to prefer full disclosure is the likelihood that disclosing some or all aspects of mental illness will reduce a worker's level of acceptance. In economic terms, there is a *trade-off* between acceptance and disclosure.

Formal economic analysis can now proceed from three assumptions: (1) utility (i.e., happiness or satisfaction) flows from two commodities, acceptance and disclosure; (2) a worker controls the level of disclosure (i.e., symptoms are concealable), subject to a constraint that specifies the relative trade-off between acceptance and disclosure; (3) the relative trade-off between acceptance and disclosure varies from one workplace to another.

Trade-off between Acceptance and Disclosure

Just as consumers face trade-offs between desirable goods, because they are constrained by a budget (e.g., I can afford a new car *or* a trip to Hawaii, but not both), workers with SMI face a trade-off between disclosure and acceptance, because they are *constrained by the culture of their workplace.* Workers with SMI may selectively reveal details about their mental illness to their employer or coworkers. Afterward, the extent to which they are accepted at work is determined by the level of disclosure they choose, and the culture of the firm in which they are employed.

For lack of a more useful metric, disclosure may be viewed as a continuum ranging from zero to one. At the lower bound of nondisclosure, the worker is not at all forthcoming, keeping their diagnosis and history of mental illness completely private. At the upper bound of full disclosure, the worker is completely forthcoming, revealing both their diagnosis and entire history of mental illness. Along the disclosure continuum, the worker is somewhat forthcoming, revealing selected pieces of information (laundered diagnoses and limited histories).

Acceptance may also be viewed as a continuum from zero to one. At the lower bound of no acceptance, the worker quits their job, is terminated, or attempts to function in a hostile work environment. At the upper bound of full acceptance, the worker is treated "just like everyone else." Being treated just like everyone else does not necessarily mean an average or normal level of acceptance, because there are social hierarchies of acceptance for all workers in every workplace. The worker with SMI may, for example, exhibit some symptoms of mental illness and therefore be regarded as "odd" or "quirky." In this context, "full acceptance" implies that the worker's behavior is judged impartially (exactly as the behavior of any "quirky" employee is judged) rather than according to the negative stereotypes of mental illness. In Charlotte, David's employer interpreted his symptoms of mental illness as signs of exuberance. Other employers might have thought that he was a little crazy, but none of them could draw inferences from a label of schizophrenia because David *chose* a disclosure of zero.

Workplace cultures vary according to the rate at which the level of acceptance decreases as more details of SMI are revealed. The nature and extent of the trade-off between disclosure and acceptance defines the firm's *culture of discrimination.*[34] Workers with no mental illness are defined as fully accepted because there are no stigmatizing characteristics other than mental illness in this hypothetical workplace. Workers with SMI who choose a disclosure level of zero are also defined as fully accepted because they are sufficiently symptom-free that their illness is not exposed involuntarily.

Under these theoretical conditions, the culture of discrimination in a workplace may be represented as a continuous variable that ranges from zero ("a person with schizophrenia would be fully accepted as a coworker") to one ("a person with schizophrenia should be kept out of this workplace"). In any workplace, the level of acceptance of a worker with SMI is functionally related to the worker's level of disclosure and the culture of that workplace. So long as there is pervasive stigma against SMI, all workplaces are characterized by some level of discrimination greater than zero.

While these conditions are theoretical, the recognition that workplace cultures vary in the tolerance of mental illness is not. In a qualitative study of the impact of bipolar disorder on an individual's quality of life, for example, one worker told researchers that disclosure is not an option for him because, in the corporate environment where he works, having a diagnosis of mental illness is "a sign of weakness" and cause for dismissal.[35]

Every possible combination of disclosure and acceptance available at a firm yields a level of utility (job satisfaction) for the worker with SMI. Utility increases with acceptance up to the level of full acceptance, because workers with SMI want to be treated "just like everyone else." Utility also increases with disclosure, but only up to a *preferred level of disclosure* that is less than complete. In other words, workers with SMI view some aspects of their history of mental illness as private and "nobody's business." They would prefer to keep these details hidden even if there were no threat of stigma or discrimination. Beyond this preferred level, disclosure is perceived as a *bad*, and the worker will only disclose more if they are required to do so. If, for example, the worker needs to request job accommodations, the ADA requires that they tell their employer something about their disability, even if their preferred level of disclosure is zero..

Utility-Maximizing Level of Disclosure

Let us suppose that a worker with SMI has accepted a job and has been employed long enough to appraise the discriminatory culture of the workplace. The worker is now in a position to choose the level of disclosure that will *maximize their utility*, in other words, the level of disclosure that will make them most content, given their preferences for acceptance and privacy, and the culture of the firm in which they are employed.

As a frame of reference, consider a completely nondiscriminatory workplace, where a worker with SMI is fully accepted no matter what level of disclosure they choose. Full disclosure is feasible, with no loss of acceptance, but the rational agent will disclose only up to their *preferred level* of disclosure. Their utility is maximized at this point because they have revealed only those details of SMI that make them most comfortable and, at the same time, they are accepted "just like everyone else."

Now consider a workplace where the worker with SMI faces a trade-off between acceptance and disclosure. Without going into technical detail, I will assume that the worker with SMI has preferences for acceptance and disclosure that are represented by a "well-behaved" utility function, and that acceptance and disclosure are both "normal goods."[36] Within this framework, the worker with SMI chooses a level of disclosure that maximizes their utility subject to the trade-off between acceptance and disclosure imposed by the culture of the firm. The utility-maximizing level of disclosure will be *less than* the preferred level of disclosure because the worker values acceptance, and some acceptance is lost when more is disclosed. The worker's maximum utility is less than it would be in a nondiscriminatory firm, because they must trade off some preferred disclosure for acceptance.

Finally, consider an employment situation where there is a *compulsory level* of disclosure (e.g., because the job is set aside for workers with particular types of disabilities, or because job placement is arranged through a vocational rehabilitation program). The compulsory level of disclosure may be greater than the preferred level of disclosure that the worker would choose, even in the absence of discrimination. In this case, the worker is doubly penalized: Their utility is reduced because they are compelled to reveal details of their illness that they would prefer to keep private, and because the disclosure of these details reduces their level of acceptance. They would be happier (i.e., achieve a higher utility level) in a competitive job, with a similar culture of discrimination, where they could choose their utility-maximizing level of disclosure. In fact, they would be happier in a competitive job, with a slightly *more discriminatory* culture, where they could choose their utility-maximizing level of disclosure.

To summarize the model, it is useful to interpret the firm's culture of discrimination as the *price* that a worker with SMI pays for disclosure. For each "unit" increase in disclosure the worker pays a price in terms of the number of "units" of acceptance lost. In firms with a strong culture of discrimination, the price of disclosure is high. As the price falls, the worker with SMI chooses more disclosure and benefits from the reduced price. Even at a price of zero, however, concerns for privacy ensure that the preferred level of disclosure for most workers with SMI is less than full. For any specific price of disclosure, the worker is worse off when forced to "pay" for a level of disclosure beyond their preferred level.

The predictions of the model can be stated as formal and testable hypotheses:

Hypothesis 1—Even in a completely nondiscriminatory workplace, workers with SMI will not voluntarily disclose their entire psychiatric history, so long as they place any subjective value on privacy.

Hypothesis 2—Workers with SMI will disclose more information about their illness, and attain greater utility, in firms where the culture of discrimination (i.e., price of disclosure) is low.

Hypothesis 3—Workers with SMI who are employed at a firm that compels a level of disclosure beyond the level they would freely choose, could attain greater utility at a more discriminatory firm that does not require a specific level of disclosure.

These hypotheses are not trivial. Beginning with a preferred level of disclosure that is less than full for any individual who values privacy, the hypotheses state that the preferred level of disclosure will apply only in a hypothetical work environment where stigma does not exist. Having to seek acceptance in a discriminatory workplace, the rational worker maximizes utility by disclosing less than the preferred level. The utility-maximizing level of disclosure decreases as the culture of discrimination intensifies. In this context there are two ways to harm an employee with SMI. One is to increase the level of discrimination in the workplace; the other is to force disclosure beyond the level the worker prefers in the absence of discrimination.

Social Model of Disability

Taken together, the hypotheses establish a logical foundation for the social model of disability. According to the social model, workers with health impairments are disabled (unable to participate fully in normal life activities) more by their environment and the attitudes of society than by their functional limitations.[37] Consider, for example, an individual who cannot walk and is unable to use the restroom because their wheelchair is wider than the doorway. The social model of disability says the individual is disabled, not because they cannot walk, but because the doorway is too narrow. Thus, we have laws that public spaces and public transportation must be accessible to persons with disabilities. We have widened doorways, built entry ramps, and installed lifts on buses so people who cannot walk can still function in society. This is good.

Now consider the situation of a worker with SMI whose symptoms are in remission or controlled by medication, so they are able to work, with or without job accommodations. The rational choice model of disclosure implies that the key factor determining employment outcomes for the worker (including their job satisfaction) is the culture of discrimination in their workplace. This prediction is the very foundation of the social construct of disability, which asserts that if the individual is disabled at work it is *not* because of their illness, but because of *the stigmatizing attitudes of others.* Sadly, we have not put the same effort into changing the negative stereotypes of mental illness that foster workplace stigma, as we have put into building wheelchair ramps.

It is a fact that many persons with SMI are working in jobs where they *must disclose* all, or part of, their history of mental illness. These include supported employment jobs set aside for persons with mental disorders, and jobs with mental health agencies providing peer support for other persons with SMI. Presumably, these jobs are found in less discriminatory firms, because the firms have an institutional commitment to hiring persons with mental illness. For some workers, however, the compulsory level of disclosure in these jobs may be greater than their preferred level. Hypothesis 3 says that, given the trade-off between acceptance and disclosure, these workers could be better off at a more discriminatory, competitive firm, where disclosure is not required. To an economist, this hypothesis is obvious. To a social worker or policy wonk, it may be a disturbing "revelation."

Postscript

In his classic book on stigma, Erving Goffman calls the phenomenon of nondisclosure, "passing" (as normal).[38] Passing is possible for persons who have a discreditable stigma, one that is subject to prejudice but not readily apparent to others. Such is the case for persons with SMI, who face a *predicament*: "to tell or not to tell; to let on or not to let on; to lie or not to lie; and in each case, to whom, how, when, and where."[39] The person who passes creates a false identity for themselves, accepting treatment as a "normal" under false pretenses. Nevertheless, the rewards to being perceived as normal are so great, that the temptation to conceal is strong, despite the practical and psychological problems it creates. Many of these problems have been discussed throughout this chapter, but Goffman describes an additional predicament that is worth noting here.

In particular, the individual who passes "will feel torn between two attachments."[40] One is to the stigmatized group that is their real identity; the other is to the normal group from which they seek acceptance. The individual "leaves himself open to learning what others *really* think" of people with SMI, because they do not know that the individual is "one of them." In these situations, the individual faces an additional predicament: to defend their real identity and betray their secret, or to endorse the negative stereotypes that (secretly) apply to themselves.

> [When my co-workers were making disparaging remarks about people with mental illness] . . . for a split second I sort of thought well I could roll my sleeves up and say "You mean someone crazy like me?" Because that always shocks people and they say "Oh well you don't look like one of them." It's like, what am I meant to look like?[41]

Persons with schizophrenia look like just anyone else, and when their symptoms are under control, they are pretty much just like anyone else. They want to be accepted, to be productive, and to keep some parts of their lives private. They can make rational decisions in their own self-interest. *They can work.* They have had experiences of illness unlike other people, but they are disabled, not so much by their illness, as by the negative stereotypes that create an invisible cage around their lives.

Chapter Eight

Finding a Good Job Match

SAVED MY LIFE

On the corner of Grand and Weldon Avenues in central Phoenix is an old Embassy Suites Hotel, which is now home for Anthony, an eighteen-year-old "graduate" of Arizona Child Protective Services. Anthony is part of an outreach program operated by the Phoenix Dream Center, which provides housing, education, emotional and spiritual support for youth who are transitioning from the foster care system to independent living. The foster youth program is only one of the ministries operated by the Dream Center, which provides housing to more than three hundred persons served by its programs in the renovated hotel.[1]

The Phoenix Dream Center was founded by Pastor Tommy Barnett in 2006 to serve as the nucleus for the outreach ministries of his church. Through its faith-based curricula and assistance with basic needs, the Dream Center aims to rescue the vulnerable, rebuild lives, and restore hope. Anthony, who had lived in foster care homes since age four, says he came to the Dream Center,

> looking for how to be independent, how to take care of myself, and be on my own. Before I came, I didn't know God. But God is really not that bad once you get to know Him.[2]

Spring 2009

David had been attending Phoenix First Assembly for nearly a year when he applied to volunteer at the Dream Center. The volunteer application required a personal testimony. David replied guardedly, saying that he had "struggled mentally," and his life "had been off track," before he found the church and felt called to serve. His application was accepted and he was put to work immediately.

I went on a tour of the Dream Center one Tuesday morning. It was something like going to Open House nights when David was in school. Once again, I was "David's mom," only now there were coworkers, instead of teachers, telling me how much they loved my son. David showed me his office and his desk, and he was as proud as any first grader to have his own workspace. I am not sure which one of us was more in need of the validation that this job provided, probably both of us.

Throughout the summer and fall of 2009, David volunteered part time in various capacities at the Dream Center. Working part time gave him the flexibility he needed to reintegrate into employment. In January he began taking courses in Christian Ministry at American Indian College (AIC), a small Christian college in the Phoenix area. I was delighted that he was motivated, and meeting people, and too busy to join me for dinner most Friday nights. Still, I waited and watched for signs of another relapse.

Winter 2010

The primary ministry at the Dream Center is its "Church on the Street" outreach program. Church on the Street is a fifteen-month discipleship program designed to help men and women recover from incarceration, substance use issues, or physical, sexual, or emotional abuse. Participants (called disciples) live on-site at the Dream Center, attend classes and worship services, and conduct more than forty outreach ministries each week on the streets of inner-city Phoenix. The program is designed to reach out to the homeless population and other needy persons in the city, as well as to teach the disciples positive coping skills, and to restore them to healthy relationships with their families. Unfortunately, for some participants there is no supportive family to welcome them home at the end of the program. For others, living with their family would simply encourage a return to the cycle of bad choices and unhealthy behavior that they are trying to escape.

Toward the end of 2009, administrators at the Dream Center decided to start a new ministry, called the "Working Men's Program," which would provide housing for some of the graduates of Church on the Street as they transitioned to paid employment. The plan was to renovate unused space at the Dream Center, to be used as apartments for graduates who had no family support system. Men who participated in the program would pay a small monthly rent from their earnings. In return, they could continue to live in the safe and familiar environment of the Dream Center, even as they began a new job in the "real world."

When the lead pastor asked David to direct the new program, he was amazed. By this time he had disclosed his diagnosis of schizophrenia to

Tommy Barnett and other pastors at the Dream Center. David could not believe that they would entrust the leadership of a new program to someone with a history of mental illness. Over 95 percent of staff members at the Dream Center are volunteers, yet the leadership team had offered David a paid job, and a set of keys. He would be earning a paycheck again, after five years out of work.

Over the next few months, David developed guidelines and eligibility criteria for the Working Men's Program, hired an assistant, created marketing materials, and supervised renovations of the living space. He enrolled the first participants in the program, managed their agreements, and collected their program fees. As the rooms filled and the program began to stabilize, David's responsibilities expanded to other ministries. He took over one of the Saturday morning outreach ministries and began preaching at the Spanish service on Sunday mornings. He helped design and renovate rooms for the foster youth program, which Anthony eventually joined.

In 2012, David invited me back to the Dream Center to see the space prepared for another new program, called the Rescue Project. The Rescue Project aims to restore the lives of women and girls who are victims of human sex trafficking, or who are dealing with crisis pregnancies.[3] The program provides medical and legal services, therapy and counseling, and opportunities to earn a high school diploma or GED, while the women live on-site at the Dream Center. David wanted me to see the new space because each suite was designed by one of the top interior decorators in the Phoenix area. The designers competed to create the dream rooms that these girls never had as children, providing a real and symbolic contrast between their old lives and the new.

If you search Google+ for the Phoenix Dream Center, you will find several reviews. One of them simply says, "Saved my life." I could add, "Saved my son."

JOB MATCHING

David was fortunate to find a perfect job match at the Dream Center, first as a volunteer, then as director of the Working Men's program. The essence of job matching is that workers with disabilities have functional limitations that affect their productivity in some, but not necessarily all, jobs. A worker with SMI whose symptoms include compulsive organizing and checking, for example, might be highly successful as a filing clerk, but virtually useless as a short-order cook. A worker whose symptoms include insomnia or hypersomnia might be perfectly capable of working as a massage therapist, with a flexible schedule, but unable to retain a position as a bank manager, with fixed hours. In general, workers with disabilities who are able to *match* themselves into jobs that minimize the impact of their functional limitations on important job functions can expect better employment outcomes (e.g., higher wages, longer job tenure) than their counterparts who are *mismatched* in jobs where their functional limitations have greater impact.

Finding a good job match can be viewed as the most basic type of job accommodation for workers with disabilities, for at least two reasons. One, the objective of job matching and job accommodation is the same, namely, to minimize the impact of functional limitations on worker productivity. Two, a good job match is the foundation that determines if other accommodations are reasonable and potentially effective. The worker who is a compulsive organizer, for example, may be an effective short-order cook if his employer hires an assistant to keep the kitchen immaculate, but no one is likely to consider such an accommodation to be *reasonable*. The bank manager who experiences insomnia or hypersomnia might be allowed to work flexible hours, but such an accommodation will not enable them to perform the *essential functions* of the job, namely, to supervise bank operations during business hours. These workers are simply mismatched in their jobs.

Job matching has received little attention in the literature on accommodating workers with disabilities. Even when finding a better job match is the most obvious way to increase a worker's productivity, it is typically not suggested. Addison's disease, for example, is a rare hormonal disorder often characterized by weight loss and sensitivity to cold. The Job Accommodation Network (JAN) offers several ways of accommodating Addison's disease, including, wearing specially designed clothing, installing space heaters, and redirecting air conditioning vents. But it neglects the obvious accommodation of transferring to a job out of the cold![4]

Among the population of persons with SMI, there are those with the skills, abilities, and interests to hold almost any job in the economy.[5] The key to their success is finding a good match between their unique skill set, the characteristics of the job, and the functional limitations associated with their illness. My purpose here is to identify the characteristics of firms, and the types of jobs, that make a good match for persons with SMI. To do so, we must first specify the nature of the functional limitations typically associated with a serious mental illness.

Functional Limitations of SMI

Persons with SMI have an *impairment* which may result in *functional limitations*. In other words, their health condition may restrict their ability to perform some of the normal functions of daily living, like concentrating, carrying on a conversation, or managing stress. If the functional limitations interfere with one or more major life activities (e.g., working) the individual is *disabled* according to the criteria of the ADA.

Serious mental illnesses are characterized by a complex array of symptoms that primarily affect an individual's cognitive, emotional, or social capacities, although physical limitations (e.g., maintaining stamina) may be apparent as well.[6] Symptoms are highly variable across patients and, at the same time, the boundaries that define specific disorders (e.g., schizoaffective disorder and bipolar disorder) are indistinct.[7] So, *patients with the same diagnosis may exhibit considerable variation* in the nature and severity of their functional limitations, and *patients with different diagnoses may exhibit similar* functional limitations. Despite the considerable variation in the manifestations of SMI, the following generalizations are useful:

- *Cognitive* limitations are highly prevalent among persons with schizophrenia, albeit to varying degrees. The limitations may be generalized, or affect specific domains of cognitive functioning, such as *working memory, attention span, processing speed, verbal fluency*, and *task flexibility*.[8] Disorganized thinking and behavior are also characteristic of schizophrenia, particularly in the acute phase, and may affect a worker's ability to *stay focused* or *meet deadlines*.
- *Emotional* withdrawal and depression are common in schizophrenia, and extreme fluctuation in emotions is the hallmark symptom of bipolar disorder. Workers with SMI may have emotional limitations that make it difficult to *maintain concentration, to manage stress and emotions*, or *to deal with changes in the workplace*.
- *Social* interactions involving a person with schizophrenia can be strained and tense, given the emotional withdrawal and paucity of language that characterize the disease. In the workplace, social limitations may create *problems working effectively with supervisors*, or *problems interacting with coworkers and customers*.

The problem of job matching is to identify a job where the worker's functional limitations have little or no impact on important job functions. An individual who has difficulty maintaining stamina, for example, may be highly productive as a part-time teacher. An individual who has difficulty interacting with people may be a superb editor, working in a private office. An individual who has difficulty dealing with stress may thrive as a data analyst producing standardized reports. By necessity, the process of job matching is highly individualized, but it *is* possible to define general characteristics of jobs that are a good match for workers with SMI.

Workplace Characteristics that affect Job Matching

Two researchers who study management processes have developed a model of the way persons with disabilities are treated within organizations, which is relevant to the job matching process for workers with SMI. According to the model, the key determinants of how an individual with disabilities is treated-within an organization are individual characteristics (e.g., functional limita-tions), environmental factors outside the control of the organization (e.g., legislation, such as ADA, mandating job accommodations for workers with disabilities), and characteristics of the organization itself (e.g., inclusiveness of the organizational culture).[9] In applying the model to job matching, I am focused particularly on organizational characteristics.

With reference to the workplace, the relevant characteristics can be parsed into three categories: the nature of the *firm* in which the individual is employed, the *relationships* the individual establishes at work, and the nature of the *job* the individual has been hired to do. To be more specific:

* *Firm characteristics* describe the type of firm (e.g., public or private sec-tor, number of employees, industry), the nature of the work environment (e.g., workplace culture, physical characteristics of the workplace, and the policies and procedures established within the firm's management proto-cols).
* *Workplace relationships* describe interactions with supervisors, cowork-ers, or customers. These relationships can be defined by the nature and extent of contact with each group, the frequency and severity of conflict, and experiences of stigma and discrimination.
* *Job characteristics* describe the essential functions of a job, as character-ized by the ADA, as well as a number of ancillary characteristics that define the employment contract (e.g., the number of work hours required; the work pace and schedule; the degree of autonomy the worker has to organize their work).

The literature is largely silent with regard to the combinations of work-place characteristics that are amenable to good job matches for workers with SMI. Some of the best evidence comes from a small focus group study that I conducted with a colleague, Rebecca White. The purpose of the study was to identify workplace characteristics that facilitate, or impede, successful em-ployment outcomes for workers with SMI.

Qualitative Study

In 2003, Professor White conducted three focus group sessions with thirteen mental health professionals working in the southwest. Mental health profes-sionals are the frontline staff in outpatient clinics or private practices, provid-ing direct services to persons with disabling mental illnesses. All of the focus group participants had at least two years of professional experience as a mental health clinician, at least five years of experience in vocational counseling, and had a history of providing services to people with SMI from a wide range of occupations. They were employed as clinical social workers, employee assistance counselors, vocational rehabilitation counselors, or private-practice therapists. All focus group participants were currently serving at least one client with SMI who was working, or seeking to work, in a competitive job.

The research was designed to identify characteristics that help a person with SMI succeed in the competitive workplace, as well as characteristics that make successful employment less likely. Dr. White posed open-ended questions that were intended to encourage discussion among participants. Two questions pertained specifically to workplace characteristics: (1) As a group, can you describe the *ideal work environment* for someone with a serious mental illness? (2) Can you describe the *worst work environment* for somebody with SMI?

The subject of job match (or mismatch) came up repeatedly in the focus group discussions. Participants were keenly aware that the probability of successful employment for workers with SMI depends not only on the skills and abilities of the worker, but also on the extent to which workplace factors accommodate the worker's functional limitations. The comments of Joe and Sarah (names have been changed to protect the participants' anonymity) are instructive:

> *Joe:* To me, it's a match. It's a game of matching the right individual with the right kind of position and the right kind of company, and trying to look at the process . . . six months to a year down the line.

> *Sarah:* The most important is to fit the personalities and the environment and the skills and then the person needs to be allowed to succeed or fail on their own merit and not on the basis of an illness or a diagnosis or what somebody did or didn't do for them.

Below, I draw further on the focus group discussions, as well as the limited research literature, to identify specific workplace factors (firm characteristics, workplace relationships, and job characteristics) that are more (or less) amenable to workers with SMI.

Firm Characteristics

Workplace Culture

One study of the relationship between workplace characteristics and employment outcomes for workers with disabilities used data from a survey conducted through the National Bureau of Economic Research.[10] The survey involved nearly thirty thousand employees of fourteen U.S. companies, at

175 individual worksites. The data did not distinguish among different types of disabilities.

Drawing on this large database, the authors identified workplace characteristics that produced better employment outcomes (e.g., wages, hours worked, job satisfaction) for workers with disabilities relative to their nondisabled counterparts. A key consideration was how employment outcomes for workers with disabilities related to differences in corporate culture across worksites. The results indicated that the worksites that were advantageous for workers with disabilities were those perceived by workers with and without disabilities as "fair" and "responsive to employee concerns." A fair and responsive workplace culture was associated with lower expected job turnover, greater loyalty to the firm, and greater job satisfaction among workers with disabilities.[11]

A smaller study, specific to workers with mental disorders, supports the findings on workplace culture. The authors conducted semi-structured interviews with seventeen mental health service users in Britain, who were participating in employment projects for persons with SMI. The purpose of the study was to identify what types of support, and what types of workplace accommodations, were needed to achieve successful work outcomes in open (competitive) employment settings. The researchers found that the extent to which clients' needs could be met revolved largely around aspects of workplace culture. In particular, "a relaxed informal atmosphere, a culture within which difference was accepted, [and] a concern for employees' welfare" were most conducive to successful work outcomes for clients.[12]

The importance of a *supportive and responsive workplace culture* is echoed in the conversations of our focus groups:

Felicity: I think the culture of the company can make a difference. I noticed with one person where the culture that was very supportive and caring and so forth and an individual worked very well, but then a militaristic-type company bought out the former company and it just made that person go into a number of manic episodes. I think the culture and the management style is critically important.

Brenda: I use the term supportive. I don't mean when other people aren't being . . . nicey-nice and stuff like that, but the protocol within the system supports people being able to do their [best and make mistakes] without having such serious repercussions that they cannot recoup and move on.

Many of the characteristics of a workplace culture that support and encourage workers with SMI are also supportive for workers with physical disabilities, and nondisabled workers. But as "Brenda" suggests, workers with SMI may have less tolerance than other workers for a culture that is bureaucratic, rigid, or insensitive to individual employees.

Physical Environment

Similarly, the physical environment of the workplace matters to workers with and without disabilities, but workers with SMI may be especially sensitive to it because of their functional limitations. [13] Workers whose functional limitations make it difficult to stay focused and meet deadlines will likely struggle in a work environment that is frenzied and hectic, such as the newsroom of a daily newspaper. When we asked our focus group participants to identify specific characteristics of the physical environment that could be challenging for workers with SMI, they said:

> *Angie:* [A workplace that is] very regimented. Loud, chaotic, always changing. . . . It's probably the same work environments that are hard for anybody. It's just the tolerance starts earlier and the ability to adapt to it. Or they just refuse to [adapt].

> *Michael:* Loud, unstructured, high demand and no real supervisory support. It's kind of like if somebody already has a lot going on with their mind, their thoughts, and then the environment is also nonstop, maybe like a cubicle kind of situation where it's that low-level din of busyness and there's noise and that can be very hard on people [with SMI].

All our focus group participants agreed that a noisy, chaotic workplace is likely not a good job match for workers with SMI. They had mixed opinions, however, when asked what size firm tends to be most supportive. Some focused on the friendlier culture of a small firm, while others emphasized the resources of large firms and the mandates of the ADA (that do not affect firms with fewer than fifteen employees):

> *Joe:* In my experience, it's usually been a small company [that is more supportive]. It's like your Mom and Pop pizza shop or a small medical office where a person can manifest their symptoms in a safe environment and people will not be freaked out.

> *Simon:* I think that the larger employers don't want to be sued by ADA and I think it's important. So it helps to have government contracts and be a big employer if you want to be mentally ill and also [it helps if you] have worked there for ten, fifteen, or twenty years!

A study conducted by researchers at Cornell University also reached mixed conclusions regarding the impact of firm size on employment outcomes for workers with disabilities. The authors collected survey data from more than eight hundred human resource professionals to examine how firms of different sizes were complying with the accommodations mandate of the ADA. The results indicated that large (greater than five hundred employees) and small firms were equally likely to provide job accommodations needed by employees with disabilities.[14] Large firms were better prepared and more experienced in providing a wide variety of accommodations, but small firms had less difficulty "changing attitudes of coworkers/supervisors," when accommodations involved workplace relationships.

Workplace Relationships

Workplace relationships are important to the success of any worker, but particularly so for workers with SMI. The relationships that a worker with SMI establishes with supervisors and coworkers can be crucial to their success.

Supervisor

The most important workplace relationship for a worker with SMI is likely to be with their immediate supervisor. This is the person who trains them, oversees their daily tasks, and evaluates their job performance. Perhaps most importantly, this is the person to whom they must disclose their mental illness if they need to request employer-provided job accommodations. Research indicates that supervisors who are a good match for workers with SMI are those who treat workers with respect, provide constructive feedback, and express genuine concern about their employees' welfare.[15]

For workers whose functional limitations include memory deficits and difficulties maintaining concentration, the best match is with a supervisor who establishes clear expectations and boundaries, provides adequate training (including a breakdown of job tasks into manageable units), and provides support when problems arise.[16] Our focus group respondents emphasized the need for supervisors to accommodate the individual needs of employees, but cautioned against supervisors who are hypervigilant in overseeing an employee's every move:

Felicity: I think if the supervisor has an understanding [that], whether it's mental illness or not, different people have different needs to operate to their capacity. Some people need a little bit of attention; other people like to be totally independent.

Anne: Well, to me structure is when there's a set job and protocol by which the job is done. Where expectations about what . . . people should be [doing] in the office, what is the general flow of the day's structure [are clear] . . . versus supervision which is a . . . manager who is really eyeballing over the shoulder on a continuous basis . . . [asking for] quality assessment reports and time studies . . . and it's like the person has to practically write down when they signed out for the bathroom and when they came back and how many minutes was that.

Coworkers and Customers

Coworker relationships can be critically important to workers with SMI in competitive jobs. Supportive coworkers can increase a worker's confidence, make them feel comfortable in the workplace, help them adjust to the requirements of their job, and provide support through periods of difficulty.[17] In contrast, coworkers who are critical and demanding, or who harass workers whom they perceive to be "different," create conflict in the workplace. Such hostility obviously makes it more difficult for a worker with SMI to succeed.

> *Felicity:* I think the term respect is the best one I can come up with. That within a work situation we all would like to be respected for what we bring to the work situation, to the work that needs to be done. Telling a group of colleagues [to] respect that someone may be having some difficulties with anxiety but that person can still get this job done and [to] focus on that rather than focusing on, "Did you know that she's leaving early every Tuesday afternoon to go see her therapist?"

Ironically, the development of respectful and supportive relationships at work can be hampered by the very functional limitations that characterize SMI. The issue is especially acute when a worker's functional limitations include emotional withdrawal or problems with anger management. So, even though a worker with SMI may need the support and understanding of coworkers, they may not have the social skills to develop a relationship that elicits those responses. One of our focus group respondents expressed the predicament this way:

> *Sandy:* In my experience you have two parts of work. You have the task that you're expected to do every day but almost as big as that is this whole thing that we do every day socially. It's the potlucks; it's who's putting in for so-and-so's baby shower; who's taking their lunch when, with whom. Workers with SMI really lack those skills and it's those skills that could get them into trouble. So if their coworkers could be inclusive and invite them into that environment, or that social aspect of work, but then also respect the fact that they might not want to be doing that. It's a fine line. It says, "Please invite me but then also understand that there may be days where I just can't do it."

Another workplace relationship that can be challenging for workers with SMI is the relationship with customers. Any job that involves dealing with angry, impatient customers will be difficult for most workers with a history of mental illness, because conflict is the nature of the job, and conflict aggravates anxiety and stress.[18] In other words, working in the customer relations department of any large organization will almost certainly be a mismatch for a worker with SMI. Our focus group respondents agreed. When asked about workplace factors that make competitive employment difficult for workers with SMI, several of our focus group respondents immediately said:

Ken: Demanding customers.

Joe: Customer service is not good. That's just my opinion.

Job Characteristics

Occupation

Surprisingly, a worker's occupation is not particularly important in defining a good job match for workers with SMI. The mental health professionals who participated in our focus groups had worked with nurses, engineers, computer programmers, technicians, plumbers, teachers, roofers, telemarketers, construction installers, janitors, phlebotomists, medical assistants, accountants, sales persons, computer repairers, executive directors, program coordinators, nurse's aides, a prep-worker in a fast-food restaurant, a radio disk jockey, in short, a vast array of occupations.

Brenda: We've run the gamut [of occupations]. That's real fun as a rehab counselor because it's then again people achieving their level of potential, utilizing their transferable skills and sometimes along the way the agency helping them with training [and] education, which we do a lot. That's fun. It's really nice.

As Brenda notes, one of the characteristics of a good job match for workers with SMI is that the job allows them *to achieve their potential.* For those whose residual symptoms are severely disabling, a part-time, low-skill job, with or without employment support, may be a sufficient challenge. But many persons who are recovering from mental illness aspire to more than entry-level work.

The desire for more challenging work was a prominent theme emerging from a study of the way persons with SMI navigate employment. Researchers conducted in-depth interviews with thirty-two persons who have significant psychiatric disabilities. Respondents expressed dissatisfaction with vocational rehabilitation counselors who offered low-wage jobs that were neither challenging nor interesting:

> I think the problem that we have with the [VR] program is that we have what is called blue-collar positions, and they probably don't have a means to place you in more difficult things. . . . When people get mentally ill they don't lose their intelligence. So there should be fields for mental illness that could use a higher IQ.[19]

Too often, well-meaning relatives, friends, or mental health providers discourage patients with SMI from seeking anything more than low-level work. The message conveyed to patients is that their future, including the kind of work they can do, is limited by the severity of their illness. Most of the study participants had received these kinds of negative messages regarding their potential work capacity.[20] Some were told by mental health providers that they would never work again. Others were placed by vocational rehabilitation counselors into low-wage, low-skill jobs, and then discouraged from seeking more challenging work because they might experience a relapse, or lose their SSDI benefits. When the focus is on the *illness* rather than the person, "often an individual's talents, abilities, and interests are simply forgotten or unwittingly relegated to the background by the concerned and well intentioned individuals around them."[21]

Work Processes

Provided that the knowledge, skills, and abilities required for a job are a good match for the skills and abilities of the worker, the job characteristics that are most critical for workers with SMI are *autonomy, flexibility,* and *consistent expectations*. These characteristics of the work process facilitate the success of almost any worker, but are particularly important for workers with SMI because of the nature of the functional limitations associated with mental illness. For workers who have difficulty with interpersonal relationships, some degree of autonomy at work is important. For workers who have difficulty dealing with change, consistency of expectations is important. For almost any worker with SMI, flexibility in the way work is accomplished is crucial, because *flexibility allows a worker to adapt their job to their specific functional limitations*. When we asked our focus groups "What characteristics make a job a good match for workers with SMI?" one participant told us:

Michael: Flexibility of schedule. [Flexibility of] work hours. I think that helps folks a lot. Part-time jobs seem to be almost ideal for a lot of folks because full time is a lot, but when there's a flexible kind of schedule and there's that lack of pressure like, "I've got to be here at this time." It helps accommodate, sometimes, a symptom flow.

With respect to other work processes, finding a good job match is a highly individual undertaking. Some workers with SMI find working alone to be intimidating; others thrive on the flexibility that comes from working by themselves. For some workers, the pressure of a job with managerial responsibilities (e.g., overseeing finances, inventories, or other people) is too stressful, but there are many individuals with SMI who are successful accountants, executives, and even kindergarten teachers! Working with computers can be daunting for some workers with SMI; others find that a computer helps them drown out symptoms and focus on job tasks:

> *Simon:* One of the things that is just amazing to me is to take a person who is very, very psychotic, with a lot of symptoms, and put them in front of a computer and it's just great! It's the focus, I think. I have found that if the job has a real focus, then a lot of the symptoms go away while they're focused.

In defining the job requirements that make a good job match for a worker with SMI, there are only a few general rules: The expectations should be consistent; the tasks should be achievable but fulfilling; and the work processes should be flexible. And the greatest of these is flexibility.

Job Matching as a Supply Side Intervention

In the United States, efforts to improve employment outcomes for workers with disabilities have focused almost exclusively on demand-side interventions in the labor market. The ADA and its amendments place the burden of providing job accommodations for workers with disabilities squarely on employers. Although well-intentioned, disability employment policies that focus on employer-provided job accommodations are inherently condescending, such policies emphasize the limitations associated with disability, and implicitly assume that workers with disabilities must be treated differently from others. Many workers with SMI reject these assumptions and choose not to request employer-provided job accommodations at all. [22]

A recurrent theme of this book is to encourage the redirection of disability employment policies to focus on the supply-side of the labor market, for example, by ensuring that persons with SMI acquire human capital that is valued by employers. Job matching is a supply-side policy because it emphasizes placing workers with SMI in jobs that minimize the impact of their functional limitations, hence increasing their value in the labor market. The topic of job matching has received hardly any attention from policy makers, funding agencies, or administrators of the mental health system. Yet the extant literature, combined with excerpts from our focus group participants, demonstrate that the process of job matching should be a critical component of any approach to accommodating workers with mental disabilities.

In fact, job matching can be viewed as the most basic accommodation for workers with disabilities. If a good job match is found, few additional accommodations will be needed. If the job has sufficient flexibility, any additional accommodations can be initiated by the worker, without the need to involve their employer or disclose their diagnosis of SMI. Hence, job matching has the potential to minimize the need for employer-provided accommodations, which impose financial costs on the employer, indirect costs on coworkers, and psychological costs on the employee with SMI.

Employment policies that focus on the supply side of the labor market are inherently empowering because they emphasize the capabilities and autonomy of the worker with SMI. By focusing on accumulation of human capital, and job placements that are a good match for both the talents and functional limitations of the worker, supply-side politics have the potential to reduce dependency on SSDI and SSI.

To promote the concept of job matching, I have identified a number of workplace characteristics that make a good match for the typical worker with SMI. These include: a *workplace* culture that is flexible and supportive; workplace *relationships* that are respectful and reflect genuine concern for individuals; and a *job* with clear and consistent expectations, flexible work processes, and tasks that are appropriate for the worker's skills and abilities. Ultimately, however, the process of finding a good job match is an individual one. Our focus group data suggest that process is happening, for some unknown number of workers with SMI, and it is effective.

> *Brenda:* I'll tell you what, the cool thing is and I don't know if it [is a change] that was conscious or something that was just happening. But [ever] since I've been in this business I know that the trend was to get individuals into entry level positions . . . get them working, get them in a job. What I've seen happen more so lately is that individuals who are getting jobs are more able to sustain themselves financially and get off of benefits and that's just been really cool, the independence and the empowerment and the transformation I've seen in individual's lives because of it.

Postscript

When David first began work at the Dream Center, he had not experienced an acute episode of psychosis for five years. He had also not held a regular job (or any job) for five years. He no longer had delusions about being God, but he was still passionate about his religious beliefs, and religion was his favorite topic of conversation. His medications made him tired, especially in the mornings. He was not accustomed to being around people, other than his parents and the few friends that he had made at church. He was anxious about returning to work and insecure about his capabilities. His cognitive abilities were intact, but he was perhaps more rigid in his opinions and less flexible with changes in routine than he was before schizophrenia. His disease was in remission and he could work, if he could find the right job.

The Dream Center was an almost ideal workplace for David. Its mission is to serve as a resource for needy populations in the City of Phoenix, including the homeless, at-risk youth, families with limited financial resources, persons with alcohol and substance use issues, and persons newly released from prison. By its very nature, the culture of the Dream Center is supportive and tolerant of differences. A person with SMI fits right in!

The Dream Center is a nonprofit organization sponsored by Phoenix First Assembly Church. All its programs are centered on the ideals of the Christian faith, and many of its staff members serve in the ministry. David's deep spiritual convictions and inclination to talk about Christianity were not unusual there. He was accepted, included, and respected by his coworkers and supervisors.

As a volunteer in a newly created position, David had considerable flexibility to set his own work hours (he usually started work after 9 a.m., and worked two to three days a week) and to work at his own pace (there were no deadlines for most of his projects). As his confidence increased, his responsibilities expanded to giving weekly tours of the Dream Center and eventually to running the Working Men's Program. He achieved his goals of launching the new program, completing his associate's degree at AIC, and serving the missionary outreach of the church. The job was full of purpose and challenge (one Christmas his wish list included several books on leadership and management).

The job at the Dream Center was *almost* ideal. The problem was that, even after David started being paid, the income was small and there were no benefits. The job was not on a career path that led to financial security or independence from government support. But it was a perfect job from which to find that path.

Chapter Nine

Job Accommodations for Workers with SMI

A LONG WAY FROM PARIS

I met Chung Choe while he was a graduate student at the University of Arizona, studying for a doctoral degree in economics. He shared my research interests in workplace discrimination and workers with disabilities and hoped that we might collaborate in the future. After graduation, Chung accepted a position at a research institute in Luxembourg. One day I received an email from him, inviting me to spend a month at the institute as part of their Visiting Professor program. "How far is it to Paris?" I wrote back. "Two hours by train," Chung replied.

And so, in June 2010, I was in Luxembourg. On a long weekend I took the train to Paris for four carefree days of art museums, croissants, cathedrals, and *joie de vivre*.

Summer 2010

Chung and I were working at the institute one stifling afternoon (the building had no air conditioning), when I realized that I had not received a single email from David for three weeks. It was odd, because we talked several times a week when I was at home. I confided to Chung that I was worried about my son. He simply smiled and said, "He's met a girl." Impossible, I thought.

Nevertheless, when I returned home in July, David introduced me to Alex. The two had met at the Dream Center that spring and planned to be married on Labor Day weekend! Alex had three young children. I liked her very much; I always liked my sons' girlfriends. (My colleagues once told me it was because my sons were smart enough to introduce me only to the girls I was sure to like.)

We had a short two months to plan a wedding. Alex had no family in the area, so I volunteered to help in any way I could. The two of us shopped for a wedding dress and wedding clothes for her daughters. We addressed and mailed the invitations. We reserved the church for the ceremony and a small reception. One day, David went along with us to order flowers. Alex and I sat down to talk with the florist, but David could not stay still. He kept jumping up, collecting flowers that he liked, experimenting with different color combinations. When he wasn't bouncing out of his chair, he was talking nonstop. I had seen this behavior before.

As we left the store, I asked if he was taking his medicine.

No, he had been off his meds for five months.

Years later, David told me how he had weaned himself off the antipsychotic drugs. In January 2009, he told his psychiatrist that he had been taking a reduced dose of medication and wanted to get off the meds entirely. His doctor agreed to help. Together, they formulated a plan: David saw the psychiatrist every three months; every six months they reduced his dosage of antipsychotics by 30 milligrams. By March 2010, David was off the drugs completely.

I was more than a little distressed by the signs of relapse, certain that David would have another psychotic episode if he did not resume the medications. My distress triggered a firestorm. Alex asked David to go back on the medications "for her sake." He said no. When she then sought my advice, I told her bluntly, "If I were you, I'd run as far away as I could." Alex broke off the engagement. I helped with the process of un-inviting guests and canceling the church and flowers. The wedding dress hung in my closet (where it remained for nearly two years). Meanwhile, I prepared to deal with the relapse that was sure to come. Paris seemed very far away and long ago.

Fall 2010

David did not seem too upset about the canceled wedding plans. He continued working at the Dream Center and attending classes at AIC. As November approached, he asked if he could invite a few friends from the college to share Thanksgiving dinner at my new condominium. I thought it might be fun to show off my new home, so I agreed to do the cooking. A few days before the holiday, I asked David how many friends he expected. "Oh, twenty to twenty-five," he said.

I bought another turkey and doubled my recipes.

What an eclectic group we had for Thanksgiving that year! There was David's favorite professor, who had recently moved to Arizona, but whose family was still back east. There were two Native American women from his classes. There was an African American man and his three teenage daughters. Twenty people in all, crammed into my little home. Before we sat down to eat, David asked everyone to join hands as he said grace.

How much fun it was to listen to the conversation around that Thanksgiving table! The Native Americans told us about their Thanksgiving traditions; the three teenagers challenged the professor with questions about God; like Socrates, he answered their questions with questions of his own. Looking back, that was the night I first had a glimpse of the man my son was becoming. He was not the same person that he would have been without schizophrenia, for he had a compassion and sensitivity that comes only with suffering and pain. He was a gracious host, and exhibited no signs of anxiety or restlessness. Still, part of me waited, and watched, for the relapse that I thought was sure to come.

It never did.

To this day, more than five years after he stopped taking his meds, David has been virtually symptom-free. I do not pretend to understand how his mind was healed, but David has no doubts. The hand of God laid out a divine plan, through the hospitals and jail, to the woman in the psychiatrist's office, to Tommy Barnett and the Dream Center. When God was ready, it was time to let go of the medications; David let go and let God.

There are others with schizophrenia who, like David, have successfully weaned themselves off antipsychotic drugs. In 2012, an article in a leading psychiatry journal asked the question, "Do all schizophrenia patients need antipsychotic treatment throughout their lifetime?" The authors followed seventy patients with schizophrenia, for up to twenty years after being hospitalized with acute psychosis. Beginning with the two-year follow-up, 34 percent of patients were taking antipsychotic medications continuously, 21 percent were not taking medications at all. Those who were not taking medications were a self-selected group, with better prognostic factors at the index hospitalization than the group that was still on antipsychotics. At the twenty-year follow-up, the group not taking medications exhibited a *significantly higher rate of recovery* than the group that was still on antipsychotic drugs.[1]

I am *not* advocating that persons with SMI stop taking their medications. Many persons with mental illness who are working in competitive jobs have told us that they *could not function* without their meds. But in response to the question posed in the article, the answer is no. Not all patients with schizophrenia need to be on antipsychotics for the remainder of their lives.

THE NATURE AND COSTS OF JOB ACCOMMODATIONS

More and more research is discrediting the negative stereotypes of persons with schizophrenia as hopeless and helpless. Not all persons recover from the

illness, but many do. Not all persons with schizophrenia are capable of independent, competitive employment, but many are. For those whose symptoms
are in remission, with or without medications, success in the labor market
depends more on the accommodations that are available, than on the constraints of their illness.

The *Oxford English Dictionary* gives some idea of the scope of what
accommodation can mean. The word *accommodate* comes from a Latin root,
meaning suited, or suitable. Today, the word means:

1. To fit things to each other; to adjust, reconcile (things or persons that
   differ), and hence, to compose, settle, their differences; to bring to
   harmony or agreement . . .
2. To fit (a person with the understood requirements of the occasion); to
   furnish (a person with something requisite or convenient); to equip,
   supply, provide . . .
3. To suit, oblige, convenience . . .
4. To adapt oneself to. . . .[2]

Definition 1 captures the very essence of Title I of the ADA, namely, that,
"qualified persons with disabilities" have a right to be treated without discrimination (harmoniously) in the workplace. This definition also captures
the essence of job matching as an accommodation, namely, *to fit* a worker
and a job *to each other.*

Definition 2 applies to the types of employer-provided accommodations
that *furnish* or *equip* persons with disabilities with items that they need in
order to function in the workplace. Wheelchair ramps for workers who cannot walk, lifting devices for workers with chronic back pain, and telecommunications devices for workers with hearing disabilities, are good examples.
Few, if any, of the job accommodations needed by workers with mental
illness fall into this category.

Definition 3, which comes directly from the Latin root, meaning *suited*, is
the one that best applies to the employer-provided accommodations recommended for workers with SMI. Typically, these accommodations involve
changes to the work environment, workplace relationships, or job characteristics that *suit* the functional limitations of workers with mental illness, or
make it more *convenient* for them to work. Allowing a worker to take un-
scheduled breaks to help cope with stress, or to move to a quieter office to
minimize distractions, are good examples.

Definition 4 fits a type of accommodation that is not mentioned in the
ADA, and has been almost completely overlooked in the literature. Specifically, workers with disabilities often find ways to *adapt themselves or their
job* to accommodate their functional limitations. These types of self-initiated

accommodations have many advantages relative to the employer-provided accommodations mandated by the ADA.

Self-Initiated Job Accommodations

More formally, *self-initiated accommodations* can be defined as ways in which workers with disabilities adapt themselves or their job to compensate for their functional limitations, on their own initiative, without involving their employer or coworkers. For example, in our qualitative study of workers with SMI, one woman told us:

> When I was working with the developmentally-disabled population and my illness was affecting me at work, I would take them out. We would go to a movie, or go bowling, or something. I kind of just redirected my attention.[3]

As another example, a massage therapist said that he compensates for the side effects of antipsychotic drugs by not scheduling morning appointments, and by canceling appointments when he is symptomatic.

One tremendous advantage of self-initiated accommodations is that there is no need to disclose a diagnosis of SMI to an employer. Thus, contrary to what appears in much of the literature, disclosure of a disability is *not* a prerequisite for accommodation to take place. The worker who can initiate accommodations on their own can avoid a potentially stigmatizing revelation, and continue to feel "just like any other worker."

Relatively simple adaptations (e.g., maintaining a calendar to keep track of deadlines or making organizational charts to help stay focused on job tasks) can be implemented by almost any worker, but most self-initiated accommodations require considerable flexibility in a job. Flexibility might include freedom to change work hours, control over specific job tasks, or mobility around the workspace. The woman working with the developmentally disabled population, for example, could choose the group's daily activities to accommodate her flow of symptoms. The massage therapist was self-employed, so he could adjust his work schedule to accommodate his illness.

In some cases, a job is such a perfect match for a worker's functional limitations that the necessary accommodations are incorporated in the job description. One worker with SMI fortunate enough to be in such a job called these "natural" accommodations:

> Some jobs that I had really had the natural accommodations built into them. One was I was developing x-ray films in the dark room and they'd be sending these films in to me and I would be by myself most of the day, and I felt that was a great job because I didn't have that pressure because I was in that particular spot I felt it was my little world.[4]

No worries about difficult workplace relationships in that job!

All in all, self-initiated accommodations are far easier to implement (because no one else is involved), and have far less potential for negative repercussions (because disclosure is not required), than accommodations that must be requested from an employer. Many workers, however, do not have sufficient autonomy to initiate accommodations on their own. When an employer becomes involved, the accommodations process becomes both more complex and more costly.

Employer-Provided Job Accommodations

Accommodating workers with SMI presents a unique set of challenges for employers, beginning with identifying the particular accommodations that suit an individual worker. There is no well-defined set of functional limitations that characterize mental illness, and no well-defined set of accommodations that apply to all workers with SMI. Workers with schizophrenia, for example, may exhibit cognitive, emotional, or social limitations, or no limitations at all. The wide range of functional limitations gives rise to a correspondingly wide range of suggested job accommodations: from providing headphones to adjusting work shifts, from sensitivity training for coworkers to providing checklists of assigned tasks, from increasing supervision, to being allowed to work from home!

The potential accommodations can be characterized by their nature (*public versus private goods*) and by their impact on coworkers (*positive versus negative externalities*). These distinctions are important because they affect how difficult and how costly it will be to implement an accommodation. In other words, they help to determine if an accommodation is *reasonable.*

Public Goods

An example will help to clarify what economists mean by a *public good.* Many years ago, while traveling in Rome, I visited the church of St. Luigi dei Francesi to view *The Calling of St. Matthew*, a masterpiece by the Italian painter, Caravaggio. All the chapels in the church were brightly lit, except the one that held the famous painting. To illuminate that chapel, visitors had to drop coins into a box on the wall. (The priests were entrepreneurs; they knew they had something of great value, and found a way to profit from it.) Most visitors were eager to contribute, even though the light illuminated the painting for everyone, whether or not they had "paid." The intensity of light did not diminish, whether ten people or one hundred were viewing the painting. The light was a *public good* and those who did not contribute were *free riders.*

Free riders are not always so fortunate: If no one contributes, a public good will not be provided. The entrepreneurial priests did not use the same tactic to illuminate other chapels because, without a famous art work to attract donations, the chapels would remain mostly dark. I mention this because profit-oriented firms provide a number of public goods that benefit their employees and customers (lighting, air conditioning, smoke alarms, etc.), without ever attempting to charge for them directly.

Like the lights in the chapels and the air conditioning in stores and factories, some job accommodations are public goods. Wheelchair ramps, for example, are available to anyone, and the value of the ramps does not diminish with use. Some of the job accommodations that are recommended for workers with SMI, such as sensitivity training for coworkers and supervisors, can be characterized as public goods as well.

Other accommodations are *private goods*, because they are provided only to an individual worker with disabilities. A desk built to exact specifications for a wheelchair user is an example, as is the set of headphones purchased for a worker with SMI.

Externalities

Job accommodations that are public by nature clearly affect other workers, but accommodations that are private goods can impact coworkers as well. If, for example, building a special desk for a wheelchair user means that another worker is displaced, the accommodation has an effect on the coworker. Economists refer to these kinds of effects as externalities, which can be positive (beneficial) or negative (harmful) to others.

The textbook example of a commodity with *positive externalities* is vaccination. Vaccination benefits those who receive the vaccine and *others who have never been vaccinated*, by reducing their likelihood of exposure to disease. Semantically, positive externalities are often attributed to public goods as a matter of emphasis. Sensitivity training may have positive externalities for every worker who has been subject to teasing or harassment, even though the training was offered to accommodate a particular worker with SMI.

The textbook example of *negative externalities* is a manufacturer that dumps waste products in a river, thereby imposing pollution on *others who may never purchase the manufacturer's products*, but happen to be located downstream. With reference to job accommodations, assigning a worker with chronic back pain to light duty (lifting loads of twenty pounds or less) imposes negative externalities on other workers who must then lift a higher proportion of heavy loads. Similarly, allowing a worker with SMI to work only day shifts imposes negative externalities on other workers who must then work the night shift more often.

As noted earlier, the characterization of job accommodations as public versus private goods, with positive versus negative externalities, has important implications for evaluating the costs of employer-provided accommodations. The characterization also provides a convenient way to classify and compare the accommodations recommended for different types of disabilities.

Taxonomies of Job Accommodations

For Serious Mental Illness

I analyzed thirty-five different types of job accommodations for workers with SMI, and classified them as private or public goods, and as goods with positive externalities, negative externalities, or no externalities. The list of accommodations was assembled from recommendations of the Job Accommodation Network[5] and the literature on accommodating persons with mental illness in the workplace.[6] According to this analysis, there are four distinct clusters of accommodations:

1. *Public goods with positive externalities.* For example, promoting a nonhostile work environment, or reducing distractions in the workplace, has benefits available to every worker without diminishing the value to others (20 percent of total).
2. *Private goods with positive externalities.* For example, transferring a worker to another supervisor is an option available only to the worker receiving the accommodation, but the arrangement may benefit coworkers by reducing conflict and tension in the workplace (less than 10 percent of total).
3. *Private goods with few if any externalities* for other workers. For example, a set of headphones provided to a worker to drown out the voices they hear neither benefits nor harms coworkers (approximately 25 percent of total).
4. *Private goods with negative externalities.* For example, allowing one worker to take longer or more frequent breaks imposes costs on coworkers who must cover for them (more than 45 percent of total).

My analysis suggests that nearly half the accommodations recommended for workers with SMI have a negative impact on other workers. These accommodations can be problematic for employers, because the negative externalities increase the real costs of the accommodation.

For Back Pain

To see if this proportion of accommodations with negative externalities is representative of other disabilities, I constructed a similar taxonomy of job accommodations recommended for workers with back pain. Like mental illness, back pain is a chronic disorder that imposes functional limitations ranging from mild to severe, and that is often characterized by periods of remission and relapse. Unlike mental illness, back pain is not stigmatized.

I found a list of twenty-four accommodations recommended for workers with back pain on the JAN,[7] and classified them as public or private goods, with positive, negative, or no externalities. Once again, the recommended accommodations fall into four clusters:

1. Twenty percent of accommodations for back pain are *public goods with positive externalities* (e.g., automatic door openers)
2. Seventeen percent are *private goods with positive externalities* (e.g., a rolling ladder, which might be provided to one worker but shared with others)
3. Forty-six percent are *private goods with no externalities* (e.g., low-task chairs, height-adjustable desks, ergonomic workstations)
4. Seventeen percent are *private goods with negative externalities* (e.g., being allowed to take frequent rest periods, or being assigned to light duty)

Compared to the accommodations recommended for workers with SMI, a greater proportion of accommodations recommended for workers with back pain create *positive* externalities for other workers (37 percent versus 30 percent), and a far smaller proportion create *negative* externalities (17 percent versus 45 percent). As shown next, the difference has important implications for evaluating the relative costs of providing job accommodations for workers with SMI versus workers with back pain.

Real Costs of Job Accommodations

Research on the subject of job accommodations for workers with disabilities indicates that most accommodations can be implemented at minimal, or even zero, cost to employers.[8] This insight would be very encouraging if it were true, or even approximately accurate. Unfortunately, the estimated costs on which the insight is based are almost always lower than the real costs of the accommodations, because some cost categories are not fully counted.

For example, the indirect costs of negative externalities are typically not included in estimates of the costs of job accommodations. These costs involve both the time costs imposed on coworkers or supervisors and the resentment that coworkers naturally feel when one worker receives a benefit for which others bear the costs. Resentment can translate into weakened morale and reduced willingness to work hard; such reactions reduce productivity, which imposes real costs on the employer.[9]

The research on job accommodations also typically ignores the cost implications of accommodations with a public goods nature. It is misleading, for example, to allocate the full cost of constructing a wheelchair ramp to the accommodation of a single worker with a mobility limitation. Other workers who have difficulty climbing stairs benefit from the ramp as well. And, if there were no ramps, there would be more stairways. To make an accurate accounting of costs, the value of the benefits to other workers (positive externalities) must be factored out of the accommodation cost.

The reader should note, however, that making an appropriate adjustment for the indirect costs of positive or negative externalities is extremely difficult. In fact, the adjustment is so difficult that it is almost never attempted. Thus, it is acceptable to count the wheelchair ramp as a cost of accommodating a physical disability, if the external benefits are duly noted: Ramps benefit other workers with mobility limitations, and also reduce the need to construct stairways.

Cost allocation is not much of an accounting problem when the accommodation is a private good. The costs of a specially constructed desk for a worker in a wheelchair, or headphones for a worker with SMI, can be directly allocated to the accommodation of a specific beneficiary.

The nature of job accommodations recommended for workers with SMI is intrinsically different from the nature of accommodations recommended for workers with physical or sensory disabilities. Accommodations for workers with SMI are less likely to involve purchases of equipment, or physical changes to the workplace, and more likely to involve workplace relationships and supervisory time. Hence, accommodations for SMI typically involve lower direct costs, but higher indirect costs, than accommodations for workers with physical or sensory disabilities.[10] The indirect costs reflect the potential loss of morale among coworkers and supervisors are likely to be far greater when an employer is trying to accommodate a worker with SMI.

Cost Categories for Job Accommodations

Suppose we view job accommodations as (nonmarket) transactions between workers with disabilities and employers, who have a legal obligation to provide reasonable accommodations under the ADA. The direct and indirect costs of each transaction can be divided into five general categories: (1) purchases of equipment or alterations to the workspace, for which the firm will have external or internal invoices; (2) negative externalities in the form of supervisory time; (3) negative externalities in the form of coworker time; (4) other negative externalities, including productivity losses associated with coworker anger and resentment; and (5) positive externalities (negative costs) if an accommodation benefits other workers.

Only the first category (equipment purchases/alterations to the workspace) involves observable costs that are relatively easy to measure. The costs of such accommodations (e.g., an ergonomic workstation or an enclosed workspace) will be documented by an accounting trail of paid invoices or service requisitions. In contrast, it is unlikely that any firm keeps an accounting record of the time costs that a job accommodation imposes on supervisors or coworkers.

The fact that a large proportion of accommodations for SMI involve negative externalities in the form of time costs, together with the lack of documentation for time costs, has helped perpetuate the myth that "the majority of job accommodations for workers with mental illness are free, or cost very little."[11] Based on this mistaken perception, one author asserts that an employer's reluctance to accommodate workers with SMI is economically "irrational."[12] In fact, there is no such thing as a free accommodation,[13] and any economically rational employer considers supervisory time as a valid cost of production.

When the accommodations recommended for workers with SMI and workers with back pain are mapped to the five cost categories, the results show that a much larger proportion of accommodations for workers with SMI involve supervisory time (51 percent versus 21 percent), coworker time (34 percent versus 8 percent), or other negative externalities (26 percent versus 17 percent). A far smaller proportion of accommodations for workers with SMI involve direct costs for equipment, or modifications to the workplace (14 percent versus 58 percent). Additionally, a smaller proportion of accommodations for workers with SMI confer positive externalities on other workers (29 percent versus 37 percent).

The preponderance of negative externalities among the job accommodations for SMI suggests that these accommodations may encounter resistance from coworkers, supervisors, and employers who bear the costs. The authors of one study asked 305 employees of a Canadian health-care organization about the appropriateness of various job accommodations for workers with mental illness. Of the seven accommodations considered, "taking time off for counselling" and "banking of overtime hours" were perceived as most appropriate; "taking longer/more frequent breaks," and "working at a slower pace," were perceived as least appropriate.[14] The results suggest that accommodations which involve special privileges *at work* are likely to breed greater coworker resentment than accommodations that involve *time off* work.

The costs associated with coworker anger and resentment tend to be aggravated when a disability is concealable. In this case, coworkers have no way to know that the worker is legally entitled to job accommodations, because the ADA prohibits an employer from disclosing the reason for the apparent special privileges. Other employees wonder why the worker is "getting away with everything" or "being allowed to complain and end up getting a nice work schedule." In our interviews of employers who have supervised workers with SMI, one respondent told us that keeping coworkers "in the dark" exacerbates such feelings of resentment:

> Some people have been wondering about where [he is] and why [he isn't] here. I think their response would have been better if I had been allowed to let them know what the problem was. [15]

Although the real costs of accommodating workers with mental illness are far from negligible, nothing in this discussion implies that the costs are prohibitive, or that the costs outweigh the benefits. In fact, the benefits of providing job accommodations to workers with SMI are numerous: the *employer* benefits through increased productivity from the worker with SMI; the *worker* benefits through improved job performance, increased job security, enhanced self-esteem, and better chances for recovery; *society* benefits through reductions in disability support payments, and increased integration of persons with SMI into the community. The cumulative benefits almost surely outweigh the costs. But it does not follow that the employer should bear *all* the costs.

One economist, who has published numerous studies on disability and work, describes the ADA as an exercise in "morality on the cheap":

> The principal charm of this Act appears to be its ability to provide some help to the disabled at no cost to the federal government. . . . The ADA compels employers to accommodate disabled workers, even [if] the costs to them of doing so exceed the benefits the firm receives. . . . [It is left] to the courts to determine the degree to which firms are required to subsidize work by the disabled. [16]

Reasonable Accommodations in the Courts

It is safe to say that "morality on the cheap" has not fared well in court. Courts have generally taken a narrow view of what is reasonable to impose on employers, acknowledging the potential hidden costs of accommodations and leading to decisions that tend to favor the defendants. The tenor of these decisions is not that the costs of accommodating workers with SMI are prohibitive or unjustified, but that *employers* should not be forced to bear the costs. The following is a review of cases that involved workers with SMI requesting: a job transfer to accommodate work-related stress, a leave of absence for medical care, and negotiated job accommodations after returning from disability-related leave.

Job Transfer

The most common reason for workers with SMI requesting a job transfer is difficulty getting along with a supervisor. [17] So long as the worker is qualified for another position that is available, a transfer can be accomplished at relatively low cost (one-time training costs) and has potential positive externalities for other workers (reduced friction). In our interviews of employers, one respondent tells how easily a request to change supervisors was accomplished for a police detective with mental illness:

> When I came over here to [this department], he was working for a different supervisor. . . . There was constant conflict. The other supervisor was very, I would say, very aggressive, very opinionated, and had a habit of embarrassing this individual. And it just wasn't going to work out. And he . . . asked me if he could come to work for me. And, I said, whatever come on. [18]

Employers are typically more resistant to requests for job transfers than this anecdote implies. Despite the economic conclusion that transfers are relatively low-cost accommodations, courts have almost universally ruled that job transfers requested because of personality conflicts are *not* reasonable. [19] The case of *Gaul vs. Lucent Technologies Inc.* is representative.

Dennis Gaul was employed by AT&T, working on the design of a cordless telephone for international markets. Gaul suffered from depression and anxiety disorders. His condition was serious enough that he had spent time in a psychiatric hospital and taken extended disability leave before returning to work on the telephone project.

Gaul worked without stress for over a year, until he was assigned a new coworker with whom he had conflicts. Gaul complained that the coworker held back information from him, took credit for his ideas, and failed to acknowledge his contributions to the project. Gaul complained to his supervisor that he was under tremendous stress, and requested that he be transferred to a less stressful position:

> *Gaul:* If you don't help me, or if you can't help me at this point, I am going to get very sick, and I'm going to pop. . . . Do you know what I mean by pop?
>
> *Supervisor:* I don't know what you mean by pop.
>
> *Gaul:* Well, I am going to have a nervous breakdown, and I wouldn't be able to come back to work.

The supervisor ignored the transfer request, and Gaul took another disability leave. He then filed suit under the ADA, alleging that AT&T had failed to accommodate his disability. The Third Circuit Court of Appeals affirmed the lower court's decision that Gaul's "request to be transferred away from individuals causing him prolonged and inordinate stress was unreasonable."

The majority opinion held that the proposed accommodation would impose an "extraordinary administrative burden" on the employer, "essentially asking this court to determine the conditions of [plaintiff's] employment, most notably with whom he will work."

In short, an employer cannot be expected to transfer a worker with disabilities whenever the worker becomes "stressed out" by a coworker or supervisor. The court granted summary judgment to the employer, declaring that "nothing in the [ADA] leads us to conclude that . . . Congress intended to interfere with personnel decisions within an organizational hierarchy."[20]

The court explicitly accounted for indirect administrative costs associated with the accommodation request, concluding that the costs placed an undue hardship on the employer. In a similar vein, courts have been hostile toward accommodation requests for a nonhostile work environment. Just as employers cannot be expected to eliminate all sources of stress in the workplace, they cannot be expected to eliminate all sources of conflict. Unfortunately, in closing the door on accommodation requests involving job transfers, the courts may have closed down negotiations that could help some workers with SMI move, relatively easily, into jobs that are a better match for their functional limitations.

Leave of Absence

The most frequently requested accommodations, by workers with any type of disability, are accommodations that involve time off work.[21] Often, the requests are compelled by the need for ongoing medical care. In the case of psychiatric disabilities, such requests range from a few hours for regular therapy visits to long-term leaves of absence for inpatient psychiatric care.

Long-term leaves are disruptive and costly. If the worker is replaced by temporary help, there may be large transaction costs, with additional costs incurred when the worker returns. If the worker is not replaced, substantial negative externalities are imposed on coworkers who must cover the worker's responsibilities. All things considered, leaves of absence tend to be more costly and fraught with substantially more uncertainty (and therefore less reasonable) than internal job transfers. In *Rascon v. U S West Communications*, however, the court ruled differently.

In 1971, after a two-year tour of duty in Vietnam, Robert Rascon began working as a network technician for US West Communications. He received superior job performance ratings, but had anger management problems in the workplace. He was repeatedly suspended, and once fired, for fighting with coworkers.

Rascon attended two posttraumatic stress disorder (PTSD) treatment programs in 1989 and 1991, but his symptoms persisted. Finally, his physician recommended more intensive, inpatient treatment at the National Center for PTSD in Menlo Park, California. Rascon requested long-term disability leave from US West to enroll in the program for an expected period of four months.

His supervisor, Lorrie Sullivan, claimed that she knew nothing about PTSD until Rascon informed her that he had "Vietnam syndrome." Sullivan told him that US West did not have sufficient information to grant him paid disability leave, but that the company would grant unpaid leave in periods of thirty days. Rascon was required to submit documentation of ongoing, beneficial treatment to extend the leave month by month. He signed a waiver allowing the physicians at Menlo Park to communicate with his employer regarding his ongoing treatment, but revoked the waiver before his treatment ended. Rascon told a coworker he "did not wish US West to know every detail regarding his disability and its treatment."

After Rascon revoked the waiver, US West refused to extend further leave and terminated his employment. He filed suit alleging failure to provide reasonable accommodations for his mental condition. US West argued that an extended leave of absence is not a reasonable accommodation because "attendance is an essential function of Mr. Rascon's job." The court sided with Rascon:

> (T)he question of whether attendance is an essential [job] function is equivalent to the question of what kind of leave policy the company has. . . . Although US West characterizes the [requested] leaves as "extraordinary" [they] were less accommodating than company policy required, and the corresponding conditions US West attached to the leaves of absence were more restrictive than company policy allowed. Thus, we conclude that leave to attend the Menlo Park treatment program was a reasonable accommodation.[22]

US West did not hire a replacement for Rascon, so coworkers probably had to cover his job duties. The court opinion did not acknowledge the negative externalities, implicitly declaring that the costs were reasonable because the leave of absence fell within established policies of the firm.

Negotiating Job Accommodations

The EEOC guidelines for administering the ADA impose an affirmative duty on supervisors to negotiate job accommodations with an employee, once the employee has identified themselves as disabled and requested accommodations. The determination of what accommodations are appropriate involves an interactive process to identify the worker's functional limitations and to explore potential accommodations.[23] In *Taylor v. Phoenixville School District*, an employer's motion for summary dismissal was denied because a supervisor failed to engage in the interactive negotiation of reasonable accommodations.

Katherine Taylor was employed as the principal's secretary in Phoenixville School District beginning in 1974. For twenty years, she worked under several different principals, with consistently positive performance evaluations. In August 1993, Ms. Taylor developed symptoms of mental illness and was forced to take a leave of absence. At the time she went on leave, she had been working with the newest principal, Christine Menzel, for one week.

Taylor was hospitalized, diagnosed with bipolar disorder, and treated with antipsychotic medications. Her family kept the school district updated on her health condition during her absence and requested reasonable accommodations when she returned from leave. In October 1993, her psychiatrist said she was able to return to work.

Upon her return, Taylor discovered that Menzel had made a number of changes to the office, including new procedures and forms, a new furniture arrangement, and new computer and filing systems. Taylor also received a new job description, nearly doubling her responsibilities. She was disoriented by the changes and felt that they made her return to work more difficult.

Menzel exacerbated the situation by documenting the secretary's every mistake. Taylor had never been disciplined in twenty years working for the district, but after returning from leave she began receiving disciplinary warnings on a monthly basis. She was eventually placed on probation for unsatisfactory job performance, and finally received a notice of termination in October 1994. Taylor sued the school district, alleging that the principal had failed to negotiate reasonable accommodations when she returned from disability leave.

The court declared that Taylor had established herself as a "qualified individual with a disability"; that the school district had been informed of her disability and associated functional limitations, and received a request for accommodations; and that the school district had failed to fulfill its obligation to engage in an interactive process to negotiate accommodations. The court reversed a prior grant of summary judgment in favor of the employer, and remanded the case for further proceedings.[24]

In this case, the principal appears to have deliberately discriminated against an employee, possibly because Ms. Taylor had been diagnosed with SMI. In contrast, the majority of supervisors that we interviewed for our qualitative study were willing to "go the extra mile" for a worker with mental illness. Their comments made it clear, however, that the demands on supervisory time can be substantial.[25]

According to the supervisors we interviewed, workers with SMI typically require more time to manage than other workers because they need more explanation of what is expected of them, and more frequent reassurance that their job performance is satisfactory. Some supervisors said that they had redone work or taken over job duties for an employee with mental illness. Others talked about dealing with unusual behaviors of a worker with SMI, or with harassment from coworkers. Overall, they indicated that managing a work group that includes a worker with mental illness can be "very stressful" for supervisors. Nevertheless, most of these supervisors expressed empathy for their employee with SMI, and wanted to help them succeed.

Postscript

Title I of the ADA was expected to open the doors to employment for persons with disabilities, with employer-provided job accommodations being the keys to unlock those doors. Instead, there was a significant *decline* in employment rates for persons with disabilities between 1990 and 1995.[26] By 2013, the employment rate for working-age men with disabilities was still less than 40 percent of that for nondisabled men.[27] Clearly, this is not the world the framers of the ADA envisioned.

Numerous pundits have tried to explain why the ADA has failed to achieve its employment goals. Some blame the courts for conservative interpretations of the act that contravened the original intentions of Congress. Others point to work disincentives inherent in public disability programs, noting the steady decline in employment of persons with disabilities as SSDI enrollment expanded after 1989.[28] The economic explanation is more straightforward: The reasonable accommodation mandates of the ADA make it more costly to employ workers with disabilities; therefore employers are less likely to hire them.[29]

Few authors have questioned the fundamental assumption of the ADA, namely, that the way to improve employment outcomes for workers with disabilities is through employer-provided job accommodations. And few authors have challenged the myth that the majority of employer-provided accommodations can be implemented at little or no cost. I have argued that the hidden costs of job accommodations can impose a substantial burden on employers, and even the most accommodating supervisor cannot rescue a worker whose functional limitations and job demands are mismatched. The story of the police detective, for example, did not have a happy ending:

> His behavior was so extreme at times that everybody here knew that something was very much wrong. I tried to help keep him afloat. First I gave him . . . some time to catch up. And he did. And he did pretty darn well at it. . . . But he was always falling behind because he had these [mental health] issues you know. I [told my staff], I want you all to pitch in and help John.

And people volunteered to take cases and help him. But soon, I realized that I couldn't . . . put this added responsibility and burden and work on everybody else continually.[30]

The detective was eventually transferred to an administrative position with regular hours and less time pressure. He worked in that position successfully for two years, but then requested to go back out on patrol. His former supervisor tried unsuccessfully to dissuade him. She told us, "I'm afraid this is a disaster waiting to happen."

All things considered, the ADA is fundamentally flawed in its emphasis on employer-provided job accommodations, and its implicit assumption that such accommodations can be implemented without undue costs for employers. The law is an exercise not only in "morality on the cheap," but in "morality without reality." The framers of the ADA did not understand the multifaceted nature of job accommodations (including job matching and self-initiated accommodations) or their real costs (including negative externalities). They were *Planners* rather than *Searchers*, and the law has failed to achieve its goals.

A smarter strategy would be to study the success stories, the stories of people with serious mental illness who are independently and gainfully employed in competitive jobs. Once we understand how *real* people with SMI have succeeded in *real* jobs in the competitive labor market, we will be better equipped to craft policies that recreate the conditions of success for other workers. The success stories are out there, if we search for them.

Chapter Ten

Beyond Schizophrenia

ALWAYS MORE MIRACLES

In December 2012, David resigned his position at the Dream Center. He had completed his associate's degree in ministry from AIC and told me, "It's time to move on." He planned to search for a job in the Phoenix area, and continue his part-time ministries in the city.

Spring 2013

Over the next few months, I helped David develop several versions of his resume. Each version had one intractable problem: an unexplained employment gap from 2005 to 2009. This would be a red flag for any personnel department, but telling the truth ("Diagnosed with schizophrenia, lived with parents after relapse of psychotic symptoms, now in recovery") was unlikely to produce many job interviews. I feared that David's job search would not go well.

After months with no good leads, my fears were confirmed. By then, however, David had decided to start his own small business providing carpentry, repair, and painting services to homeowners. He had construction experience working with my brother during college and, more recently, he had worked part time for several friends who were licensed contractors. He had acquired a set of *transferable skills* in construction; he had a talent for visualizing the final product of a construction job, and he enjoyed the variety and independence of construction work. Most importantly, he could set his own hours and work at his own pace.

We supported the small business idea enthusiastically and, over the next few months, provided capital to help with start-up costs. The business was officially established in August 2013. David acquired his first paying client in September and by March 2014, he was fully licensed, bonded, and in-sured.

One of David's first major projects was to re-paint our deck. We expected it to be a small job, but did not fully appreciate the training he had received from Uncle Gordon. David discovered that several support beams were dete-riorating and many of the surface boards had been damaged by weather. With our approval, he made the necessary repairs before starting to paint. After four days, my husband asked, "Do you suppose he will ever finish? This deck will be here for the next fifty years!" I smiled and replied, "Yes, dear," recalling that Gordon's deck had withstood a hurricane.

Fall 2014

By the end of year one, David was working steadily and needed more help. He found a ready supply of labor among the men who were living at the Dream Center. David had come full circle: from being out of work, to orga-nizing the Working Men's program for the Dream Center, to being an em-ployer himself. For him, the construction company was more than a business; it was part of his ministry.

David found other ways to minister as well. Every Sunday night, as part of Alongside Ministries, he preaches to men in the Maricopa County Jail. On Wednesday evenings, he preaches at the House of Healing, a nondenomina-tional ministry in central Phoenix, specializing in healing, teaching, and de-liverance.

One Wednesday night, I visited the House of Healing to hear David preach. I had a queasy feeling in my stomach, like the butterflies I had when he was six and played goalie for his soccer team. Could my little boy really defend that big goal all by himself? Could my little boy really preach a sermon?

David's topic that evening was "Out of Captivity and Hope for a Future." Preaching from the book of Joshua, his message was to keep moving for-ward, no matter what the obstacles. God, he said, is bigger than any problem we might encounter.

> God will never take something away from you that he does not return some-thing better. There is always more to God, more revelation, and more miracles to come.[1]

I was amazed—my little boy could really preach. I sat back and watched the miracle unfold.

EXTRAORDINARY LIVES

How many other miracle stories are out there, of people who have recovered from schizophrenia to find gainful competitive employment? The literature does not say. Psychosocial rehabilitation studies have focused mainly on barriers encountered by persons with SMI who are seeking employment, on increasing access to vocational rehabilitation programs, and on identifying best practices among supported employment programs.[2] There is almost nothing in the research literature about the career paths of persons with SMI who support themselves through independent competitive employment.

Such information cannot be gleaned from large-scale, nationally representative surveys designed to measure employment or health outcomes for the U.S. population. Several national databases provide detailed information on employment and earnings (e.g., the Survey of Income and Program Participation), but these data have limited information on health and health conditions. Likewise, databases that provide detailed information on health conditions (e.g., the Medical Expenditure Panel Survey) have limited information on employment and earnings. In short, nationally representative data that describe employment experiences unique to workers with SMI (e.g., stigma, disclosure, and job accommodations) do not exist. Nearly ten years ago, Steven Marcus and I set out to collect the data ourselves.

The Survey

The first challenge was how to obtain a representative sample of persons with SMI, who were gainfully employed in competitive jobs. We called them the "hidden population" because the problem stymied us for several years. Screening for the hidden population by random sampling would be prohibitively expensive because the prevalence of employed persons with schizophrenia (or other SMI) is so low. Asking employers to identify their workers with SMI would be fruitless because an employer would not necessarily know about an employee's history of mental illness and could not reveal the information if they did. The screening problem seemed insurmountable, until a chance encounter at a research conference.

In a casual conversation with a stranger, I mentioned that I was a health economist. She told me that her employer, Truven Health Analytics, conducts an ongoing survey (the PULSE), to collect information on health conditions, health insurance, and utilization of health services. The PULSE gathers data from large, random samples of the U.S. population by conducting telephone interviews with a new set of nine thousand households each month.[3] Most importantly, researchers can contract with Truven to add their own questions to the survey.

Could we add questions to the PULSE to screen for our target population? Could we then call back and ask additional questions specific to their employment experiences? Yes, PULSE interviewers ask all participants if they are willing to be called back for other surveys. Approximately 60 percent give permission to be called again, and follow-up surveys are routine. When I returned home, I called Steven. "I know how to find the hidden population!" I told him.

We contracted with Truven to screen for our target population over an eight-month period in 2012–2013. They identified households where someone had been diagnosed with serious mental illness *and* that person was currently employed in a competitive job or had been employed in a competitive job for at least six months post-onset of SMI.

Over the screening period, Truven identified 677 households in which a resident reportedly met our screening criteria and the survey participant was willing to be called back.[4] We were able to contact and verify eligibility for 377 households. A separate survey firm completed interviews with 230 eligible participants, for a 61 percent response rate.[5]

The survey generated information on *hours and earnings* in the worker's current job or, if not currently employed, their most recent job post-onset of SMI, as well as information about the *work environment, workplace relationships,* and *job characteristics.* The survey also included questions about *disclosure* of SMI, *job accommodations* requested and received, current *symptoms and treatment* history, investments in *human capital* (e.g., education or job training), and *support* from family, friends, or government programs.

The results presented here provide the first-ever information on the experiences of workers with SMI in competitive jobs, from a representative sample of persons with SMI who are capable of mainstream competitive employment. To add context to the survey data presented below, I include several case studies of extraordinary lives—people whose lives have been disrupted by mental illness but who are now gainfully employed in competitive jobs.

Ben's Story

Ben Rinaudo grew up in the Republic of Niger, where his parents were development workers. Ben aspired to a career in international development, and completed the coursework for a degree in development studies from the University of Melbourne. While he was writing his honors thesis on female slavery in West Africa, he developed the first symptoms of mental illness. He became anxious and depressed, his thinking became confused, and he developed feelings of disorientation, even in familiar settings. Within a few months, his symptoms escalated to paranoia, panic attacks, racing thoughts, and hallucinations.

Ben's family took him to a hospital emergency room, where he was transferred to a psychiatric inpatient unit. Like many first-time patients, Ben felt both relief and fear. He was treated with antipsychotics and antidepressants, which controlled the most overt symptoms of mental illness, but the medications left him feeling lethargic, bored, and hopeless. One year after his release from the hospital, with little accomplished since he became ill, Ben felt a tremendous sense of grief and guilt over his lost ambitions. He asked his psychiatrist, "Will I be like this forever?"

During the following year, Ben's mood improved. His energy returned sufficiently to begin a supported education course offered by Mental Illness Fellowship (a coalition of organizations across Australia, working to facilitate recovery from mental illness). Toward year's end, Ben's uncle offered him a part-time job with his piano tuning and restoration business. Ben had been out of work for nearly two years, and the thought of working regular hours was overwhelming to him. The part-time job, with flexible hours and a sympathetic employer, was ideal.

A few months later, Ben took on a second part-time job helping a friend who was a self-employed gardener. When his friend left the area, Ben took over the business. The coursework, piano tuning, and gardening business gave Ben a renewed sense of purpose for his life.

In due course, Ben completed three Graduate Education Certificates with the Mental Illness Fellowship, where he was eventually offered part-time employment. At the time his story was written in 2012, Ben was working full time at the fellowship, managing peer and community education, advocacy efforts, and community outreach. He was completing a fourth graduate certificate in mental health services, with the long-term goal of helping to improve mental health treatment in developing countries. In this way he planned to return to his original ambition of a career in community development.[6]

Survey Results I

There are striking similarities between Ben's story and David's. Both young men became ill while they were in college, returned to school when their acute symptoms were in remission, completed their college degrees, were absent from the workforce for a significant period of time, found an entrée back to work with a flexible employer, and became self-employed in a services occupation. How typical is this story? Is self-employment a common pathway back to work? Is it significant that both young men earned a college degree? Our survey was designed to answer exactly these types of questions.

Employment Status

Among the persons we interviewed, 27 percent said that they were currently working in a competitive job. Three-quarters of current workers were *gain-*

fully employed (i.e., not receiving disability benefits). Among those who were not working, over half (52 percent) had left their most recent job for reasons unrelated to mental illness (e.g., to care for a child or return to school). (That result is strikingly similar to the findings of another, smaller study, in which participants with SMI were asked why they had left each job they held post-onset of mental illness. More than half—53 percent—of the time participants had resigned a job for reasons unrelated to their illness.[7])

We are particularly interested in two comparison groups: those who are currently employed, and those who left their jobs because of their mental illness. We define as successfully employed the sixty-one persons working in a competitive job on the date of interview, and refer to them as *stayers*. The eighty persons who left their most recent competitive job because of their mental illness we define as unsuccessfully employed, and refer to them as *leavers*. In subsequent analyses, we aim to identify characteristics that distinguish the two groups, and that may guide policy makers in developing ways to improve employment outcomes for this population.

Twenty percent of current workers (stayers) were self-employed at the time of our survey. Their jobs ranged from housekeeper to financial planner; one owned a pottery school. The rate of self-employment in this group was almost twice that of the U.S. workforce (20 percent versus 11 percent) at the time.[8] Accordingly, the survey findings are consistent with the hypothesis that *self-employment is a good job match for workers with SMI,* possibly because it offers the ultimate potential for flexibility.

Occupation

We asked all respondents about their occupation in their current or most recent job. Their responses ran the entire gamut of occupations: nurses, teachers, cooks, cleaners, home health-care workers, cashiers, receptionists, salespersons, construction workers, machinists, production workers. The survey is concrete evidence that *among the population of persons with SMI, there are those with the skills, abilities, and interests to hold almost any job in the economy.*

The distribution of our sample across major occupational categories was, however, quite different from that of the general workforce. Compared to all U.S. workers, those in our sample were overrepresented in professional or service occupations (57 percent versus 40 percent) and underrepresented in managerial and sales occupations (26 percent versus 39 percent).[9] The differences in occupational distributions are consistent with the idea that workers with SMI are matching into jobs that minimize the impact of their functional limitations. The workers in our survey appear to avoid managerial and sales occupations, where interpersonal interactions are essential, in favor of professional and service occupations, which offer greater autonomy.

Human Capital

Both David and Ben had education and job training that provided an entrée to the competitive labor market. David acquired construction skills as an "apprentice" to his uncle and returned to school to complete a degree in ministry. Ben acquired piano tuning and gardening skills on-the-job, and completed graduate certificates in mental health services. The survey results provide objective evidence that, on average, investments in human capital improve employment outcomes for persons with SMI.

Our sample had higher average educational attainment than the U.S. population as a whole at the time the data were collected (2012–2013). Over 80 percent of respondents reported at least some postsecondary education, compared to only 58 percent of all U.S. adults. [10] Inasmuch as schizophrenia does not disproportionately affect the intelligent and well-educated, education evidently raises the probability that a person with SMI returns to independent competitive employment (and was eligible for our sample).

Although respondents to our survey were more likely to have *attended* college than U.S. adults overall, they were also more likely to have *dropped out* of college (47 percent versus 27 percent). The reason for the disproportionately high dropout rate is obvious. Onset of SMI often strikes young adults of college age. The symptoms disrupt, and all too often end, progress toward a college degree. Consequently, the proportion of our survey respondents with a college degree was similar to the proportion in the U.S. population overall (roughly one-third), even though many more of the persons in our sample had some postsecondary education.

Comparing the stayers and leavers in our sample, there is a clear education gap, which multiplies during the college years. Stayers were 15 percent more likely to attend college than leavers, but *twice as likely* to complete a four-year college degree, and *five times more likely* to complete a postgraduate degree. Thus, a key distinguishing characteristic between the two groups is that *stayers found a way to complete their education.*

We asked all respondents about investments in job training. We were particularly interested in job coaching, transitional work training, or any other form of supported employment. Only 15 percent of respondents said they had participated in a supported employment program. Stayers were more likely to have participated in supported employment than leavers (20 percent versus 13 percent), suggesting that supported employment helps some workers transition to independent, competitive jobs. That inference is tentative, however, because the number of workers in our sample who had experience with supported employment is so small. Of course, that is a key point: 80 percent of stayers said that they had never participated in supported employment, casting doubt on the claim that "the single best predictor of competitive employment for patients with schizophrenia is enrollment in IPS, or evidence-based supported employment."[11]

Kurt's Story

Kurt Snyder was a good student in high school and doing well in college until he began to experience symptoms of mental illness. The first manifestation was grandiose thinking; Kurt believed he was destined to discover a mathematical principle that would transform our understanding of the universe. He spent so much time focusing on his principle that his grades suffered. He eventually dropped out of college at age twenty-four.

After leaving school, Kurt made several attempts at starting a business (as a computer graphics designer and as a handyman), but each attempt failed. He began to experience feelings of paranoia, to the point that he believed he was under continuous surveillance and being followed whenever he went outside.

With the aid of a friend, Kurt was able to obtain a job as a repairman for a large telecommunications firm. However, the high-security worksite, with ever-present surveillance cameras, intensified Kurt's feelings of paranoia. He began experiencing hallucinations: hearing clicking noises that did not exist and seeing car doors lock and unlock themselves. He wondered if he was living in an alternate universe or had been drugged with hallucinogens.

The paranoia forced Kurt to quit his job. He stayed at home, afraid to go outside. Eventually, the self-isolation relieved his feelings of paranoia and he decided to take a train trip, both as a vacation and a chance to ponder his great mathematical principle. Almost as soon as Kurt boarded the train, however, the paranoid thoughts returned. When the train stopped, he abruptly disembarked, with no luggage and nowhere to go. By now his psychotic symptoms were so blatant that his family was notified and he was hospitaized. A psychiatrist prescribed antipsychotics, which Kurt refused to take.

Three months later, Kurt was hospitalized again. A psychiatrist prescribed an atypical antipsychotic, which Kurt again refused to take. This time the psychiatrist told Kurt he would not continue to treat him, unless he took his medications. Kurt relented and agreed to try the meds. The hallucinations ceased almost immediately. The delusions and paranoia faded over time.

With the acute symptoms of mental illness under control, Kurt returned to school to earn a certificate in database management. Upon completion of the program, he found a job as a database administrator with the state of Maryland. At the time his story was written (2007), he was working full time for the state and performing volunteer work with the local fire department. He was thirty-six years old.[12]

Survey Results II

As Kurt's story shows, a workplace filled with surveillance cameras is a poor job match for someone with paranoid schizophrenia. Kurt finally found a good match as a computer programmer; David and Ben found good matches in self-employment. In chapter 8, I identified a number of work-related characteristics that make a good job match for workers with SMI, based on theory and anecdotal evidence. The survey data are consistent with all these predictions.

Work-Related Characteristics

With respect to firm characteristics, I argued that a *supportive culture* and *calm environment* were important to the success of workers with SMI. In our survey, workers who were successfully employed reported a less hostile and less stressful work environment than those who left their job for reasons related to SMI. Stayers were less likely than leavers to report that, because of their mental illness, they had been teased, bullied, or harassed at work (21 percent versus 29 percent), or had been treated unfairly (26 percent versus 45 percent). Stayers were also less likely to say that their job involved working at high speed (43 percent versus 60 percent), or working to tight deadlines (51 percent versus 58 percent).

With respect to workplace relationships, I argued that *supportive supervisors* and *sympathetic coworkers* were important. Indeed, workers who were successful in their most recent job were more positive about their workplace relationships than those who were unsuccessful. Exactly the same proportion (41 percent) of each group said that their employer did not know about their mental illness, but stayers were less likely than leavers to say that the main reason for not disclosing was "fear of what their supervisor would do" or "fear of how coworkers would react" (8 percent versus 34 percent). Stayers were also less likely than leavers to say that stigma had affected their relationships with coworkers (18 percent versus 38 percent).

Finally, with respect to job characteristics, I argued that the most important features of a good job match were consistency, autonomy, and flexibility. Shift work may be the ultimate inconsistency in job requirements. As expected, stayers were less likely than leavers to say that their job involved working in shifts (44 percent versus 62 percent). Stayers also reported greater autonomy and flexibility across multiple dimensions of their jobs. Relative to leavers, stayers were more likely to say that they could choose/change their order of tasks (70 percent versus 53 percent), choose/change their methods of work (68 percent versus 42 percent), choose/change their speed of work (69 percent versus 58 percent), and take their break when they wished (54 percent versus 34 percent). Stayers were also more likely to have influence over the choice of a working partner (32 percent versus 18 percent).

Some specific results cited previously (e.g., those pertaining to tight dead-lines or speed of work) fall short of accepted criteria for statistical significance. Nonetheless, the collectivity of results are highly supportive of the job matching hypotheses in that the quantitative measures *all point in the expected direction*. Overall, the survey provides the first quantitative evidence suggesting that a good match between functional limitations and job characteristics is important to successful employment outcomes for workers with SMI.

Illness and Treatment

Anecdotal evidence, like the testimony of Elyn Saks, indicates that many persons with SMI who are successfully employed in competitive jobs still experience symptoms of mental illness. In our survey data, some proportion of both stayers and leavers reported current symptoms and corresponding functional limitations associated with their illness. However, the proportion was smaller among stayers.

With respect to negative symptoms, the proportion of workers who reported difficulties with interpersonal relationships was twice as high among leavers as among stayers. The limitations related to difficulties "carrying on a conversation," "dealing with strangers," and "making/keeping friendships." One striking example is that nearly three-fourths of leavers said they had "difficulty joining in community activities," compared to only one-third of stayers. This result suggests that the leavers may have had similar difficulties assimilating at work.

Regarding cognitive deficits, the most frequently reported limitation was "difficulty concentrating on a task for more than ten minutes." However, stayers were far less likely than leavers to report difficulty concentrating (57 percent versus 83 percent). Stayers were also less likely to report "difficulty remembering to do important things" (52 percent versus 69 percent), "difficulty understanding what is going around them" (26 percent versus 59 percent), and "difficulty learning new things" (23 percent versus 47 percent). Clearly, the differences in prevalence of functional limitations distinguishes between stayers and leavers in our sample. Still, substantial numbers of stayers reported functional limitations associated with the symptoms of SMI, demonstrating that *it is not necessary to be symptom-free to be successfully employed*.

Nor is it *necessary* to be taking antipsychotic medications to be able to work in a competitive job. Within our survey sample, the majority of both stayers and leavers said they were taking their medications as prescribed, but the proportion following their prescribed medication regimen was *smaller* among stayers (75 percent versus 90 percent). Moreover, 20 percent of stayers (compared to only 6 percent of leavers) said that they were not taking antipsychotic medications at all. Surprisingly, stayers had poorer adherence to their medications as a group than leavers, but stayers reported fewer symptoms of SMI—and the stayers were still working.

The results are consistent with at least one prior study that identifies a cohort of persons who recover from SMI in every sense of the word: They do not take antipsychotic drugs; they are virtually symptom-free; and, on average, they function at least as well as others with the same illness who are taking their medications.[13] Brett Hartman is one of these.

Brett's Story

Brett Hartman was a college freshman when he first experienced symptoms of mental illness. As images tumbled through his brain, he thought that he was receiving messages from God, that the moon was transmitting messages from God, and that perhaps the moon was God. Upon admission to a psychiatric unit, he was treated with a first-generation antipsychotic. After a month, he was discharged with a diagnosis of "adjustment reaction to adolescence," a "less pejorative" label than schizophrenia.

At home and experiencing the drowsiness and lethargy that are side effects of the antipsychotic, Brett decided to stop taking it. When the delusions returned, his psychiatrist warned him to get back on the meds. Brett followed the advice, but when he shook the bottle of pills, three tablets fell out. He thought the number three must be symbolic, so he took them all. He tried the "experiment" again and again until he had taken six times his usual daily dose.

Brett was readmitted to a psychiatric unit. This time he expected to be discharged quickly; when he was not, he became belligerent. He was placed in restraints, in seclusion, and his medication was forcibly administered. He was soon submissive enough to move out of seclusion, then to an unlocked unit. There he became friends with an older patient named Arthur. One day on the fitness track, Brett asked Arthur how he managed to deal with the hardships in his life. "Walking, keep on walking. Whatever you do, that'll help." Brett thought, "this is the kind of simplistic nonsense I can do without." Tired of waiting to be discharged, he left the hospital on his own. Police returned him to the locked psychiatric unit. When he finally was discharged, the diagnosis was unequivocal: "acute schizophrenia."

The pattern of delusions, hospitalization, belligerence, restraints, and forcible administration of antipsychotics, continued until Brett had "escaped" from hospitals four times. When he at last realized there was no escape, he became deeply depressed. One sleepless night, he remembered Arthur's advice. The next morning he began to walk, deliberately and purposefully, up and down the halls. The walking had a calming effect. (Is this why the staff member at UNC walked round and round with her patient?)

Brett's outlook improved and he was released from a psychiatric unit for the last time. Now he began the arduous process of rebuilding his life. He returned to college and a full courseload. He soon realized that he couldn't maintain that pace while taking antipsychotics, so he stopped his meds once again. His grades improved, but he worried about a relapse of psychotic symptoms. The relapse never happened, and he graduated with honors.

After graduation, Brett applied to several prestigious univerisities offering doctoral degrees in psychology. He disclosed his history of mental illness on the applications, thinking his firsthand experience would be a plus. It was not—every school rejected his appliction. Two years later, he applied to another university without revealing his history of schizophrenia. This time, he was accepted. When he published his story in 2005, Dr. Hartman was working as a licensed psychologist in upstate New York.[14]

Survey Results III

Disclosure and Accommodations

Brett learned firsthand the risks of disclosing a history of mental illness. Anecdotal evidence suggests that most workers with SMI are reluctant to volunteer information about their illness, for fear of stigma and discrimination.[15] Our survey provides the first-ever representative data on disclosure rates of SMI in the workplace, among individuals who are capable of independent, competitive employment. The results are surprising. More than half (59 percent) of the workers in our survey sample said that their employers knew about their mental illness; in three-quarters of those cases, the workers informed their employer themselves. (The exact circumstances and extent of disclosure were not reported.)

Stayers were far more likely to have informed their employer themselves (83 percent versus 59 percent). This result suggests that *voluntary disclosure* is correlated with more successful work outcomes, but the nature of the causality, and even whether or not there is a causal relationship is unclear. It could be that stayers were more likely to voluntarily disclose because they anticipated a more favorable response from their employer, or stayers may have received a more favorable response because they chose to voluntarily disclose. Alternatively, the mere fact that the workers stayed with the firm implies a comfort level that is conducive to disclosure.

We also asked our survey respondents about sixteen different types of job accommodations that they might have requested for their mental illness. Overall, sixty-five workers (28 percent) asked their employer for some type of accommodation in their current or most recent job. Among those who requested an accommodation, 40 percent requested a change to their work schedule (i.e., a flexible schedule, part-time work, or different work hours).

No other single accommodation was requested by more than 15 percent of workers who asked for an accommodation.

Stayers were somewhat *less likely* to have requested job accommodations than leavers (26 percent versus 35 percent), possibly because they had fewer functional limitations. Alternatively, stayers may have found a better job match, where they either did not need accommodations, or could initiate accommodations themselves. (Recall that stayers had far more flexibility and autonomy in their jobs than leavers.) On the other hand, stayers were *more likely* to have received the accommodations they requested. Here, the differences are startling. Among those who requested schedule changes, *100 percent* of stayers said that their employer granted their request, compared to only 50 percent of leavers. This could be one of the primary reasons that the workers left their jobs.

Overall, the responses on disclosure and job accommodations suggest that stayers were employed in firms where the workplace culture was more supportive, and their supervisor was more accepting, than leavers. These are exactly the results that the theory of job matching would predict.

Support Networks

In each of the foregoing case studies, the support of family and friends played a crucial role in the patient's return to competitive employment. My husband and I provided startup capital for David's business. Ben's uncle gave him a job restoring and tuning pianos; a friend started him in the gardening business. Kurt had a friend who bought him a computer and paid for one of his classes in database management. Brett's father helped him pay for graduate school.

Consistent with the case studies, a majority of our survey participants said that family and friends supported their return to work. Stayers were only *slightly* more likely than leavers to acknowledge support from family members (72 percent versus 66 percent), but *considerably* more likely to report support from friends (81 percent versus 66 percent). (Recall that leavers reported more difficulty making and maintaining friendships than stayers.)

Most of the participants said that they had a social circle of family and friends with whom they maintained contact. Only 35 percent lived alone. When asked if they had frequent ("almost daily" or "a few times a week") contact with others, stayers were less likely than leavers to report frequent contact with family members (43 percent versus 58 percent), but more likely to report frequent contact with friends (45 percent versus 37 percent).

The results reinforce the belief that support from family members and friends plays an important role in recovery from SMI.[16] Most of our survey respondents had supportive relationships, but the social circle of those who were currently employed was more balanced between family and friends.

Could this be another indicator of recovery? I observed the same pattern with David. As he became more involved with work and made friends at the Dream Center, his cell phone started ringing again.

Postscript

Although the inferences drawn from the survey remain in the "preliminary" stage, they collectively form a consistent whole. The story that emerges from both case studies and survey responses is not one of stigma and intimidation, but one of empowerment and success. The first crucial element of success is *control of the acute symptoms of SMI*. Persons who are experiencing acute psychotic symptoms cannot work in any meaningful way. They deserve the best medical care available. Today, that means short-term hospitalization and stabilization on antipsychotic medications.

The second element of success is *education and skills training*. Schizophrenia is a cruel disease in many ways, not the least of which is timing. It strikes most often when a young adult is in college or just entering the labor force, disrupting their acquisition of human capital. The impact upon future earnings and employment is tremendous. Contrary to the stereotype of incompetency, many persons with SMI are capable of completing advanced skills training and college degrees. These investments in human capital help to ameliorate the negative impact of functional limitations on work outcomes.

Third, in the wake of deinstitutionalization, we depend on families to be primary caregivers for persons who are recovering from SMI. In his lowest moments, when Brett Hartman thought everyone else might abandon him, he could still rely on his mother to bring him milkshakes every week.[17] Families can provide crucial support on the path to competitive employment. Policy makers take note: If the emotional and financial burdens of caregiving become overwhelming, so that family members "give up" on their relative with SMI, an important support network for return to work may be lost.

Finally, finding a good job match is crucial to employment outcomes for workers with SMI. In defining a good match, the single most important characteristic appears to be flexibility. David is self-employed; Ben was self-employed and now works in mental health services; Kurt works as a database administrator; Brett travels across New York State conducting disability evaluations. All of these jobs give workers considerable control over their job tasks and their pace of work. In our survey data, measures of job flexibility clearly distinguish workers with SMI who are employed from those who have left their jobs because of their mental illness.

There are many stories of super-extraordinary people who suffered from schizophrenia or other SMI, yet made brilliant contributions to the arts, sciences, and humanities. John Nash, mathematics prodigy and winner of the

Nobel Prize in economics, is one example. Vincent Van Gogh is another. Robert Lowell, U.S. Poet Laureate from 1947 to 1948, and twice winner of the Pulitzer Prize for Poetry, is another. In fact, there are so many names on the list that the concept of the "mad genius" has become a stereotype in fiction and research. But a person need not be a genius to be a productive and contributing member of society after a diagnosis of schizophrenia. In the throes of mental illness, Brett Hartman wrote:

> I could shine before and I remember what it was like to shine. Now I've lost it, and the reality of the loss goes deep. To regress this way, with full awareness of the regression, seems unmatched as far as life's frutsrations go. [18]

We all deserve our chance to shine. With appropriate mental health policies, there can be a full life and productive work after schizophrenia.

Chapter Eleven

Toward a More Rational
Mental Health Policy

IT

During the years I struggled to help my son recover from mental illness, I did not think of schizophrenia as merely a disease. To me, it was the enemy. Like the clown-monster in Stephen King's *It*, schizophrenia lurked at the corners of our lives, threatening to snatch my son away at any time:

> What he saw then was terrible enough to make his worst imaginings of the thing in the cellar look like sweet dreams; what he saw destroyed his sanity in one clawing stroke.[1]

With every passing year, I become more confident that David has defeated the enemy. We had some lucky breaks along the way, but there were stumbling blocks as well.

The first obstacle was my complete failure to recognize that David was suffering from SMI. As the symptoms of schizophrenia developed, David's personality and behavior changed radically. I thought he was using drugs, or excited about starting college, or just being insufferable. Looking back, I wonder if I was too uninformed to recognize the signs of mental illness, or if I closed my mind to a possibility that was too frightening to face. "We lie best when we lie to ourselves."[2]

After David was diagnosed, he was fortunate to be enrolled in a research study under the direction of Diana Perkins. It was not, however, blind luck that led us to her. David had health insurance, which allowed him to be admitted to the psychiatric unit at UNC Hospital, rather than the state hospital near Durham. I had contacts in the psychiatric research community, who strongly recommended Dr. Perkins. When it came time to sign the informed consent, I requested that she be David's physician and made that a condition for his participation in the study. *Excellent care for SMI is available within the U.S. health care system, if patients and their families have the knowledge and resources to access it.*

The medical staff at UNC Hospital was incredibly supportive of David during the early years following his diagnosis. In contrast, UNC administrators made the path to completing his college degree more difficult. When I contacted the Disability Services Office about readmission after his first episode of psychosis, the response I received ("when your son got in trouble . . .") made me determined never to contact that office again. Had we been unaware of our son's rights under the ADA, David might not have been readmitted to school. I expect the response to parents of a student with schizophrenia would have been similar at almost any university in the country. This is tragic, because *graduating from college gives persons with SMI options in the labor market that can help them accommodate their mental illness and succeed in gainful employment.*

The disaster in Charlotte was avoidable. David's psychiatrist was either unable or unwilling to refer David for inpatient care, even though David was experiencing acute symptoms of mental illness. Later, the CMHC refused to admit David, even though he was exhibiting psychotic symptoms and willing to be hospitalized. Social services, community mental health services, and the local police could not or would not intervene. As David became increasingly psychotic, quit his job, ran up huge credit card bills, and began intimidating his roommates, there was nothing we could do, except wait and watch as his life crumbled, and bail him out of jail when he finally crashed.

In resolving the felony charges, we had three pieces of good fortune: (1) North Carolina has a jail diversion program for defendants with mental illness. (2) We found an attorney who specialized in disability law and was determined that David should participate in the diversion program, despite the fact that he was living out of state. (3) I found a Searcher at the Treatment Assessment Screening Center in Phoenix, who volunteered to organize and manage a diversion plan for David.

Once again, it was not all blind luck. We had no experience with the criminal justice system, but we had the financial resources to hire a knowledgable attorney, and the connections to find him. We had no knowledge of alternative sentencing rules, but we had the wherewithal to search for a rehabilitation program in Arizona that could substitute for jail diversion, and the imagination to think that a program designed for drug offenders might work for someone with SMI. Completing the diversion program meant that the charges against David were expunged. He was fortunate, because *a criminal record makes it more difficult for persons with SMI to return to the labor force, yet prison has become a de facto substitute for the mental hospital for many persons with SMI.*

Once he was living in Arizona, David became eligible for psychiatric care and medications through the public mental health system, at no out-of-pocket cost. The medical care was more than adequate, but the vocational services were abysmal ("he could collect coins from vending machines"). David spent four long years doing virtually nothing before he found a godsend at the Dream Center. What the church program could do, that the public mental health system could not, was return David to the real world.

Schizophrenia takes a terrible toll on family members. When David returned to live with us in Arizona, I was emotionally exhausted. We had invested years helping him rebuild his life after that first psychotic episode; now we had to begin all over again. All the problems he faced—the legal issues, the credit card bills, the mental illness, the depression—were ours to solve. I remember telling my therapist, "Maybe I can handle him living with us for six months, but absolutely no longer than that." It was three years before he moved out to live with his father. Somehow, I survived:

> [Schizophrenia] was, after all, only a [disease]. Perhaps at the end, when the masks of horror were laid aside, there was nothing with which the human mind could not cope.[3]

MENTAL HEALTH POLICY

Prior to the introduction of antipsychotic medications in the 1950s, the best outcome most patients with SMI (and their families) could hope for was, to *survive*. In fact, E. Fuller Torrey's *Surviving Schizophrenia* was my textbook in the early days of David's illness. Today, many persons with even the most serious mental illnesses can live independently and work in gainful employment. The tragedy is that so many do not. Too many persons with SMI are homeless, in jail, or dependent on government entitlement programs. Our mental health policy has failed to keep up with the possibilities our medical system has created.

The ADA and its amendments are the primary federal policies designed to improve employment outcomes for workers with disabilities. The acts prohibit discrimination against otherwise qualified persons with disabilities in decisions regarding hiring, compensation, promotion, and other employee benefits. To say that the ADA has failed to achieve its promise for workers with SMI is an understatement. The amended act may have a greater impact, but many legal analysts are skeptical.[4]

Why, with improved treatments and tougher laws, have we not observed better employment outcomes for this population? One part of the problem is the persistent stigma against mental illness, which cannot be legislated away.

Another part of the problem is the exclusive focus of disability employment policy on the demand side of the labor market. The ADA imposes a mandate on employers to offer equal employment opportunities to *qualified* workers with mental disorders, but there are no complementary policies to ensure that persons with mental disorders have opportunities to *become qualified* for the jobs that are now open to them.

In particular, current policies do not address the functional limitations and human capital losses that stand between a person with SMI and sustainable employment. Current policies do little to help persons with SMI acquire general human capital, which is *the* entrée to good jobs in the contemporary labor market. Finally, current policies are not geared to support the families, who support the recovery, of persons with SMI. The root cause of these failures is that mental health policy has been driven by Planners committed to an ideology, rather than by Searchers who are close to the problems that need to be solved.

Background

According to the *Oxford English Dictionary*, the word "policy" derives from the Greek "polis," meaning city-state, the unit of government in ancient Greece. Policy was once a verb with a meaning equivalent to "police." Today, the word is a noun, meaning:

> A course of action pursued by a government, party, ruler, statesman, etc.; any course of action adopted as advantageous or expedient.[5]

The definition makes clear that policy should be welfare-enhancing (advantageous). In a democracy, the welfare to be enhanced (at least in theory) is that of the city-state.

Government policy has the potential to increase social welfare in situations where free markets fail to achieve socially desirable outcomes, such as when there are negative externalities (as with untreated mental illness). In theory, government actions can enhance welfare in such situations because government has the authority to coerce socially desirable behavior from its citizens. It does so by enacting *laws*, by establishing *rights*, or by exercising the *authority* of local, state or federal governments.[6]

Laws motivate desirable behavior by creating incentives in the form of rewards (granted for compliance with a policy) or penalties (imposed for noncompliance).[7] The Mental Health Parity and Addiction Equity Act of 2008, for example, requires health insurers to establish equity between coverage for mental/substance use disorders and coverage for medical/surgical disorders. The act carries substantial penalties for noncompliance (up to $100 per covered member, per day).[8]

Declarations of *rights* establish claims to certain privileges on behalf of a designated group. A relevant example is the United Nations Convention on the Rights of Persons with Disabilities. Among many enumerated rights, the convention states that:[9]

- Persons with disabilities have the right to enjoy the highest attainable standard of heath, without discrimination on the basis of disability. [Article 25]
- Health care professionals [shall] provide the same quality of care to persons with and without disabilities, including on the basis of free and informed consent. [Article 25]
- The existence of a disability shall in no case justify a deprivation of liberty. [Article 14]

Finally, the power of government rests on its *authority* to act in the interests of the society. In the United States, authority may be shifted among local, state, and federal governments to achieve particular policy objectives. The State Care Acts, passed at the end of the nineteenth century, are a good example. The acts shifted responsibility for the care of persons with SMI from local authorities to state mental hospitals, where state officials believed patients would receive higher-quality care.

Unfortunately, the shift of authority to state mental hospitals did not evolve as planned, nor did the subsequent shift to federal authority under the Community Mental Health Act of 1963. The result is today's chaotic mental health system, wherein the welfare of patients and their families are too often sacrificed to the ideologies of Planners with Big Goals. Not since the moral treatment model of the 1700s has mental health policy been driven by persons who actually lived with someone suffering from SMI. It makes a difference.

What kinds of policies are needed to ensure that persons with schizophrenia and other SMI have the highest possible quality of life, including the opportunity for gainful, competitive employment if they are capable? In the following, I set forth a package of proposals, designed to remove barriers to successful employment for this population, to the extent that is possible within the bounds of current medical knowledge.

The proposals fit into three broad categories: restoration of health capital, investments in higher education, and training in transferable skills. For each category, there is a conventional wisdom, or ideology, that confines persons with SMI within negative stereotypes of incompetence and hopelessness. The foundation underlying the proposals is that the negative stereotypes can best be combatted, and the objectives of mental health policy can best be achieved, by Searchers who are close to the problems they aim to solve. Hence, wherever possible, authority for developing solutions should be shifted away from the federal government, to the states, communities, and families, who struggle with It every day.

Restoring Health Capital

Anyone who surveys the landscape of U.S. mental health services in 2015 must conclude that our mental health policies do not meet the standards of the UN Convention on Disability Rights. In particular, current policy does not support the rights of persons with SMI to the *highest attainable health.* Many vulnerable patients receive substandard treatment or none at all, because effective systems for treating them in the community never materialized.[10] Today, the mental health system imposes barriers that make it difficult, or even impossible, to get patients the treatment they need. The barriers are legal, economic, and systemic.

Legal Barriers

The central legal issue is how to obtain care for patients who have acute symptoms of SMI, but do not believe they need treatment at all. Legislation in many states prohibits involuntary inpatient treatment of persons with mental illness, unless they pose "an imminent danger to themselves or others," or are "gravely disabled" (i.e., they are in physical danger because they have neglected their basic needs). Only eighteen states allow involuntary hospitalization on the basis of a demonstrable "need for treatment."[11]

These well-intentioned laws are designed to protect vulnerable persons from lengthy and unjustified confinement to a psychiatric institution. In the real world, the laws make it virtually impossible for family caregivers to obtain appropriate care for their relatives until *after* they become dangerous. A recent study reveals the anguish that the "imminent danger" provision imposes on families. The authors interviewed mothers caring for a child with SMI who had exhibited violent or threatening behavior toward their parent. The study describes the period of frustrated waiting until the police could be called:

> While their children decompensated right before their eyes, mothers waited for the inevitable point at which their children would meet criteria to be hospitalized involuntarily. Their living environments were filled with stress and growing tension. Mothers knew that their children needed help, but had no other option than to wait until something dangerous, even life threatening, happened. One woman said, "So what do I have to do? Do I have to sit here and wait and wait and wait and wait until that explosion happens?"[12]

Economic Barriers

In one sense, the "imminent danger" criterion is a crude mechanism for rationing inpatient psychiatric beds that are in short supply. The diversion of funding away from state mental hospitals that accompanied the community mental health movement spurred a drastic reduction in the number of inpatient psychiatric beds. In 1970, there were 525,000 psychiatric beds in the United States, by 2002 there were fewer than 212,000.[13] In a 2006 survey, more than two-thirds of state mental health authorities reported a shortage of inpatient beds for acute psychiatric care.[14] The shortages mean that patients who enter an emergency room with an acute psychiatric crisis may wait days or weeks for a bed, inmates who qualify for psychiatric care may wait in jail for several months before a bed becomes available, and patients who are admitted to a psychiatric hospital are often released too soon, in order to make room for other patients.[15]

Psychiatric inpatient beds are rationed among patients according to a priority status determined largely by forces external to the mental health system. Patients whose treatment is mandated by a court have the highest priority; patients who are referred to the system by a family member or physician have the lowest.[16] Police officers familiar with the mental health system say that they take offenders who are exhibiting signs of mental illness to jail rather than to an emergency room, because jail is the more likely route to the mental health services they need.[17]

Systemic Barriers

In spite of Robert Felix's acknowledgment that his vision of community-based care and prevention of mental illness had failed, federal policy makers continue with *more of the same.* The inefficient allocation of funding in today's mental health system, and ideological biases within the agencies that receive those funds, create systemic barriers to providing the best possible care for persons with SMI. In fiscal year 2014, for example, the Substance Abuse and Mental Health Services Administration (SAMHSA), the agency that directs federal mental health policy, allocated more than $480 million in Mental Health Block Grants to states for *community care and prevention.*[18] The funding increases annually despite the demonstrable failure of Community Mental Health Centers to provide adequate treatment for persons with the most serious mental illnesses, and despite the fact that we do not know how to predict or prevent SMI.

Appallingly, some federal mental health funds are used to support efforts to *withhold* necessary treatment from patients with SMI. In particular, the 2014 SAMHSA operating plan includes $36 million to support the Protection and Advocacy for Individuals with Mental Illness (PAIMI) Program.[19] In fiscal year 2012, the program investigated serious allegations of abuse, neglect, or civil rights violations on behalf of approximately eleven thousand persons, but performed proactive advocacy on behalf of *more than twenty-four million.*[20] In effect, "advocacy efforts" focus on ensuring that no one receives treatment for mental illness without their free and informed consent, even if the individual's decision-making capacity is impaired by acute symptoms of SMI. Such efforts often directly undermine the best interests of the patients, their families, and the community.[21] Can you imagine funding a program that advocates for children who do not want to attend school, or for elderly persons who want to keep driving even though their eyesight is failing? Funding for PAIMI continues, despite the fact that advocacy efforts outnumber protection efforts by more than two thousand to one, and despite the fact that patient advocates express no responsibility, and plan no change in tactics, following tragedies like the murder of Amy Bruce.

Flawed Ideology

If jail is the most direct route to mental health services for persons with SMI, current mental health policy warrants serious reconsideration. Current policy has failed because it has been driven by flawed ideologies, namely, that: (1) treatment for mental illness without a patient's consent is a violation of the patient's civil rights; and (2) community-based care is capable of treating and preventing acute cases of SMI.

The first ideology ignores the simple fact that mental illness attacks the brain. The brain is the center of rational thought, the organ that enables a person to understand stimuli, evaluate options, and make rational decisions. When a person is experiencing acute symptoms of SMI, their brain does not function properly; often they do not understand that they are ill, do not appreciate that treatment can help, and neither seek nor accept the care that they need. Asking a person with acute symptoms of mental illness to make rational decisions about their treatment is like asking a person in a wheelchair to get up and walk. *They cannot.* Society has an obligation to protect persons in acute phases of mental illness from the consequences of refusing treatment that can restore their health. Laws that prohibit involuntary treatment essentially deny treatment to persons with SMI who lack insight into their condition. It is this *failure to treat* that violates their right "to enjoy the highest attainable standard of health."[22]

With respect to the second ideology, fifty years of experience with community-based care has demonstrated that outpatient services cannot substitute for short-term hospitalization when a person is experiencing acute symptoms of SMI. A minimum fourteen-day period of treatment is necessary to stabilize a patient on antipsychotic medications.[23] The best way, sometimes the only way, to ensure that a patient adheres to the medication regimen is by admitting them for a short-term hospital stay. But beds are in such short supply that the only way to guarantee inpatient care is by court order.

A revised mental health policy should focus on solutions that promote both the welfare of the individual and the security of the community. Individuals have a right to be protected from making poor choices when their decision-making capacity is impaired by mental illness, and communities have a right to be protected from the potential dangers posed by persons whose symptoms of SMI are untreated. Contrary to the prevailing ideology, *there is no fundamental right to be mentally ill.*

Solutions

A bill introduced by Representative Tim Murphy (R-PA) in the 114th Congress proposes changes to federal mental health policy designed to improve access to mental health services for patients with SMI and their families.[24] If the bill becomes law, it will be a good beginning, but only a beginning. The U.S. mental health system is in need of fundamental reforms that *focus the system on the problems of persons with the most serious mental illnesses,* and *shift decision-making authority to Searchers who understand those problems.* To those ends:

(1) Congress should revamp the structure, administration, and mission of SAMHSA to focus on promoting the welfare of the agency's core constituencies (persons with SMI or substance use disorders), through activities that increase their access to high-quality mental health services.

   a. To ensure that services reflect the specific needs and research-based best practices for each constituency, SAMSHA should be replaced by two agencies: a Substance Abuse Administration and a Mental Health Services Administration (MHSA). The new organizational structure aligns the service agencies with the structure of the NIH, where research on substance abuse is supported by the National Institutes on Drug and Alcohol Abuse and research on mental disorders by the National Institute of Mental Health (NIMH).

   b. To ensure that leadership is highly qualified, Congress should mandate that the director of the MHSA be a physician with recognized expertise in treating SMI. No one among the current leadership team at SAMHSA has a medical degree. In contrast, the current director of NIMH (Dr. Thomas Insel) is a physician, former professor of psychiatry at Emory University, and respected research scientist.

c. To ensure that programs directed by the MHSA concentrate on the most serious and disabling mental illnesses, the agency's mission statement should reflect that focus. The current SAMHSA mission, "To reduce the impact of mental illness and substance abuse on America's communities"[25] has no focus and no measurable outcomes. One imagines an agency that expects little of itself, and accomplishes little as a result. Here is an alternate suggestion: "To increase and actively promote access to high-quality mental health services for persons with serious mental illness, with the goal of restoring each person to their maximum attainable mental health, and best possible quality of life."

(2) This mission can best be accomplished by supporting Searchers, at the state and community levels, who work closely with the target population and understand the problems they face. Hence, the locus of decision-making authority for public mental health services should be decentralized to reside with state mental health authorities.

a. To ensure that state mental health systems are adequately funded, MHSA should direct a major portion of its budget to State Mental Health Grants in support of its revised mission.
b. To ensure that states have freedom to innovate and develop best practices in the delivery of mental health services, the Mental Health Grants should have minimal restrictions, that define *what* is to be accomplished (improve access to high-quality mental health services) and for *whom* (persons with SMI), but place no restrictions on *how* the goals are to be accomplished.
c. To ensure that best practices in mental health services are disseminated nationwide, MHSA should collect a standard set of objective performance and expenditure measures from all states. Analyses of the data will identify the most cost-effective approaches to the delivery of mental health services, which MHSA should be responsible for disseminating.

(3) The federal government should adopt policies aimed at eliminating economic, legal, and systemic barriers to short-term inpatient care for persons experiencing acute symptoms of SMI.

a. To address economic barriers, the Centers for Medicare and Medicaid Services should eliminate restrictions that prohibit states from covering the costs of inpatient psychiatric care for Medicaid insureds. The policy creates disparities between persons with SMI covered by Medicaid (who may need hospital care for their mental illness but cannot get it) and persons with SMI covered by private insurance (who can).

b. To address legal barriers, the MHSA should draft, and provide incentives for states to adopt, a Model Involuntary Treatment Law. The law should make it possible for caregivers or mental health providers to obtain necessary *short-term* care for persons who have diminished decision-making capacity because of the acute symptoms of mental illness. In particular, the Model Law should expand the criteria for treatment without consent to include, with appropriate safeguards, *any person who is in need of medical treatment who is not mentally capable of understanding that need.*[26]

c. To address systemic barriers, Congress should de-fund the Patient Advocacy Program and replace it with an office empowered only to field complaints of abuse, neglect, or civil rights violations on behalf of persons with mental disorders. There is abundant evidence that the Advocacy Program *reduces* social welfare by depriving persons with SMI of the medical care they need, jeopardizing the welfare and security of family members, and imposing unnecessary costs on the social services and criminal justice systems.[27]

When we left David in Charlotte, after unsuccessful efforts to bring him back to Arizona or have him hospitalized, my greatest fear was that he would hurt himself or someone else. I was not concerned about deliberate acts of violence (David had never been threatening to anyone), but about poor judgment. I imagined a fatal car accident, a fight in a bar, David sleeping on the street, or becoming the victim of violent crime. There was nothing I could do except wait for the inevitable disaster, and pick up the pieces afterward. A functional mental health system would facilitate intervention before the disaster occurred.

Investing in Higher Education

The onset of SMI occurs most often in late adolescence, exactly when many young adults are making significant investments in human capital at a college or university. For the unlucky ones who become afflicted, the shock of SMI can derail their plans for graduation, career, and future. Students with bipolar I disorder, for example, are 70 percent more likely to drop out of college than students with no mental disorder.[28] The loss of human capital is tragic.

Structural Discrimination

Prior to the discovery of antipsychotic medications, it would have been almost unthinkable for a person with mental illness to aspire to a college education. The uncontrolled symptoms of SMI would be too great an obstacle to success. Now that we have treatments that control the acute symptoms for many patients, many college students with a diagnosis of SMI can return to school and complete their degrees. The primary obstacles to their success are the pervasive stigma against mental illness, the diminished self-confidence associated with a diagnosis of SMI, and the lack of necessary resources and support.[29]

At most U.S. colleges and universities, students with SMI are more likely to encounter structural discrimination than structural support. *Structural discrimination* is defined as a set of institutional practices that marginalize a disadvantaged group (e.g., students with mental illness).[30] Colleges and universities are not immune from such practices, even though they exist primarily for the purpose of promoting education and enlightenment. Examples of potential structural discrimination in higher education include: a disability services office that serves students with physical disabilities, but is unable or unwilling to support students with SMI; admission/readmission standards that are more stringent for students with SMI than for other students; campus residency policies that restrict the housing choices of students with SMI, solely on the basis of their illness.

The federal government provides no incentive or mandate to colleges and universities to eliminate structural discrimination against students with mental illness. In contrast, the government expends millions of dollars on higher education programs for other disadvantaged groups.[31] There are programs to support postsecondary education for blacks, Hispanics, migrants, Native Americans, and other minorities. There are programs to support special institutions of higher education for persons who are blind or deaf. But for persons with mental illness, there is vocational rehabilitation, supported employment, and SSDI.

Flawed Ideology

The structural discrimination against students with SMI on college and university campuses is fueled by negative stereotypes of persons with mental illness as dangerous, disruptive, and somehow responsible for their illness. Recall the college administrator who characterized my son's illness as "getting into trouble." Such discrimination would not be tolerated if it were directed at a member of another minority group.

Research shows that gender (male) and ethnicity (Hispanic) are stronger predictors of violent behavior than SMI.[32] Do colleges and universities have more stringent readmissions standards for Hispanic men (with no history of violence) than for other students? Of course not. Violent behavior among persons with SMI is strongly linked to acute psychotic symptoms.[33] There is simply no justification for universities to discriminate against students with mental illness who have no history of violence, who are responsive and adherent to medication, and who are not experiencing acute symptoms.

The failure of the federal government to establish any higher education programs for persons with SMI, one of the most disadvantaged and stigmatized of minority groups, suggests that policy makers are also driven by negative stereotypes. Why create policies or programs to support higher education services for persons with SMI, if you believe that they are incompetent and incapable of taking care of themselves? In fact, the stereotype is false. There are many examples of persons with schizophrenia and other serious mental illnesses who have completed college and postgraduate degrees.

Colleges and universities are in a unique position to help students with SMI acquire the human capital they need, both to qualify for stable jobs in the primary labor market and to find jobs that are a good match for their residual functional limitations. Colleges and universities are also in a position of authority, from which they can provide incentives (i.e., the opportunity to stay in school) for students with SMI to adhere to their prescribed treatment. Thus, public policies that encourage institutions of higher education to support their students with SMI can enhance the welfare of the students, increase equity in the market for higher education, and improve long-term employment outcomes for this population.

Solutions

The NIMH is ideally poised to create incentives for universities to provide supported education services for students with SMI. In fiscal year 2014, NIMH awarded more than $927 million in research grants to U.S. institutions of higher education.[34] In addition to supporting basic and clinical research that will develop better treatments for mental disorders, the funds support interventional research aimed at developing (emphasis added):

> new and better interventions that incorporate the diverse needs and circumstances of persons with mental illness, . . . allowing those who may suffer from these disorders to *live full and productive lives.*[35]

The vast amount of research funds awarded by NIMH give the institute considerable leverage to motivate welfare-enhancing behavior from grant recipients. NIMH already uses its leverage to ensure that research protocols have adequate protections for human and animal subjects, include appropriate representation of women and minorities, and provide training opportunities for undergraduate and graduate students. It is perfectly consistent with the strategic objectives of NIMH to ensure that its partner universities support their students with SMI. In fact, it is ironic that institutions can accept millions of dollars of grant support from NIMH to study mental disorders, but have no reciprocal obligation to provide educational supports for their students with mental illness. Therefore:

(4) The NIMH should use existing grant mechanisms to force U.S. universities to offer supported education programs for students with SMI. Qualifying programs should be designed to attain significant increases in graduation rates for this population.

a. To ensure that supported education services are widely available, NIMH should require all funding applications from universities to include a detailed statement regarding on-campus services provided for students with SMI. The services should be aimed at encouraging and supporting return to school, academic achievement, graduation, and job placement.

b. To encourage innovation in supported education services for students with SMI, NIMH should issue a special Request for Applications (RFA) for projects that develop, test, and disseminate best practices in providing educational services to university students with mental illness. The RFA is appropriate under the Child and Adolescent Research Program, which aims to "accelerate the implementation of evidence-based services for youth within and across service sectors" (including schools), and to support the "integration of mental health services across sectors" (including education).[36] Consistent with the idea that solutions will be developed by Searchers, the RFA should allow broad scope for innovation in the nature of services delivered, provided that those services are delivered in integrated settings *on-campus* (so that students with SMI are not marginalized), and that the expected outcome measure is *graduation*.

The proposed MHSA provides another mechanism to promote supported education services for students with SMI. As set forth previously, a primary mission of the agency should be to ensure that persons with SMI have the best possible quality of life. That mission naturally includes the opportunity to complete their education. Hence:

(5) Once established, the MHSA should fund targeted grants to states, public universities, and local community colleges to develop supported education services for students with SMI. Qualifying programs should be designed to attain significant increases in graduation rates for this population.

a. To ensure that grantees have maximum flexibility to develop effective interventions, targeted grants should have few restrictions beyond the basic objectives to eliminate structural discrimination, and provide pro-active, on-campus support, for students with SMI who are enrolled in regular university degree programs.

b. To ensure that best practices are encouraged and disseminated, the MHSA should collect data from grantees on particulars of the programs and outcomes attained (admission/readmission rates, retention rates, graduation rates, employment rates, earnings, etc.). Results should be distributed and posted on the agency's website, both to encourage the spread of on-campus supported education, and to counteract negative stereotypes of persons with SMI as incapable of earning a college degree.

Parents, university administrators, and others may raise concerns that increasing access to higher education for students with SMI will create risks for the campus community. What if a student stops treatment and suffers a relapse of psychotic symptoms? The risk is slight because, even among persons with SMI who are suffering acute symptoms of psychosis, only a small fraction will commit acts of violence. The risk can be minimized even further if NIMH and MHSA require colleges and universities to include strategies for monitoring a student's adherence to their prescribed medications. For students with SMI, the *privilege* of attending college should include the *responsibility* of adhering to treatment.

Training in Transferable Skills

Vocational training for persons with SMI is dominated by models of supported employment, and the current gold standard is the Individual Placement and Support (IPS) model. The consensus in the literature is that IPS out-performs other models of vocational rehabilitation in terms of job placement, hours worked per month, and monthly earnings.[37] Still, IPS, like other models of supported employment, has almost no impact on moving participants off disability benefits and into gainful competitive employment.

Evaluation of IPS

In 2005, the SSA launched a study to determine if a combination of IPS, systematic medication managment, and behavioral health services could succeed in moving persons with SMI off SSDI. The Mental Health Treatment Study (MHTS) enrolled more than 2,200 SSDI recipients, with schizophrenia or affective disorders, at twenty-three sites across the United States.[38] Subjects were randomized to either an intervention group, which received IPS vocational services plus medication management and behavioral health services, or a control group, which received the usual mental health services covered by Medicare.

Vocational services provided to the intervention group adhered to the core principles of IPS:

- *Eligibility based on consumer choice*, with no exclusions for treatment noncompliance, co-occurring substance use disorders, lack of work readiness, etc.
- *Integration of employment service*s with mental health services
- A *focus on competitive employment*, meaning jobs in regular work settings, paying at least the minimum wage
- *Rapid job search* beginning immediately upon admission to the program
- *Individual employment support*, as needed, after job placement
- *Job placement based on client preferences* rather than availability of jobs
- *Benefits counseling* to mitigate the impact of employment on government entitlements such as SSDI and Medicaid[39]

The MHTS tracked employment outcomes for participants over a two-year period. The intervention group attained significantly better outcomes, on average, than the controls.[40] Nevertheless, those among the intervention group who obtained a job typically worked less than half the months in the follow-up period, with mean weekly earnings of $192.[41] Only 8 percent of the intervention group attained earnings above the level for "substantial, gainful activity."

The MHTS is stark evidence of the problems with current vocational services for persons with SMI. IPS is the best model of supported employment we have, but it is not successful in placing persons with SMI in *full and gainful competitive employment*. One analyst summarizes the "take-home messages" as follows (emphasis added):

> People with severe mental illness often want to work and to feel socially included, and the MHTS demonstrated an ability to improve those outcomes. The MHTS also establishes strongly that the best we have will have only a small effect on employment and earnings and essentially *no effect on exit from SSDI into mainstream economic life.*[42]

Many thousands of persons with SMI are capable of full and gainful competitive employment but are disadvantaged by disruptions to schooling and gaps in work experience that leave them with diminished human capital. Participation in IPS-type supported employment programs will not provide the *transferable skills* they need to succeed in today's competitive labor market. The broad eligibility criteria (no exclusions) and rapid job placements characteristic of IPS virtually condemn clients to low-skill, low-wage jobs, where any human capital they acquire is job-specific. Such jobs do not lead to long-term stable employment.

Flawed Ideology

Better models of vocational training are needed for persons with SMI who are capable of independent, competitive work. We are not, however, *searching* for new and different ways to provide vocational services to this population. Research in the area of vocational rehabilitation is dominated by studies of the outcomes of IPS, the relative merits of IPS versus other models of supported employment, and the degree to which IPS programs maintain fidelity to its core principles. In the vocational services literature, the commitment to IPS has become almost an ideology in itself.

Paradoxically, some of the core principles of IPS reinforce negative stereotypes of persons with SMI that create barriers to successful employment. Providing individual employment supports after job placement suggests that persons with SMI are incapable of independent work. Counseling to ensure that disability benefits continue suggests that persons with SMI will always be dependent on government support. Rapid job placement without training suggests that persons with SMI are incapable of holding more than menial jobs. Allowing participation of those who are not work-ready suggests that persons with SMI must be exempted from normal work requirements.

For reasons cited throughout this book, work is an important part of recovery from a serious mental illness. Accordingly, there is a role for IPS in providing employment opportunities for persons who are so severely disabled by mental illness that they are unable to succeed in independent, competitive jobs. But, continuing the *exclusive* focus on IPS is prejudicial and counterproductive, because it creates the mindset that all persons with SMI are so severely work-limited. New models of vocational services need to be developed to ensure that all persons with SMI achieve their maximum potential at work. Policy solutions should aim to increase efficiency in the labor market by enhancing the general human capital (transferable skills) of workers with SMI, and placing those who are capable of gainful employment in stable and well-paying competitive jobs.

Solutions

New models of vocational training for persons with SMI are being piloted in both Canada and Australia. In Ontario, Frontenac County Mental Health Services and St. Lawrence Community College jointly developed a retail skills training program to improve competitive employment outcomes for persons with SMI.[43] The focus of the program was on retail skills because skilled retail workers were in demand (the retail sector was expanding in

Ontario) and because many clients expressed interest in careers in retail sales (and had related work experience). The training program consisted of twelve weeks of classroom instruction, and a three-week community work placement.

> Eleven individuals enrolled in the inaugural program. All expressed great enthusiasm for the program, based on the novelty of being in school, connecting to the world of work, and feeling more a part of the community at large. The group formed friendships and acquired new learning. All completed the rigorous classroom training. [44]

By 2010, the Skills for Retail training program had been offered three times, to a total of twenty-nine participants. Twenty graduates (69 percent) were working in competitive retail sales positions, with job tenure ranging from six to twenty-four months. [45]

In Australia, the Division of Mental Health Services for Liverpool and Fairfield Counties partnered with the Southwestern Sydney Institute of Technical and Further Education to offer trainings in horticulture, hospitality, and computer literacy for clients with SMI. Classes were taught by instructors from the institute, with counseling and support services provided by an occupational therapist from the Division of Mental Health. Sixty-one clients participated in one or more trainings. Most clients (nearly 90 percent) had diagnoses of schizophrenia, schizoaffective disorder, or bipolar disorder. No client who expressed an interest in the training was excluded. The overall course completion rate was 72 percent. Within six to twelve months of completion, two-thirds of graduates were either employed in mainstream "open" employment (18 percent), or had continued on with further education (51 percent). [46]

These programs are too small to provide more than illustrative evidence of what might be accomplished with vocational services targeted at developing the general human capital of persons with SMI. However, they demonstrate that people with even the most serious mental illnesses can aspire to more than menial employment and can acquire skills of value in the labor market. There is no indication in the literature that programs like these are even being pondered in the United States. The almost exclusive focus of research on supported employment models appears to have crowded out other models that can enhance the productive potential of persons with SMI. Hence:

(6) The federal government should direct grant monies appropriated to the National Institute of Disability and Rehabilitation Research (NIDRR) and NIMH to support research aimed at developing and evaluating new models of vocational skills training for persons with SMI. These vocational services are not intended to supplant the IPS

model, but to serve the "hidden population" of persons with SMI who are capable of supporting themselves in competitive jobs, but have thus far been ignored. To ensure that new training models serve the target population and maximize their productive potential, the following core principles should be applied:

- *Eligibility is based on the capacity for independent and gainful employment*, meaning that the most acute symptoms of SMI are controlled, with or without antipsychotic drugs.
- *The focus is on gainful competitive employment*, in other words, mainstream jobs, not set aside for persons with disabilities, which provide sufficient income for financial independence.
- *Education and/or vocational skills training* is provided to enhance the general human capital of participants before job placement.
- *Job placement is focused on finding a good match* between the client's skills, abilities and functional limitations, and the requirements of a potential job.
- The expectation is that clients will *not need long-term support from government entitlements* such as SSDI or Medicaid.

(7) Once established, the MHSA should provide funding to state mental health authorities to develop vocational services programs consistent with these principles.

(8) The MHSA should also provide funding to states to support ventures in *entrepreneurship and self-employment* for the target population. Self-employment is a good job match for many persons with SMI, because of the flexibility that comes with being in charge. One participant in our qualitative study, for example, told us that:

> One of my major decisions was to get out of real estate and go back to school and become a massage therapist. [Now] if I am not feeling well I don't have to worry about the whole anxiety attack to have to call in and explain to somebody that I am not feeling well and that I can't come to work. So if I am sick, I am sick and I don't have to answer to no one, but me. . . . And so, just knowing that I can have time to do what I need to do for myself with my new career is just worth its weight in gold.[47]

In a recent twenty-year update on the IPS model of supported employment, two of its ardent proponents stated:

> Some professionals in many countries, including the U.S., persist in believing that many people [with SMI] cannot work and need to be protected in sheltered settings. These latter arguments recall paeans for long-term institutional-

ization in the 1970s and, like those cries, are likely to become historical anachronisms.[48]

The authors continue on to say that (emphasis added):

Current research on IPS supported employment shows that the majority [of people disabled by psychiatric disorders] can succeed as *steady part-time workers*.[49]

The statement implies that the best a person with SMI can hope for, in the competitive workplace, is a steady, part-time job. I look forward to the day when *that belief* becomes an historical anachronism.

Postscript

The history of mental health policy in the United States has been a series of well-intentioned attempts by Planners to solve problems they did not fully understand. The policies have been implemented with little accountability, a general lack of foresight regarding unintended consequences, and sometimes a callous disregard for the well-being of persons with SMI and their families. The outcomes have been largely unsuccessful and, in some cases, tragic.

Current mental health policy is rife with irony and inconsistency. Government policy turns family members into default caregivers for persons with SMI, but denies them decision-making authority or access to medical information in times of crisis. Policy makers fund patient advocates to ensure that persons with mental illness are not hospitalized against their will, then decry the fact that the criminal justice system is overrun by persons with mental illness who ought to be hospitalized. Researchers and policy makers who insist that persons with SMI can make competent decisions about treatment when they are ill seem to believe these same persons are incapable of full employment when they are well.

With the vision of a more rational mental health system in mind, my policy proposals are designed to improve employment outcomes for persons with SMI. In the belief that solutions will come from visionary Searchers rather than ideologically-driven Planners, I have identified policies that shift decision-making authority for mental health services away from the federal government and empower Searchers at the state and local levels to develop creative solutions.

Some readers will criticize these policies as overly paternalistic (e.g., involuntary hospitalization based on the "need for treatment," or adherence to treatment as a condition for attending a college or university). Therefore, let me reiterate the logic that led to these proposals: Mental illness is a disease of the *brain*, which compromises a person's *decision-making capacity*. Adherence to prescribed treatment in the first five years after onset of

SMI is critical to prevent relapse, to increase the probability of recovery, and to minimize the subsequent loss of functional capacity. Investments in general human capital can protect individuals from some of the disabling effects of mental illness, and significantly increase the probability of gainful, competitive employment. Thus, policy interventions that optimize the health, functional capacities, and employment prospects of persons with SMI, are both justifiable and humane. *There is no fundamental right to be mentally ill.*

My faith in the creative problem-solving power of Searchers comes from both research and experience. For the past fifteen years, the overriding purpose of my life has been to help my son reclaim his life from schizophrenia. It has been my greatest challenge. I have had family, friends, and colleagues for support; access to the best physicians and lawyers; and a lot of luck. But in the end, the solutions have come, not from others and not from chance, but from intuition, determination, and desperation to save my son. "Once you get into cosmological [muck] like this, you got to throw away the instruction manual."[50]

Chapter Twelve

Life Reclaimed

EPILOGUE

Summer 2012

In June 2012, I was back in Luxembourg working at the Research Institute and enjoying my European lifestyle: commuter train to and from work, daily shopping trips to the village market, and occasional weekend trips to Paris. I didn't hear much from David, but I wasn't particularly worried this time. He was busy too. He had his own friends, and his job at the Dream Center, and classes at American Indian College.

Still, I always worried about David's future. We revised our will, setting up a trust to ensure that he had an income after we were gone. Aaron knew that it would eventually be his responsibility to make sure David was never homeless or alone. Sometimes, I imagined the kind of wife I wished David could find. She would be confident, decisive, and organized, but compassionate and caring. Of course, this was all an impossible dream. I never expected David to marry. I grieved for the life he had lost, and the grandchildren I would never see.

But, when I returned home from Europe that summer, David had a surprise for me. "Let's have lunch," he suggested. "Someplace special, Mom, because there's someone I want you to meet." And so Megan walked into our lives. She was everything I had imagined in my wishful thinking, and more. She loved my son, which is really the only important selection criteria for a daughter-in-law, and he was obviously in love with her. They planned to be married in December.

When I returned home from lunch, I told my fiancé that David was engaged. "You don't seem very excited," he said. "You don't understand," I

197

told him, "I've been down this path before." And I worried that the stress of an impending marriage would trigger a relapse of psychotic symptoms again.

Others were worried as well. When Megan's family learned about David's diagnosis of schizophrenia they were, understandably, concerned. (I have to admit, a man with SMI is not most parents' idea of the perfect son-in-law.) David and Megan scheduled an intervention with her family to discuss their objections to the marriage. David told them, "I'm glad you raised your concerns. I want to have everything out in the open about my illness. Ask me whatever questions you like." Brother Mike, David's pastor at the House of Healing, mediated the session. After David finished answering questions, Mike told Megan's family about David's healing from mental illness. To their great credit, they were able to see past the stereotypes of schizophrenia, and accept David into their family.

It was delightful to watch Megan plan her wedding. She knew exactly where she wanted to be married, but it was outside her budget. So she planned the wedding for a Thursday, when there was less demand, and negotiated a rate she could afford. About two months before the wedding, she went shopping for a dress. Sales clerks at the bridal shop were appalled; "You can't possibly order a dress and have it altered in time." They did not know Megan. She found her perfect dress and took it home that day. In short, Megan had all the details of the wedding under control. The only thing for me to do was choose a song for my dance with David.

Winter 2012

David and Megan were married in December, outdoors, in view of Camelback Mountain in Phoenix. Aaron's children were flower girl and ring bearer. Little Zachary (age four) at first refused to participate. When he tried on his tuxedo, however, he decided he liked his ring-bearer "costume" and agreed to walk down the aisle with sister, Audrey. Pastor Tommy Barnett conducted the ceremony, and Brother Mike was part of the wedding party. One of my favorite moments was when Megan's brother toasted the newlyweds during the reception. He said that, even at a young age, older sister Megan was clearly in charge. "I was more afraid of getting in trouble with Megan than getting in trouble with my mother."

David and Megan planned to honeymoon in Mexico. My husband offered his time-share points to rent a condo for them. When they told Allan where they wanted to stay, he said to me, "Do you know how many points this is costing me?" "Welcome to parenthood," I told him.

Spring 2015

One year ago, with his construction business bringing in a steady income, David wrote to the Social Security Administration to inform them that he no longer needed monthly checks from SSDI. The letter he received in reply said, "You are not eligible to withdraw from SSDI at this time." He waited six months and tried again. This time, SSA agreed. David received his last government check in February 2015—in March, his construction business multiplied four-fold and he had to hire additional workers to keep up with the demand.

Last December, David and Megan celebrated their second wedding anniversary. She works for Phoenix First Assembly as their event planner, where she manages all the weddings. David preaches every Sunday evening at the state prison. Since he met Megan, he is more relaxed, more accepting, and better dressed. Gradually, I am beginning to relax as well, and to believe that David's victory over *It* is real. The song I chose? "The Impossible Dream."

Notes

1. A DISEASE UNLIKE ANY OTHER

1. Rajiv Tandon, Matcheri S. Keshavan, and Henry A. Nasrallah, "Schizophrenia, 'Just the Facts' What We Know in 2008. 2 Epidemiology and Etiology," *Schizophrenia Research* 102 (2008): 3–4.

2. Tandon, Keshavan, and Nasrallah, "Epidemiology and Etiology," 4–5.

3. R. Walter Heinrichs, "Historical Origins of Schizophrenia: Two Early Madmen and Their Illness," *Journal of the History of the Behavioral Sciences* 39 (2003): 357.

4. Heinrichs, "Historical Origins of Schizophrenia."

5. Heinrichs, "Historical Origins of Schizophrenia," 356.

6. Heinrichs, "Historical Origins of Schizophrenia," 354.

7. Heinrichs, "Historical Origins of Schizophrenia," 354.

8. Celeste Silveira, Joao Marques-Teixeira, and Antonio Jose de Bastos-Leite, "More Than One Century of Schizophrenia: An Evolving Perspective," *Journal of Nervous and Mental Disease* 200 (2012): 1054.

9. Rajiv Tandon, Matcheri S. Keshavan, and Henry A. Nasrallah, "Schizophrenia, 'Just the Facts' 4. Clinical Features and Conceptualization," *Schizophrenia Research* 110 (2009): 2.

10. Michael D. Hunter and Peter W. R. Woodruff, "History, Aetiology and Symptomatology of Schizophrenia," *Psychiatry* 4 (2005): 2; Nick Craddock and Michael J. Owen, "The Kraepelinian Dichotomy—Going, Going . . . But Still Not Gone," *British Journal of Psychiatry* 196 (2010): 92.

11. Silveira, Marques-Teixeira, and Bastos-Leite, "One Century of Schizophrenia," 1054; Hunter and Woodruff, "History, Aetiology and Symptomatology," 3.

12. Silveira, Marques-Teixeira, and Bastos-Leite, "One Century of Schizophrenia," 1054.

13. Rajiv Tandon, Henry A. Nasrallah, and Matcheri S. Keshavan, "'Just the Facts': Meandering in Schizophrenia's Many Forests," *Schizophrenia Research* 128 (2011): 5. Pathoplastic factors are factors, like personality, that can affect the way an illness is expressed.

14. Tandon, Keshavan, and Nasrallah, "Clinical Features and Conceptualization," 2.

15. Heinrichs, "Historical Origins," 352.

16. Tandon, Keshavan, and Nasrallah, "Clinical Features and Conceptualization," 4–5.

17. Tandon, Keshavan, and Nasrallah, "Clinical Features and Conceptualization," 6.

18. Matcheri S. Keshavan et al., "Schizophrenia, 'Just the Facts': What We Know in 2008 Part 3: Neurobiology," *Schizophrenia Research* 106 (2008): 90–96.

19. Manfred Bleuler, "A 23-Year Longitudinal Study of 208 Schizophrenics and Impressions in Regard to the Nature of Schizophrenia," *Journal of Psychiatric Research* 6 (1968, Supplement 1): 10.

20. Tandon, Keshavan, and Nasrallah, "Epidemiology and Etiology," 6.

21. John H. Gilmore, "Understanding What Causes Schizophrenia: A Developmental Perspective," *American Journal of Psychiatry* 167 (2010): 8.

22. Tandon, Keshavan, and Nasrallah, "Epidemiology and Etiology," 12.

23. K. H. Nuechterlein et al., "The Vulnerability/Stress Model of Schizophrenic Relapse: A Longitudinal Study," *Acta Psychiatrica Scandinavica* 89 (1994): 58–60.

24. Elaine F. Walker and Donald Diforio, "Schizophrenia: A Neural-Diathesis Stress Model," *Psychological Review* 104 (1997): 677–79.

25. Keshavan et al., "Schizophrenia, 'Just the Facts' 6. Moving Ahead with the Schizophrenia Concept: From the Elephant to the Mouse," *Schizophrenia Research* 127 (2011): 7.

26. Keshavan et al., 4–7.

27. Keshavan et al.

28. Francisco Lopez-Munoz and Cecilio Alamo, "The Consolidation of Neuroleptic Therapy: Janssen, the Discovery of Haloperidol and Its Introduction into Clinical Practice," *Brain Research Bulletin* 79 (2009): 133.

29. Lopez-Munoz and Alamo, "The Consolidation of Neuroleptic Therapy," 134–35.

30. Rajiv Tandon, Henry A. Nasrallah, and Matcheri S. Keshavan, "Schizophrenia, 'Just the Facts' 5. Treatment and Prevention Past, Present, and Future," *Schizophrenia Research* 122 (2010): 2–6.

31. Tandon, Nasrallah, and Keshavan, "Treatment and Prevention"; George Foussias and Gary Remington, "Antipsychotics and Schizophrenia: From Efficacy and Effectiveness to Clinical Decision-Making," *Canadian Journal of Psychiatry* 55 (2010): 117–23.

32. Foussias and Remington, "Antipsychotics and Schizophrenia," 121–22.

33. Tandon, Nasrallah, and Keshavan, "Treatment and Prevention," 5.

34. Eric Q. Wu et al., "The Economic Burden of Schizophrenia in the United States in 2002," *Journal of Clinical Psychiatry* 66 (2005): 1125–26.

35. Marjorie L. Baldwin and Steven C. Marcus. "Labor Market Outcomes of Persons with Mental Disorders," *Industrial Relations* 46 (2007): 481–96.

2. THE MARK OF SCHIZOPHRENIA

1. Nathaniel Hawthorne, *The Scarlet Letter* (Reprint, New York: Simon & Schuster, 2004), 62.

2. *Oxford English Dictionary*, 1st ed., s.v. "stigma."

3. Emory Bogardus, "A Social Distance Scale," *Sociology and Social Research* 17 (1933): 269.

4. Erving Goffman, *Stigma: Notes on the Management of Spoiled Identity* (Englewood Cliffs, NJ: Prentice-Hall, 1963), 3.

5. Goffman, *Stigma*, 4–18.

6. Mary T. Westbrook, Varoe Legge, and Mark Pennay, "Attitudes towards Disabilities in aMulticultural Society," *Social Science and Medicine* 36 (1993): 617.

7. Westbrook, Legge, and Pennay, "Attitudes towards Disabilities in a Multicultural Society," 619.

8. John. L. Tringo, "The Hierarchy of Preference toward Disability Groups," *Journal of Special Education* 4 (1970): 299; Gary Albrecht, Vivian G. Walker, and Judith A. Levy, "Social Ddistance from the Stigmatized: A Test of Two Theories," *Social Science and Medicine* 16 (1982): 1323.

9. Bruce Link et al., "Public Conceptions of Mental Illness: Labels, Causes, Dangerousness, and Social Distance," *American Journal of Public Health* 89 (1999): 1331–32.

10. Caroline E. Mann and Melissa J. Himelein, "Factors Associated with Stigmatization of Persons with Mental Illness," *Psychiatric Services* 55 (2004): 186–87; Ross Norman, Deborah

Windell, and Rahul Manchanda, "Examining Differences in the Stigma of Depression and Schizophrenia," *International Journal of Social Psychiatry* 58 (2012): 74.

11. Marc Franchot Weiss, "Children's Attitudes toward the Mentally Ill: A Developmental Analysis," *Psychological Reports* 58 (1986): 12.

12. Marc Franchot Weiss, "Children's Attitudes toward the Mentally Ill: An Eight-Year Longitudinal Follow-Up," *Psychological Reports* 74 (1994): 52.

13. Weiss, "Children's Attitudes toward the Mentally Ill," 55.

14. Weiss, "Developmental Analysis," 16.

15. Matthias C. Angermeyer and Herbert Matschinger, "Public Beliefs about Schizophrenia and Depression: Similarities and Differences," *Social Psychiatry and Psychiatric Epidemiology* 38 (2003): 529.

16. Patrick W. Corrigan, "Mental Health Stigma as Social Attribution: Implications for Research Methods and Attitude Change," *Clinical Psychology: Science and Practice* 7 (2000): 51–54; Bernard Weiner, Raymond P. Perry, and Jamie Magnusson, "An Attributional Analysis of Reactions to Stigmas," *Journal of Personality and Social Psychology* 55 (1988): 738–39.

17. Bernard Weiner, "On Sin versus Sickness: A Theory of Perceived Responsibility and Social Motivation," *American Psychologist* 48 (1993): 959–61.

18. Corrigan, "Stigma as Social Attribution," 52.

19. Corrigan, "Stigma as Social Attribution," 50–57.

20. Craig Hemmens et al., "The Consequences of Official Labels: An Examination of the Rights Lost by the Mentally Ill and Mentally Incompetent Ten Years Later," *Community Mental Health Journal* 38 (2002): 132–34.

21. Patrick Corrigan et al., "An Attribution Model of Public Discrimination towards Persons with Mental Illness," *Journal of Health and Social Behavior* 44 (2003): 166; Angermeyer and Matschinger, "Public Beliefs," 529.

22. Nava R. Silton et al., "Stigma in America: Has Anything Changed? Impact of Perceptions of Mental Illness and Dangerousness on the Desire for Social Distance: 1996 and 2006," *Journal of Nervous and Mental Disease* 199 (2011): 363; Bernice A. Pescosolido et al., "'A Disease Like Any Other?' A Decade of Change in Public Reactions to Schizophrenia, Depression, and Alcohol Dependence," *American Journal of Psychiatry* 167 (2010): 1324.

23. Ross Norman et al., "The Role of Perceived Norms in the Stigmatization of Mental Illness," *Social Psychiatry and Psychiatric Epidemiology* 43 (2008): 855.

24. Matthias C. Angermeyer and Herbert Matschinger, "Labeling—Stereotype—Discrimination: An Investigation of the Stigma Process," *Social Psychiatry and Psychiatric Epidemiology* 40 (2005): 393.

25. Norman et al., "Perceived Norms," 855.

26. Angermeyer and Matschinger, "Labeling—Stereotype—Discrimination," 393.

27. David B. Feldman and Christian S. Crandall, "Dimensions of Mental Illness Stigma: What about Mental Illness Causes Social Rejection?" *Journal of Social and Clinical Psychology* 26 (2007): 145–46; Matthias C. Angermeyer, Michael Beck, and Herbert Matschinger, "Determinants of the Public's Preference for Social Distance from People with Schizophrenia," *Canadian Journal of Psychiatry* 48 (2003): 666.

28. Corrigan et al., "An Attribution Model," 165.

29. John Read, "Why Promoting Biological Ideology Increases Prejudice against People Labelled 'Schizophrenic.'" *Australian Psychologist* 42 (2007): 118.

30. Pescosolido et al., "A Disease Like Any Other?" 1322–24.

31. Lisa Wood et al., "Public Perceptions of Stigma towards People with Schizophrenia, Depression, and Anxiety," *Psychiatry Research* 220 (2014): 605–6.

32. Pescosolido et al., "A Disease Like Any Other?" 1324; G. Schomerus et al., "Evolution of Public Attitudes about Mental Illness: A Systematic Review and Meta-Analysis," *Acta Psychiatrica Scandinavica* 125 (2012): 446.

33. Wood et al., "Public Perceptions of Stigma," 606.

34. Read, "Promoting Biological Ideology," 121–23.

35. Matthias C. Angermeyer et al., "Biogenetic Explanations and Emotional Reactions to People with Schizophrenia and Major Depressive Disorder," *Psychiatry Research* 220 (2014): 702–3.

36. Wood et al., "Public Perceptions of Stigma," 606.

37. Silton et al., "Stigma in America," 363.

38. Pescosolido et al., "A Disease Like Any Other?" 1324.

39. Corrigan et al., "Newspaper Stories as Measures of Structural Stigma," *Psychiatric Services* 56 (2005): 552–53.

40. Corrigan et al., "Newspaper Stories," 554.

41. Pamela J. Taylor, "Psychosis and Violence: Stories, Fears and Reality," *Canadian Journal of Psychiatry* 53 (2008): 647.

42. Patrick W. Corrigan and Amy C. Watson, "Findings from the National Comorbidity Survey on the Frequency of Violent Behavior in Individuals with Psychiatric Disorders," *Psychiatry Research* 136 (2005): 156–57.

43. Linda A. Teplin et al., "Crime Victimization in Adults with Severe Mental Illness," *Archives of General Psychiatry* 62 (2005): 914.

44. Gary S. Becker, *Economics of Discrimination*, 2nd ed. (Chicago: University of Chicago Press, 1971), 39–40, 55–56, 75–77.

45. Marjorie L. Baldwin and William G. Johnson, "Labor Market Discrimination against Men with Disabilities in the Year of the A.D.A.," *Southern Economic Journal* 66 (2000): 558.

46. Marjorie L. Baldwin, "The Effects of Impairments on Employment and Wages: Estimates from the 1984 and 1990 SIPP," *Behavioral Sciences and the Law* 17 (1999): 20–23; Melanie K. Jones, Paul L. Latreille, and Peter J. Sloane, "Disability, Gender, and the British Labour Market," *Oxford Economics Papers* 58 (2006): 434; Baldwin and Marcus, "Labor Market Outcomes," 496–502.

47. Baldwin and Marcus, "Labor Market Outcomes."

48. Marjorie L. Baldwin and Steven C. Marcus. "Perceived versus Measured Stigma among Workers with Serious Mental Disorders," *Psychiatric Services* 57 (2006): 390.

49. Janice Hunter Jenkins and Elizabeth A. Carpenter-Song, "Awareness of Stigma among Persons with Schizophrenia," *Journal of Nervous and Mental Disease* 197 (2009): 522.

50. Jenkins and Carpenter-Song, "Awareness of Stigma among Persons with Schizophrenia," 524.

51. Patrick W. Corrigan and Amy C. Watson, "The Paradox of Self-Stigma and Mental Illness," *Clinical Psychology: Science and Practice* 9 (2002): 35–36.

52. Beate Schulze and Matthias C. Angermeyer, "Subjective Experiences of Stigma: A Focus Group Study of Schizophrenic Patients, Their Relatives and Mental Health Professionals," *Social Science and Medicine* 56 (2003): 303–4.

53. Marjorie L. Baldwin and Rebecca M. B. White. "Workplace Accommodations That Work for Persons with Mental Illness." In *Perspectives on Disability and Accommodation*, edited by Kelly Williams-Whitt and Daphne G. Taras (Victoria, BC: National Institute of Disability Management and Research, 2010), 123.

54. Corrigan and Watson, "Paradox of Self-Stigma," 40.

55. Goffman, *Stigma*, 7–9.

56. Amy C. Watson, Frederick E. Miller, and John S. Lyons, "Adolescent Attitudes toward Serious Mental Illness," *Journal of Nervous and Mental Disease* 193 (2005): 771–72.

57. Corrigan and Watson, "Paradox of Self-Stigma," 44.

58. Schulze and Angermeyer, "Subjective Experiences of Stigma," 303–304.

59. Corrigan and Watson, "Paradox of Self-Stigma," 40.

60. Kristin Viana. "People That Have Won," *Soundings East* 17 (1993): 11.

61. Schulze and Angermeyer, "Subjective Experiences of Stigma," 303.

62. Sara Kvrgic et al., "Therapeutic Alliance in Schizophrenia: The Role of Recovery Orientation, Self-Stigma, and Insight," *Psychiatry Research* 209 (2013): 15–16.

3. LIFE INTERRUPTED

1. Edward L. Glaeser et al., "An Economic Approach to Social Capital," *Economic Journal* 112 (2002): F438.

2. Rafael Gomez and Eric Santor, "Membership Has Its Privileges: The Effect of Social Capital and Neighbourhood Characteristics on the Earnings of Microfinance Borrowers," *Canadian Journal of Economics* 34 (2001): 960–61; Michael Bernabé Aguilera, "The Impact of Social Capital on Labor Force Participation: Evidence from the 2000 Social Capital Benchmark Survey," *Social Science Quarterly* 83 (2002): 864–68.

3. Richard C. Baron and Mark S. Salzer, "Accounting for Unemployment among People with Mental Illness," *Behavioral Sciences and the Law* 20 (2002): 588.

4. Christopher J. L. Murray et al., "Disability-Adjusted Life Years (DALYs) for 291 Diseases and Injuries in 21 Regions, 1990–2010: A Systematic Analysis for the Global Burden of Disease Study 2010," *Lancet* 380 (2012): 2197.

5. Joshua Salomon et al., "Common Values in Assessing Health Outcomes from Disease and Injury: Disability Weights Measurement Study for the Global Burden of Disease Study 2010," *Lancet* 380 (2012): 2131–37.

6. Salomon et al., "Common Values in Assessing Health Outcomes."

7. Harvey A. Whiteford et al., "Global Burden of Disease Attributable to Mental and Substance Use Disorders: Findings from the Global Burden of Disease Study 2010," *Lancet* 382 (2013): 1578.

8. Christopher J. L. Murray et al., "DALYs for 291 Diseases and Injuries," 2216.

9. Harvey A. Whiteford et al., "Burden of Disease Attributable to Mental Disorders," 1578.

10. Theo Vos et al., "Years Lived with Disability (YLDs) for the 1160 Sequelae of 289 Diseases and Injuries 1990–2010 . . . ," *Lancet* 380 (2012): 2184.

11. Christopher J. L. Murray et al., "DALYs for 291 Diseases and Injuries," 2204–209.

12. Murray et al., "DALYs for 291 Diseases and Injuries," 2207.

13. Harvey A. Whiteford et al., "Burden of Disease Attributable to Mental Disorders," 1582.

14. Christopher J. L. Murray and Alan D. Lopez, eds., *Global Burden of Disease: A Comprehensive Assessment of Mortality and Disability from Diseases, Injuries and Risk Factors* (Cambridge, MA: Harvard School of Public Health, 1996), 415.

15. Joshua Salomon et al., "Disability Weights Measurement Study," *Lancet* 380 (2012): 2136.

16. "Where Next with Psychiatric Illness?" *Nature* 336 (1988): 95.

17. Baron and Salzer, "Accounting for Unemployment," 589.

18. Robert Rosensheck et al., "Barriers to Employment for People with Schizophrenia," *American Journal of Psychiatry* 163 (2006): 414; David Salkever et al., "Measures and Predictors of Community-Based Employment and Earnings of Persons with Schizophrenia in a Multisite Study," *Psychiatric Services* 58 (2007): 318–19.

19. Hector W. H. Tsang et al., "Review on Vocational Predictors: A Systematic Review of Predictors of Vocational Outcomes among Individuals with Schizophrenia," *Australian and New Zealand Journal of Psychiatry* 44 (2010): 499.

20. Kevin Hollenbeck and Jean Kimmel, "Differences in the Returns to Education for Males by Disability Status and Age of Disability Onset," *Southern Economic Journal* 74 (2008): 719–20.

21. Michael Spence, "Job Market Signaling," *Quarterly Journal of Economics* 87 (1973): 356–58.

22. Goffman, *Stigma*, 10.

23. Chung Choe and Marjorie L. Baldwin, "Onset of Disability, Job Matching, and Employment Outcomes," MPRA Paper No. 63805 (January 2015): 12-14, http://mpra.ub.uni-muenchen.de /63805/.

24. Lachlan J. Best, Megan Still, and Grant Cameron, "Supported Education: Enabling Course Completion for People Experiencing Mental Illness," *Australian Occupational Therapy Journal* 55 (2008): 65–66.

25. Best, Still, and Cameron, "Supported Education," 65.

26. Carol T. Mowbray et al., "Supported Education for Adults with Psychiatric Disabilities: An Innovation for Social Work and Psychosocial Rehabilitation Practice," *Social Work* 50 (2005): 12.

27. Gary R. Bond et al., "A Randomized Controlled Trial Comparing Two Vocational Models for Persons with Severe Mental Illness," *Journal of Consulting and Clinical Psychology* 75 (2007): 969.

28. Cathaleene Macias et al., "What Is a Clubhouse? Report on the ICCD 1996 Survey of USA Clubhouses," *Community Mental Health Journal* 35 (1999): 181.

29. Macias et al., "What Is a Clubhouse?" 186–88.

30. Bond et al., "A Randomized Controlled Trial," 969.

31. Gary R. Bond and Robert E. Drake, "Predictors of Competitive Employment among Patients with Schizophrenia," *Current Opinion in Psychiatry* 21 (2008): 362.

32. Bond and Drake, "Predictors of Competitive Employment," 365.

33. Bond and Drake, "Predictors of Competitive Employment"; Gary R. Bond, Robert E. Drake, and Deborah R. Becker, "An Update on Randomized Controlled Trials of Evidence-Based Supported Employment," *Psychiatric Rehabilitation Journal* 21 (2008): 284–86.

34. Kikuko Campbell, Gary R. Bond, and Robert E. Drake, "Who Benefits from Supported Employment: A Meta-Analytic Study," *Schizophrenia Bulletin* 37 (2011): 374.

35. Bond and Drake, "Predictors of Competitive Employment," 365.

36. Anna M. Lucca et al., "Evaluation of an Individual Placement and Support Model (IPS) Program," *Psychiatric Rehabilitation Journal* 27 (2004): 253–54.

37. Anthony F. Lehman et al., "Improving Employment Outcomes for Persons with Severe Mental Illnesses," *Archives of General Psychiatry* 59 (2002): 170.

38. Morris D. Bell et al., "Neurocognitive Enhancement Therapy with Vocational Services: Work Outcomes at Two-Year Follow-up," *Schizophrenia Research* 105 (2008): 19.

39. Bell et al., "Neurocognitive Enhancement Therapy with Vocational Services," 26.

40. Abraham Rudnick and Maya Gover, "Combining Supported Education with Supported Employment," *Psychiatric Services* 60 (2009): 1690.

41. Rudnick and Gover, "Combining Supported Education with Supported Employment."

4. THE SUPPLY OF MENTAL HEALTH SERVICES

1. E. Fuller Torrey, *American Psychosis* (Oxford: Oxford University Press, 2014), 124.

2. Henry J. Steadman et al., "Prevalence of Serious Mental Illness among Jail Inmates," *Psychiatric Services* 60 (2009): 764.

3. William Easterly, *The White Man's Burden* (New York: Penguin Books, 2006), 5–6.

4. Sijo J. Parekattil and Michael E. Moran, "Robotic Instrumentation: Evolution and Microsurgical Applications," *Indian Journal of Urology* 26 (2010): 398.

5. Paul Janssen, "The Social Chemistry of Pharmacological Discovery: The Haloperidol Story," *International Journal of the Addictions* 27 (1992): 331.

6. Hiroko Beck et al., "50th Anniversary of the First Successful Permanent Pacemaker Implantation in the United States," *American Journal of Cardiology* 106 (2010): 810.

7. R. Shennach et al., "Insight in Schizophrenia—Course and Predictors during the Acute Treatment Phase of Patients from a Schizophrenia Spectrum Disorder," *European Psychiatry* 27 (2012): 626.

8. Gerald N. Grob, "Mad, Homeless and Unwanted: A History of the Care of the Chronically Mentally Ill in America," *Psychiatric Clinics of North America* 17 (1994): 542.

9. "Diseases of the Mind: Highlights of American Psychiatry through 1900, Early Psychiatric Hospitals and Asylums," *U.S. National Library of Medicine*, last modified September 13, 2013, http://www.nlm.nih.gov/hmd/diseases/early.html.

10. Albert R. Roberts and Linda Farris Kurtz, "Historical Perspectives on the Care and Treatment of the Mentally Ill," *Journal of Sociology and Social Welfare* 75 (1987): 79.

11. Shomer S. Zwelling, *Quest for a Cure: The Public Hospital in Williamsburg: 1773–1885* (Williamsburg, VA: Colonial Williamsburg Foundation, 1985): 13–18.

12. Joseph P. Morrissey and Howard H. Goldman, "Care and Treatment of the Mentally Ill in the United States: Historical Developments and Reforms," *Annals of the American Academy*

of Political and Social Science 484 (1986): 14–17; Clifford Farr, "Benjamin Rush and American Psychiatry," *American Journal of Psychiatry* 151 (1994): 72.

13. Roberts and Kurtz, "Historical Perspectives," 79.

14. Roberts and Kurtz, "Historical Perspectives."

15. Gerald N. Grob, "Mental Health Policy in the Liberal State: The Example of the United States," *International Journal of Law and Psychiatry* 31 (2008): 90.

16. Grob, "Mad, Homeless and Unwanted," 548.

17. Grob, "Mad, Homeless and Unwanted," 545–46, 90.

18. Howard Goldman and Gerald N. Grob, "Defining 'Mental Illness' in Mental Health Policy," *Health Affairs* 25 (2006): 739.

19. Roberts and Kurtz, "Historical Perspectives," 80.

20. Clifford Whittingham Beers, *A Mind That Found Itself: An Autobiography* (Garden City, NY: Doubleday, 1965), 228.

21. Roberts and Kurtz, "Historical Perspectives," 81.

22. Barbara A. Dreyer, "Adolf Meyer and Mental Hygiene: An Ideal for Public Health," *American Journal of Public Health* 66 (1976): 998–1000.

23. Morrissey and Goldman, "Care and Treatment of the Mentally Ill," 18.

24. Beers, "Mind That Found Itself," 263.

25. Morrissey and Goldman, "Care and Treatment of the Mentally Ill," 18.

26. Dreyer, "Adolf Meyer," 1000.

27. Roberts and Kurtz, "Historical Perspectives," 82.

28. Easterly, *White Man's Burden*, 12–20.

29. Zigmond M. Lebensohn, "General Hospital Psychiatry U.S.A.: Retrospect and Prospect," *Comprehensive Psychiatry* 21 (1980): 500.

30. Morrissey and Goldman, "Care and Treatment of the Mentally Ill," 22.

31. Grob, "Mad, Homeless and Unwanted," 550.

32. Torrey, *American Psychosis*, 22–23.

33. Grob, "Mental Health Policy," 92–93.

34. Torrey, *American Psychosis*, 17.

35. Grob, "Mental Health Policy," 93.

36. Torrey, *American Psychosis*, 62.

37. William Gronfein, "Psychotropic Drugs and the Origins of Deinstitutionalization," *Social Problems* 32 (1985): 441.

38. Gronfein, "Psychotropic Drugs," 443.

39. Robert H. Noce, David B. Williams, and Walter Rapaport, "Reserprine (Serpasil) in the Management of the Mentally Ill and Mentally Retarded," *Senate Interim Committee Report on the Treatment of Mental Illness* 20 (1956): 30–31.

40. Noce, Williams, and Rapaport, "Reserprine (Serpasil) in the Management of the Mentally Ill and Mentally Retarded."

41. Gronfein, "Psychotropic Drugs," 440.

42. Gronfein, "Psychotropic Drugs."

43. Grob, "Mental Health Policy," 94–95.

44. Joe Parks and Alan Q. Radke, eds., *The Vital Role of State Psychiatric Hospitals* (Alexandria, VA: National Association of State Mental Health Program Directors, 2014), 9.

45. Grob, "Mental Health Policy," 94.

46. Stephen M. Rose, "Deciphering Deinstitutionalization: Complexities in Policy and Program Analysis," *Milbank Memorial Fund Quarterly* 57 (1979): 447.

47. Gronfein, "Psychotropic Drugs," 440.

48. Saleem A. Shah, "Legal and Mental Health System Interactions: Major Developments and Research Needs," *International Journal of Law and Psychiatry* 4 (1981): 224; Grob, "Mental Health Policy," 94.

49. Morrissey and Goldman, "Care and Treatment of the Mentally Ill," 22.

50. Easterly, *White Man's Burden*, 12.

51. Grob, "Mental Health Policy," 93.

52. Bernard E. Harcourt, "From the Asylum to the Prison: Rethinking the Incarceration Revolution," *Texas Law Review* 84 (2006): 1759.

53. Harcourt, "From the Asylum to the Prison."

54. Grob, "Mental Health Policy," 92.

55. Richard G. Frank and Sherry A. Glied, *Better but Not Well: Mental Health Policy in the United States since 1950* (Baltimore: Johns Hopkins University Press, 2006): 60.

56. Torrey, *American Psychosis*, 77.

57. Richard D. Lyons, "How Release of Mental Patients Began," *New York Times*, October 30, 1984, C1.

58. Grob, "Mental Health Policy," 92.

59. Morrissey and Goldman, "Care and Treatment of the Mentally Ill," 26.

60. Torrey, *American Psychosis*, 87.

61. Grob, "Mental Health Policy," 96.

62. New Freedom Commission on Mental Health, *Achieving the Promise: Transforming Mental Health Care in America.* DHHS Pub. No. SMA-03-3832 (Rockville, MD: 2003), 3.

63. Ronald C. Kessler, "The Prevalence and Correlates of Untreated Serious Mental Illness," *Health Services Research* 36 (2001): 993.

64. New Freedom Commission, *Achieving the Promise*, 1.

65. New Freedom Commission, *Achieving the Promise*, Letter to President Bush from Michael F. Hogan, Chairman.

66. New Freedom Commission, *Achieving the Promise*, 4–7.

67. New Freedom Commission, *Achieving the Promise*, 57.

68. New Freedom Commission, *Achieving the Promise*, 35.

69. New Freedom Commission, *Achieving the Promise*, 44.

70. Janssen, "The Haloperidol Story," 331.

71. Janssen, "The Haloperidol Story," 339.

72. Janssen, "The Haloperidol Story," 335–36.

73. Janssen, "The Haloperidol Story," 341–45.

74. Easterly, *White Man's Burden*, 5–18, 100–116.

75. Janssen, "The Haloperidol Story," 335.

76. Fuller, *American Psychosis*, 66.

77. Fuller, *American Psychosis*, 15.

78. John C. Burnham, "A Clinical Alternative to the Public Health Approach to Mental Illness: A Forgotten Social Experiment," *Perspectives in Biology and Medicine* 49 (2006): 222–29.

5. DEFAULT CAREGIVERS

1. Grob, "Mental Health Policy," 93.

2. E. Fuller Torrey, *Surviving Schizophrenia: A Manual for Families, Patients, and Providers.* 5th ed. (New York: HarperCollins, 2006), 409.

3. Helen J. Stain et al., "Understanding the Social Costs of Psychosis: The Experience of Adults Affected by Psychosis Identified within the Second Australian National Survey of Psychosis," *Australian and New Zealand Journal of Psychiatry* 46 (2012): 884; Joshua E. Wilk et al., "Family Contact and the Management of Medication Non-adherence in Schizophrenia," *Community Mental Health Journal* 44 (2008): 378.

4. Elizabeth Bernstein and Nathan Koppel, "A Death in the Family: Aided by Advocates for the Mentally Ill, William Bruce Left the Hospital—Only to Kill His Mother," *Wall Street Journal*, August 16, 2008, A1.

5. George A. Awad and Lakshimi Voruganti, "The Burden of Schizophrenia on Caregivers," *PharmacoEconomics* 26 (2008): 152.

6. Susana Ochoa et al., "Do Needs, Symptoms or Disability of Outpatients with Schizophrenia Influence Family Burden?" *Social Psychiatry and Psychiatric Epidemiology* 43 (2008): 613; L. Magliano et al., "Family Burden in Long-Term Diseases: A Comparative Study in Schizophrenia vs. Physical Disorders," *Social Science and Medicine* 61 (2005): 314.

7. Awad and Voruganti, "Burden of Schizophrenia," 156–57.

8. Deborah D. Franks, "Economic Contribution of Families Caring for Persons with Severe and Persistent Mental Illness," *Administration and Policy in Mental Health* 18 (1990): 12; "Median Income for Four-person Families, by State," *U.S. Bureau of the Census*, last modified, April 3. 2015, http://www.census.gov/hhes/www/income/data/statistics/4person.html.

9. Franks, "Economic Contributions of Families," 14–16.

10. B. Lowyck et al., "A Study of the Family Burden of 150 Family Members of Schizophrenic Patients," *European Psychiatry* 19 (2004): 398.

11. Lowyck et al., "A Study of the Family Burden."

12. Katerina Koutra, "Family Functioning in Families of First-Episode Psychosis Patients as Compared to Chronic Mentally Ill Patients and Healthy Controls," *Psychiatry Research* 45 (2014): 486–87.

13. Koutra, "Family Functioning in Families of First-episode Psychosis Patients," 492–93.

14. Jana C. Saunders and Michelle M. Byrne, "A Thematic Analysis of Families Living with Schizophrenia," *Archives of Psychiatric Nursing* 16 (2002): 222.

15. Saunders and Michelle M. Byrne, "A Thematic Analysis of Families Living with Schizophrenia."

16. Anniqa Foldemo et al., "Quality of Life and Burden in Parents of Outpatients with Schizophrenia," *Social Psychiatry and Psychiatric Epidemiology* 40 (2005): 136; Sally K. Gallagher and David Mechanic, "Living with the Mentally Ill: Effects on the Health and Function of Other Household Members," *Social Science and Medicine* 42 (1996): 1695–96; Frank D. Gianfrancesco, Ruey-hua Wang, and Elaine Yu, "Effects of Patients with Bipolar, Schizophrenic, and Major Depressive Disorders on the Mental and Other Healthcare Expenses of Family Members," *Social Science and Medicine* 61 (2005): 307–8.

17. Gianfrancesco, Wang, and Yu, "Effects of Patients with Bipolar, Schizophrenic, and Major Depressive Disorders," 307–10.

18. Sandy M. Magaña et al., "Psychological Distress among Latino Family Caregivers of Adults with Schizophrenia: The Roles of Burden and Stigma," *Psychiatric Services* 58 (2007): 382.

19. Awad and Voruganti, "Burden of Schizophrenia," 155; Lowyck, "Study of Family Burden," 398; Foldemo et al., "Quality of Life," 135.

20. Lowyck, "Study of Family Burden," 398.

21. Diana Clarke and Joanne Winsor, "Perceptions and Needs of Parents during a Young Adult's First Psychiatric Hospitalization: 'We're All on This Little Island and We're Going to Drown Real Soon,'" *Issues in Mental Health Nursing* 31 (2010): 244.

22. Clarke and Winsor, "First Psychiatric Hospitalization," 244.

23. Saunders and Byrne, "Families Living with Schizophrenia," 220.

24. Magliano et al., "Family Burden in Long-Term Diseases," 316–18. The physical disorders were diabetes, brain disease, heart disease, lung disease, and renal disease.

25. Magliano et al., "Family Burden in Long-Term Diseases."

26. Clarke and Winsor, "First Psychiatric Hospitalization," 245.

27. Awad and Voruganti, "Burden of Schizophrenia," 154; Magaña et al., "Distress among Latino Caregivers," 380; Ochoa et al., "Needs, Symptoms, or Disability," 616 .

28. Ochoa et al., "Needs, Symptoms, or Disability," 615.

29. Anne Maria Möller-Leimkühler and Andreas Wiesheu, "Caregiver Burden in Chronic Mental Illness: The Role of Patient and Caregiver Characteristics," *European Archives of Psychiatry and Clinical Neuroscience* 262 (2012): 158–61.

30. Ochoa et al., "Needs, Symptoms, or Disability," 613–17; Michael G. McDonell et al., "Burden in Schizophrenia Caregivers: Impact of Family Psychoeducation and Awareness of Patient Suicidality," *Family Process Journal* 42 (2003): 98; Magaña et al., "Distress among Latino Caregivers," 381.

31. Ochoa et al., "Needs, Symptoms, or Disability," 613–17.

32. Awad and Voruganti, "Burden of Schizophrenia," 155; Ochoa et al., "Needs, Symptoms, or Disability," 615; Saunders and Byrne, "Families Living with Schizophrenia," 220–21.

33. McDonnell et al., "Burden in Schizophrenia Caregivers," 93–94.

34. McDonnell et al., "Burden in Schizophrenia Caregivers," 98.

35. Brian A. Palmer, V. Shane Pankratz, and John Michael Bostwick, "The Lifetime Risk of Suicide in Schizophrenia: A Reexamination," *Archives of General Psychiatry* 62 (2005): 249.

36. Merete Nordentoft, Trine Madsen and Izabela Fedyszyn, "Suicidal Behavior and Mortality in First-Episode Psychosis," *Journal of Nervous and Mental Disease* 203 (2015): 387–88.

37. L. Magliano et al., "Social and Clinical Factors Influencing the Choice of Coping Strategies in Relatives of Patients with Schizophrenia: Results of the BIOMED I Study," *Social Psychiatry and Psychiatric Epidemiology* 33 (1998): 413.

38. McDonnell et al., "Burden in Schizophrenia Caregivers," 96.

39. Magliano et al., "Family Burden in Long-Term Diseases," 313–14; Anthony F. Lehman et al., *Practice Guideline for the Treatment of Patients with Schizophrenia*, 2nd ed. (Arlington, VA: American Psychiatric Association, 2010): 10.

40. L. Magliano et al., "Burden on the Families of Patients with Schizophrenia: Results of the BIOMED I Study," *Social Psychiatry and Psychiatric Epidemiology* 33 (1998): 409–11.

41. Magliano, et al., "Choice of Coping Strategies," 418.

42. Awad and Voruganti, "Burden of Schizophrenia," 155.

43. Magliano et al., "Family Burden in Long-Term Diseases," 317–19.

44. Clarke and Winsor, "First Psychiatric Hospitalization," 244.

45. Lehman et al., *Practice Guideline for Schizophrenia*, 10.

46. Lehman et al., *Practice Guideline for Schizophrenia*.

47. Lehman et al., *Practice Guideline for Schizophrenia*, 12–15.

48. Elizabeth Kuipers, "Family Interventions in Schizophrenia: Evidence for Efficacy and Proposed Mechanisms of Change," *Journal of Family Therapy* 28 (2006): 76–77; M. Giron et al., "Efficacy and Effectiveness of Individual Family Intervention on Social and Clinical Functioning and Family Burden in Severe Schizophrenia," *Psychological Medicine* (2009): 9; Jacqueline Sin and Ian Norman, "Psychoeducational Interventions for Family Members of People with Schizophrenia: A Mixed-Method Systematic Review," *Journal of Clinical Psychiatry* 74 (2013): 1159; Phyllis E. Smerud and Irwin S. Rosenfarb, "The Therapeutic Alliance and Family Psychoeducation in the Treatment of Schizophrenia," *Journal of Consulting and Clinical Psychology* 76 (2008): 505; Amy N. Cohen et al., "Implementation of a Family Intervention for Individuals with Schizophrenia," *Journal of General Internal Medicine* 25 (2009): S32.

49. Merrie J. Kaas, Suzanne Lee, and Carol Peitzman, "Barriers to Collaboration between Mental Health Professionals and Families in the Care of Persons with Serious Mental Illness," *Issues in Mental Health Nursing* 24 (2003): 744–45; Clarke and Winsor, "First Psychiatric Hospitalization," 244–45.

50. Frank and Glied, *Better but Not Well*, 49.

51. Frank and Glied, *Better but Not Well*, 49–51.

52. Frank and Glied, *Better but Not Well*, 72–89.

53. Frank and Glied, *Better but Not Well*, 90.

54. Frank and Glied, *Better but Not Well*, 69.

55. NC Division of Mental Health, Developmental Disabilities and Substance Abuse Services, "Exploring the Costs and Feasibility of a New Psychiatric Facility" (Raleigh: North Carolina Department of Health and Human Services, 2013), 2.

56. Behavioral Health Centers, "CMC Randolph: Annual Mental Health Report Mecklenburg County" (Charlotte, NC: Carolinas HealthCare System, 2005), 15.

57. NC Division of Mental Health, *Feasibility of a New Psychiatric Facility*, 2.

58. Tina Marshall et al., "Provider and Family Beliefs Regarding the Causes of Severe Mental Illness," *Psychiatric Quarterly* 74 (2003): 232.

59. Marshall et al., "Provider and Family Beliefs," 230.

60. Marshall et al., "Provider and Family Beliefs," 232.

61. Marshall et al., "Family and Provider Beliefs," 232.

62. Cohen et al., "Family Intervention for Schizophrenia," S35.

63. Kaas, Lee, and Peitzman, "Barriers to Collaboration," 747–49.

64. U.S. Congress, House Committee on Energy and Commerce, *Examining SAMHSA's Role in Delivering Services to the Severely Mentally Ill: Hearings before the Subcommittee on Oversight and Investigations*, 113th Cong., 1st sess., May 22, 2013 (statement of Robert "Joe" Bruce and exhibits): 2–3.

65. Bernstein and Koppel, "A Death in the Family," A1.

66. *Oxford English Dictionary.* 1st ed., s.v. "burden."

67. Möller-Leimkühler and Wiesheu, "Caregiver Burden," 161; Rita Bauer et al., "Burden, Rewards and Coping—The Ups and Downs of Caregivers of People with Mental Illness," *Journal of Nervous and Mental Disease* 200 (2012): 932–33; Sandeep Grover, "Comparative Study of the Experience of Caregiving in Bipolar Affective Disorder and Schizophrenia," *International Journal of Social Psychiatry* 58 (2011): 619–20.

6. WORK FIRST

1. Miles Rinaldi et al., "First Episode Psychosis and Employment: A Review," *International Review of Psychiatry* 22 (2010): 148.

2. Elyn R. Saks, "Successful and Schizophrenic," *New York Times*, January 27, 2013, SR5.

3. Baldwin and White, "Workplace Accommodations That Work," 122.

4. Ronni Michelle Greenwood, Ana Stefancic, and Sam Tsemberis, "Pathways Housing First for Homeless Persons with Psychiatric Disabilities: Program Innovation, Research, and Advocacy," *Journal of Social Issues* 69 (2013): 648.

5. Thomas DeLeire, "The Wage and Employment Effects of the Americans with Disabilities Act," *Journal of Human Resources* 35 (2000): 701; Daron Acemoglu and Joshua D. Angrist, "Consequences of Employment Protection? The Case of the Americans with Disabilities Act," *Journal of Political Economy* 109 (2001): 917.

6. Civil Rights Act of 1964, U.S. Code 42 (1964) § 2000 e-2.

7. Americans with Disabilities Act of 1990, U.S. Code 42 (1990), § 12101–12117.

8. 135 Cong. Rec. S10617 (1989), statement by Senator Hatch.

9. 135 Cong. Rec. E3644 (1989), statement by Representative Bereuter.

10. 135 Cong. Rec. S11173 (1989), statement by Senator Armstrong.

11. 135 Cong. Rec. S10734 (1989), statement by Senator Helms.

12. James Concannon, "Mind Matters: Mental Disability and the History and Future of the Americans with Disabilities Act," *Law and Psychology Review* 36 (2012): 91.

13. Americans with Disabilities Act, § 12112.

14. Americans with Disabilities Act, § 12102.

15. Equal Employment Opportunity Commission, Regulations to Implement the Equal Employment Provisions of the Americans With Disabilities Act, as Amended, 29 C.F.R. 1630 (March 25, 2011): 17000.

16. Americans with Disabilities Act, § 12211.

17. Americans with Disabilities Act, § 12211.

18. Concannon, "Mind Matters," 96.

19. Amy L. Allbright, "2001 Employment Decisions under the ADA Title I—Survey Update," *Mental and Physical Disability Law Reporter* 26 (2002): 394–95.

20. Allbright, "2001 Employment Decisions under the ADA," 398.

21. Susan Stefan, *Hollow Promises: Employment Discrimination against People with Mental Disabilities* (Washington, D.C.: American Psychological Association, 2002), 76; *Schwartz v. the Comex and New York Mercantile Exchange*, DC SNY, No. 96, Civ. 3386.

22. *Sutton v. United Airlines*, 527 U.S. 471 (1999).

23. Allbright, "2001 Employment Decisions under the ADA," 395.

24. *Jacques v. DiMarzio, Inc.*, 386 F.3d 192, 203–04 (2d Cir. 2004); *Carlson v. Liberty Mut. Ins. Co.*, 237 F. App'x 446 (11th Cir. 2007); *Littleton v. Wal-Mart Stores, Inc.*, 231 F. App'x 874, 877 (11th Cir. 2007).

25. Stefan, *Hollow Promises*, 74–75.

26. Patrick A. Hartman, "'Interacting with Others' as a Major Life Activity under the Americans with Disabilities Act," *Seton Hall Circuit Review* 2 (2005): 157–58.

27. *Soileau v. Guilford of Me., Inc.*, 105 F.3d 12, 15 (1st Cir. 1997).

28. *McAlindin v. County of San Diego*, 192 F.3d 1226 (9th Cir. 1999); *Jacques v. DiMarzio, Inc.*, 386 F.3d 192 (2d Cir. 2004).

29. ADA Amendments Act of 2008, Public Law 110-325, *U.S. Statutes at Large* 122 (2008): 3555.

30. ADA Amendments Act, 3555.

31. ADA Amendments Act, 3556.

32. John Petrila, "Congress Restores the Americans with Disabilities Act to Its Original Intent," *Psychiatric Services* 60 (2009): 879; Concannon, "Mind Matters," 105.

33. ADA Amendments Act, 3554.

34. Concannon, "Mind Matters," 107.

35. Stephen F. Befort, "An Empirical Examination of Case Outcomes under the ADA Amendments Act," *Washington and Lee Law Review* 70 (2013): 2046–55.

36. Concannon, "Mind Matters," 113–14.

37. *Oxford English Dictionary.* 1st ed., s.v. "work."

38. Rinaldi et al., "First Episode Psychosis," 148.

39. Simon Winchester, *The Professor and the Madman: A Tale of Murder, Insanity, and the Making of the Oxford English Dictionary* (New York: HarperCollins, 1998): 2–21.

40. Winchester, *The Professor and the Madman.*

41. Winchester, *The Professor and the Madman,* 113.

42. Winchester, *The Professor and the Madman,* 133.

43. Winchester, *The Professor and the Madman,* 167.

7. THE DISCLOSURE PREDICAMENT

1. Wilkie Collins, *No Name*, Penguin Classics (London: Penguin Group, 1995), 34.

2. Wilkie Collins, *Woman in White*, Penguin Classics (London: Penguin Group, 1994), 235.

3. Wilkie Collins, *Man and Wife*, Oxford World's Classics (New York: Oxford University Press, 1995), 312.

4. "Our Mission," Phoenix First, accessed April 14, 2014, http://www.phoenixfirst.org/about-us/mission-values.

5. "Our Mission."

6. Amanda M. Jones, "Disclosure of Mental Illness in the Workplace: A Literature Review," *American Journal of Psychiatric Rehabilitation* 14 (2011): 223–25.

7. Susan G. Goldberg, Mary B. Killeen, and Bonnie O'Day, "The Disclosure Conundrum: How People with Psychiatric Disabilities Navigate Employment," *Psychology, Public Policy and Law* 11 (2005): 467; Jones, "Disclosure of Mental Illness," 217.

8. *Oxford English Dictionary.* 1st ed., s.v. "disclose."

9. Jones, "Disclosure of Mental Illness," 220; Gerald O'Brien and Melinda S. Brown, "Persons with Mental Illness and the Americans with Disabilities Act: Implications for the Social Work Profession," *Social Work in Mental Health* 7 (2009): 446–47.

10. Stephenie R. Chaudoir and Jeffrey D. Fisher, "The Disclosure Process Model: Understanding Disclosure Decision Making and Post-disclosure Outcomes among People Living with a Concealable Stigmatized Identity," *Psychological Bulletin* 136 (2010): 239.

11. Melanie Boyce et al., "Mental Health Service Users' Experiences of Returning to Paid Employment," *Disability and Society* 23 (2008): 80.

12. Patrick W. Corrigan and John R. O'Shaughnessy. "Changing Mental Illness Stigma as It Exists in the Real World," *Australian Psychologist* 42 (2007): 92.

13. Vicky Nithsdale, Jason Davies, and Paul Croucher, "Psychosis and the Experience of Employment," *Journal of Occupational Rehabilitation* 18 (2008): 178.

14. Rebecca Spirito Dalgin and Dennis Gilbride, "Perspectives of People with Psychiatric Disabilities on Employment Disclosure," *Psychiatric Rehabilitation Journal* 26 (2003): 308.

15. Goldberg, Killeen, and O'Day, "Disclosure Conundrum," 477.

16. Goldberg, Killeen, and O'Day, "Disclosure Conundrum," 463.

17. Steven Marwaha and Sonia Johnson, "Views and Experiences of Employment among People with Psychosis: A Qualitative Descriptive Study," *International Journal of Social Psychiatry* 51 (2005): 309.

18. Chaudoir and Fisher, "Disclosure Process Model," 237–42. The model is developed for any type of concealable stigmatized identity, but easily applies to persons with serious mental illness.

19. For a more detailed discussion of the pros and cons of disclosing SMI at work, refer to Chaudoir and Fisher, "Disclosure Process Model," 244–49, or John E. Pachankis, "The Psychological Implications of Concealing a Stigma: A Cognitive-Affective-Behavioral Model," *Psychological Bulletin* 133 (2007): 331–37.

20. Marsha Langer Ellison et al., "Patterns and Correlates of Workplace Disclosure among Professionals and Managers with Psychiatric Conditions," *Journal of Vocational Rehabilitation* 18 (2003): 4.

21. Marwaha and Johnson, "Views and Experiences," 309.

22. Sokratis Dinos et al., "Stigma: The Feelings and Experiences of 46 People with Mental Illness: Qualitative Study," *British Journal of Psychiatry* 184 (2004): 178.

23. Schulze and Angermeyer, "Subjective Experiences of Stigma," 307.

24. Schulze and Angermeyer, "Subjective Experiences of Stigma," 307–8.

25. Mary B. Killeen and Bonnie L. O'Day, "Challenging Expectations: How Individuals with Psychiatric Disabilities Find and Keep Work," *Psychiatric Rehabilitation Journal* 28 (2004): 161.

26. Several studies provide quantitative evidence on disclosure of mental illness in supported employment settings in the United States. In particular, see Becky R. Banks et al., "Disclosure of a Psychiatric Disability in Supported Employment: An Exploratory Study," *International Journal of Psychosocial Rehabilitation* 11 (2007): 78–83; and Angela L. Rollins et al., "Social Relationships at Work: Does the Employment Model Make a Difference?" *Psychiatric Rehabilitation Journal* 26 (2002): 53–59.

27. Ellison et al., "Patterns of Disclosure," 7–9.

28. Anand Pandya et al., "Perceived Impact of the Disclosure of a Schizophrenia Diagnosis," *Community Mental Health Journal* 47 (2011): 614.

29. Pandya et al., "Perceived Impact," 616.

30. E. W. Howe, *Ventures in Common Sense* (New York: Alfred A. Knopf, 1919), 80.

31. Goldberg, Killeen, and O'Day, "Disclosure Conundrum," 485.

32. Goldberg, Killeen, and O'Day, "Disclosure Conundrum," 479.

33. Dinos et al., "Stigma: Feelings and Experiences," 177.

34. Gary Becker (chapter 3) refers to these stigmatizing preferences as "tastes for discrimination."

35. Erin E. Michalak et al., "The Impact of Bipolar Disorder upon Work Functioning: A Qualitative Analysis," *Bipolar Disorders* 9 (2007): 136.

36. In the language of economics, the utility function yields convex, two-dimensional indifference curves, and the quantity demanded of each good is negatively correlated with its price.

37. Sophie Mitra, "The Capability Approach and Disability," *Journal of Disability Policy Studies* 16 (2006): 237.

38. Goffman, *Stigma*, 73–91.

39. Goffman, *Stigma*, 42.

40. Goffman, *Stigma*, 87.

41. Debbie Peterson, Nandika Currey, and Sunny Collings, "'You Don't Look Like One of Them': Disclosure of Mental Illness in the Workplace as an Ongoing Dilemma," *Psychiatric Rehabilitation Journal* 35 (2011): 146.

8. FINDING A GOOD JOB MATCH

1. "About Us," Phoenix Dream Center, accessed June 3, 2014, http://www.phxdreamcenter.org /about_us.

2. John W. Kennedy, "Phoenix Dream Center Opens Program for Foster Youth," *Pentecostal Evangel*, December 12, 2013, http://ag.org/top/news/.

3. The Rescue Project has since been renamed "Where Hope Lives." "Rescuing Victims of Human Trafficking," Where Hope Lives, accessed May 20, 2015, http://www.rescueprojectphx.org/index.php.

4. "Accommodation Ideas for Addison's Disease," Job Accommodations Network, accessed June 3, 2014, https://askjan.org/soar/Other/addisons.html.

5. Sheila K. Akabas, "Workplace Responsiveness: Key Employer Characteristics in Support of Job Maintenance for People with Mental Illness," *Psychosocial Rehabilitation Journal* 17 (1994): 95.

6. Kendra M. Duckworth, "Employees with Psychiatric Impairments," Accommodation and Compliance Series: The ADA Amendments Act of 2008, U.S. Department of Labor, last modified, December 17, 2008, https://askjan.org/bulletins/adaaa1.htm.

7. Tandon, Keshavan, and Nasrallah, "Clinical Features and Conceptualization," 2.

8. Tandon, Keshavan, and Nasrallah, "Clinical Features and Conceptualization," 5–6.

9. Dianna L. Stone and Adrienne Colella, "A Model of Factors Affecting the Treatment of Disabled Individuals in Organizations," *Academy of Management Review* 21 (1996): 354–57.

10. Lisa Schur et al., "Is Disability Disabling in All Workplaces? Workplace Disparities and Corporate Culture," *Industrial Relations* 48 (2009): 387–403.

11. Schur et al., "Is Disability Disabling in All Workplaces?"

12. Jenny Secker and Helen Membrey, "Promoting Mental Health through Employment and Developing Healthy Workplaces: The Potential of Natural Supports at Work," *Health Education Research* 18 (2003): 212.

13. Akabas, "Workplace Responsiveness," 95.

14. Suzanne Bruyère, William A. Erikson, and Sara A. VanLooy, "The Impact of Business Size on Employer ADA Response," *Rehabilitation Counseling Bulletin* 49 (2006): 199.

15. Secker and Membrey, "Promoting Mental Health," 213–14; Schur et al., "Workplace Disparities and Corporate Culture," 399.

16. Akabas, "Workplace Responsiveness," 94.

17. Secker and Membrey, "Promoting Mental Health," 211.

18. Secker and Membrey, "Promoting Mental Health," 209.

19. Goldberg, Killeen, and O'Day, "Disclosure Conundrum," 475.

20. Mary B. Killeen and Bonnie L. O'Day, "Challenging Expectations: How Individuals with Psychiatric Disabilities Find and Keep Work," *Psychiatric Rehabilitation Journal* 28 (2004): 158–59.

21. Killeen and O'Day, "Challenging Expectations," 159.

22. Baldwin and White, "Workplace Accommodations That Work," 126.

9. JOB ACCOMMODATIONS FOR WORKERS WITH SMI

1. M. Harrow, T. H. Jobe, and R. N. Faull, "Do All Schizophrenia Patients Need Antipsychotic Treatment Continuously Throughout Their Lifetime? A 20-Year Longitudinal Study," *Psychological Medicine* 42 (2012): 2146–48.

2. *Oxford English Dictionary.* 1st ed., s.v. "accommodate."

3. Baldwin and White, "Workplace Accommodations that Work," 123.

4. Dalgin and Gilbride, "Perspectives of People with Psychiatric Disabilities," 307–8.

5. Duckworth, "Employees with Psychiatric Impairments," https://askjan.org/bulletins/adaaa1.htm.

6. Stefan, *Hollow Promises*, 169–70; Heather Peters and Travor C. Brown, "Mental Illness at Work: An Assessment of Co-worker Reactions," *Canadian Journal of Administrative Sciences* 26 (2009): 41; Gerald V. O'Brien, and Melinda S. Brown. "Persons with Mental Illness and the Americans with Disabilities Act: Implications for the Social Work Profession," *Social*

Work in Mental Health 7 (2009): 450; Samantha Fairclough et al., "In Sickness and in Health: Implications for Employers When Bipolar Disorders Are Protected Disabilities," *Employee Responsibilities and Rights Journal* 25 (2013): 285.

7. Beth Loy, "Employees with Back Impairments," U.S. Department of Labor, last modified, March 4, 2013, https://askjan.org/bulletins/adaaa1.htm.

8. Stefan, *Hollow Promises*, 169.

9. Fairclough et al., "In Sickness and in Health," 284.

10. Helen A. Schartz, D. J. Hendricks, and Peter Blanck, "Workplace Accommodations: Evidence Based Outcomes," *Work* 27 (2006): 346.

11. Peters and Brown, "Mental Illness at Work," 41; Rebecca Spirito Dalgin, "Impact of Title I of the Americans with Disabilities Act on People with Psychiatric Disabilities," *Journal of Applied Rehabilitation Counseling* 32 (2001): 47.

12. Stefan, *Hollow Promises*, 168–69.

13. Fairclough et al., "In Sickness and in Health," 284.

14. Peters and Brown, "Mental Illness at Work," 45.

15. Baldwin and White, "Workplace Accommodations That Work," 125.

16. Richard V. Burkhauser, "Morality on the Cheap: The Americans with Disabilities Act," *Regulation* 13 (1990): 48–49, 53.

17. Stefan, *Hollow Promises*, 177–78.

18. Interview with supervisor, June 29, 2004. All interviews were conducted in confidentiality and the names of interviewees are withheld per the informed consent agreements with participants.

19. Stefan, *Hollow Promises*, 178.

20. *Gaul v. Lucent Technologies*, 134 F.3d 576 (3rd Cir. 1998).

21. Stefan, *Hollow Promises*, 182.

22. *Rascon v. US West Communications Inc.* 143 F.3d 1324 (10th Cir. 1998).

23. Equal Employment Opportunity Commission, Interpretive Guidance on Title I of the Americans with Disabilities Act, 29 C.F.R. 1630 App. (July 1, 2012): 403–4.

24. *Taylor v. Phoenixville School District*. 184 F.3d 296 (3rd Cir. 1999).

25. Baldwin and White, "Workplace Accommodations That Work," 126.

26. DeLeire, "Wage and Employment Effects of the ADA," 701.

27. "Labor Force Statistics (CPS)," Bureau of Labor Force Statistics, accessed July 12, 2014, http://www.bls.gov/webapps/legacy/cpsatab6.htm.

28. Nicole Maestas, Kathleen J. Mullen, and Alexander Strand, "Does Disability Insurance Receipt Discourage Work? Using Examiner Assignment to Estimate Causal Effects of SSDI Receipt," *American Economic Review* 103 (2013): 1798, 1818–23.

29. DeLeire, "Wage and Employment Effects of the ADA," 708.

30. Interview with supervisor, June 29, 2004.

10. BEYOND SCHIZOPHRENIA

1. David Baldwin, preaching at the House of Healing, October 8, 2014.

2. Richard C. Baron and Mark S. Salzer, "The Career Patterns of Persons with Serious Mental Illness: Generating a New Vision of Lifetime Careers for Those in Recovery," *Psychiatric Rehabilitation Skills* 4 (2000): 139.

3. "Pulse Healthcare Survey," Truven Health Analytics, accessed January 19, 2015. http://truven health.com/portals/0/assets/HOSP_12463_0313_PULSEHealthcareSurvey_WEB_032913.pdf.

4. The screening sample represented 1.6 percent of households that agreed to participate in follow-up interviews.

5. The survey was conducted by the Behavior Research Center in Phoenix, Arizona. http://www.brc-research.com/.

6. Ben Rinaudo and Priscilla Ennals, "Mental Illness, Supported Education, Employment and Recovery: Ben's Story," *Work* 43 (2012): 100–102.

7. Baron and Salzer, "Career Patterns of Persons with SMI," 142.

8. "Employed Persons by Occupation, Sex, and Age—2013," Bureau of Labor Statistics, accessed January 19, 2015, http://www.bls.gov/cps/tables.htm#empstat.

9. Calculations by the author. Text descriptions of respondents' occupations were matched to 2010 Standard Occupational Classification (SOC) codes (http://www.bls.gov/ soc/2010/ soc_alph.htm#N). The occupational distribution of the survey sample was compared to the occupational distribution of the U.S. workforce in April–June 2013, using data from the Bureau of Labor Statistics (http://www.bls.gov/cps/cpsaat09.pdf).

10. "Educational Attainment in the United States—2013 Detailed Tables," U.S. Census Bureau, accessed January 19, 2015, http://www.census.gov/hhes/socdemo/education/ data/ cps/ 2013/ tables.html.

11. Bond and Drake, "Predictors of Competitive Employment," 364.

12. Kurt Snyder, *Me, Myself, and Them* (Oxford: Oxford University Press, 2007), 1–4, 19–40, 53–67, 79–84, 103–8.

13. Harrow, Jobe, and Faull, "Do All Schizophrenia Patients Need Antipsychotic Treatment," 2146–50.

14. Brett Hartman, *Hammerhead 84* (Niskayuna, NY: Graphite Press, 2004), 44–50, 81–95, 117–23, 190–91, 226–47, 272–74, 321.

15. Goldberg, Killeen, and O'Day, "Disclosure Conundrum," 476–79.

16. Magliano et al., "Family Burden in Long-Term Diseases," 313; Lehman et al., *Practice Guideline for Schizophrenia*, 105–6.

17. Hartman, *Hammerhead 84*, 188.

18. Hartman, *Hammerhead 84*, 213.

11. TOWARD A MORE RATIONAL
MENTAL HEALTH POLICY

1. Stephen King, *It* (New York: Viking Penguin, 1986), 14.

2. King, *It*, 439.

3. King, *It*, 1075.

4. Concannon, "Mind Matters," 112–14.

5. *Oxford English Dictionary.* 1st ed., s.v. "policy."

6. Deborah Stone, *Policy Paradox* (New York: W.W. Norton, 2012), 289–90, 331–56.

7. Anna D. Sinaiko and Thomas McGuire, "Patient Inducement, Provider Priorities and Resource Allocation in Public Mental Health Systems," *Journal of Health Politics, Policy and Law* 31 (2006): 1087.

8. Steve Melek, Clare Miller, and Irvin L. Muszynski, "Employer Guide for Compliance with the Mental Health Parity and Equity Addiction Act." Partnership for Workplace Mental Health. December 2012, 3. http://www.workplacementalhealth.org/erguide.

9. George Szmukler, Rowena Daw, and Felicity Callard, "Mental Health Law and the UN Convention on the Rights of Persons with Disabilities," *International Journal of Law and Psychiatry* 37 (2014): 246–50. The Convention passed the U.N. General Assembly in 2006, and has since been signed by 155 countries, including the United States in 2009. United Nations Enable, accessed September 30, 2014, http://www.un.org/disabilities /countries.asp?id=166.

10. Torrey, *American Psychosis*, 113–28.

11. Brian Stettin et al., "Mental Health Commitment Laws: A Survey of the States" (Treatment Advocacy Center, 2014): 4–7. http://www.tacreports.org/storage/documents/2014-state-survey-abridged.pdf.

12. Darcy Ann Copeland and Mary Sue V. Heilemann, "Getting *to the Point*: The Experience of Mothers Getting Assistance for Their Adult Children Who Are Violent and Mentally Ill," *Nursing Research* 57 (2008): 139.

13. Steven S. Sharfstein and Faith B. Dickerson, "Hospital Psychiatry for the Twenty-first Century," *Health Affairs* 28 (2009): 685–86.

14. Sharfstein and Dickerson, "Hospital Psychiatry," 686.

15. Stettin et al., "Mental Health Commitment Laws," 19–20.

16. Sinaiko and McGuire, "Patient Inducement," 1084–85.

17. Testa and West, "Civil Commitment," 34.

18. "Operating Plan for FY 2014," Substance Abuse and Mental Health Services Administration, accessed September 23, 2014, http://beta.samhsa.gov/budget/fy-2014-budget.

19. "Operating Plan for FY 2014."

20. "Protection and Advocacy for Individuals with Mental Illness Program (PAIMI)," National Disability Rights Network, accessed October 21, 2014, http://www.ncmhr.org/ downloads/ PAIMI-fact-sheet-2013.pdf.

21. Amanda Peters, "Lawyers Who Break the Law: What Congress Can Do to Prevent Mental Health Patient Advocates from Violating Federal Legislation," *Oregon Law Review* 89 (2010): 135.

22. Szmukler, Daw, and Callard, "Mental Health Law," 250.

23. Stettin et al., "Mental Health Commitment Laws," 9.

24. Helping Families in Mental Health Crisis Act of 2013, H.R. 3717, 113th Cong. (2013).

25. "About Us," Substance Abuse and Mental Health Services Administration, accessed September 26, 2014. http://www.samhsa.gov/about-us.

26. Szmukler, Daw, and Callard, "Mental Health Law," 247–50.

27. Peters, "Lawyers Who Break the Law," 164–72; Bernstein and Koppel, "A Death in the Family," A1; "Provisions in HR 3717 that Improve Protection and Advocacy for Individuals with Mental Illness (PAIMI) Program," Mental Health Policy Organization, accessed June 7, 2015, http://www.mentalillnesspolicy.org/hr3717/paimiexplanationhr3717.html.

28. Justin Hunt, Daniel Eisenberg, and Amy M. Kilbourne, "Consequences of Receipt of a Psychiatric Diagnosis for Completion of College," *Psychiatric Services* 61 (2010): 402.

29. Jackie Stoneman and Rosemary Lysaght, "Supported Education: A Means for Enhancing Employability for Adults with Mental Illness," *Work* 36 (2010): 257.

30. Patrick W. Corrigan, Fred E. Markowitz, and Amy C. Watson, "Structural Levels of Mental Illness Stigma and Discrimination," *Schizophrenia Bulletin* 30 (2004): 481.

31. "Fiscal Year 2014 Budget: Summary and Background Information," Department of Education, accessed October 27, 2014, 56–65. http://www2.ed.gov/about/overview/budget/ budget14/ summary/14summary.pdf.

32. Corrigan and Watson, "Frequency of Violent Behavior," 160.

33. Taylor, "Psychosis and Violence," 651.

34. "NIMH Awards to Domestic Higher Education," National Institutes of Health, accessed June 7, 2015, http://report.nih.gov/award/index.cfm.

35. *National Institute of Mental Health Strategic Plan*, NIH Publication No. 08-6368 (Washington, D.C.: U.S. Department of Health and Human Services, 2008), 18.

36. "Child and Adolescent Services Research Program," National Institute of Mental Health, accessed October 26, 2014. http://www.nimh.nih.gov/about/organization/dsir/services-research-and-epidemiology-branch/child-and-adolescent-services-research-program.shtml.

37. Bond, Drake, and Becker, "Update on Randomized Controlled Trials," 284–86; Lehman et al., "Improving Employment Outcomes," 168.

38. Robert E. Drake et al., "Assisting Social Security Disability Insurance Beneficiaries with Schizophrenia, Bipolar Disorder, or Major Depression in Returning to Work," *American Journal of Psychiatry* 170 (2013): 1434.

39. William D. Frey et al., *Mental Health Treatment Study: Final Report* (Rockville, MD: Westat, 2011), chap. 1; 2.

40. Frey et al., *Mental Health Treatment Study*, chap. 4: 3; Richard G. Frank, "Helping (Some) SSDI Beneficiaries with Severe Mental Illness Return to Work," *American Journal of Psychiatry* 170 (2013): 1380.

41. Frey et al., *Mental Health Treatment Study*, chap. 4: 7, 29.

42. Frank, "Helping (Some) SSDI Beneficiaries," 1380.

43. Stoneman and Lysaght, "Supported Education," 257–58.

44. Stoneman and Lysaght, "Supported Education."

45. Stoneman and Lysaght, "Supported Education," 259.

46. Best, Still, and Cameron, "Supported Education," 66–67.

47. Interview with patient, October 25, 2003.

48. Robert E. Drake and Gary R. Bond, "IPS Support Employment: A 20-Year Update," *American Journal of Psychiatric Rehabilitation* 14 (2011): 156.

49. Drake and Gary R. Bond, "IPS Support Employment," 160.

50. King, *It*, 1054.

Bibliography

Acemoglu, Daron, and Joshua D. Angrist. "Consequences of Employment Protection? The Case of the Americans with Disabilities Act." *Journal of Political Economy* 109 (2001): 915–57.

Aguilera, Michael Bernabé. "The Impact of Social Capital on Labor Force Participation: Evidence from the 2000 Social Capital Benchmark Survey." *Social Science Quarterly* 83 (2002): 853–74.

Akabas, Sheila K. "Workplace Responsiveness: Key Employer Characteristics in Support of Job Maintenance for People with Mental Illness." *Psychosocial Rehabilitation Journal* 17 (1994): 91–101.

Albrecht, Gary, Vivian G. Walker, and Judith A. Levy. "Social Distance from the Stigmatized: A Test of Two Theories." *Social Science and Medicine* 16 (1982): 1319–27.

Allbright, Amy L. "2001 Employment Decisions under the ADA Title I—Survey Update." *Mental and Physical Disability Law Reporter* 26 (2002): 394–98.

Andreasen, Nancy C., William T. Carpenter, Jr., John M. Kane, Robert A. Lasser, Stephen R. Marder, and Daniel R. Weinberger. "Remission in Schizophrenia: Proposed Criteria and Rationale for Consensus." *American Journal of Psychiatry* 162 (2005): 441–49.

Angermeyer, Matthias C., and Herbert Matschinger. "Labeling—Stereotype—Discrimination: An Investigation of the Stigma Process." *Social Psychiatry and Psychiatric Epidemiology* 40 (2005): 391–95.

Angermeyer, Matthias C., and Herbert Matschinger. "Public Beliefs about Schizophrenia and Depression: Similarities and Differences." *Social Psychiatry and Psychiatric Epidemiology* 38 (2003): 526–34.

Angermeyer, Matthias C., Aurélie Millier, Mokhtar Kouki, Tarek Refaï, Georg Schomerus, and Mondher Toumi. "Biogenetic Explanations and Emotional Reactions to People with Schizophrenia and Major Depressive Disorder." *Psychiatry Research* 220 (2014): 702–4.

Angermeyer, Matthias C., Michael Beck, and Herbert Matschinger. "Determinants of the Public's Preference for Social Distance from People with Schizophrenia." *Canadian Journal of Psychiatry* 48 (2003): 663–68.

Awad, A. George, and Lakshimi Voruganti. "The Burden of Schizophrenia on Caregivers." *PharmacoEconomics* 26 (2008): 149–59.

Baldwin, Marjorie L. "The Effects of Impairments on Employment and Wages: Estimates from the 1984 and 1990 SIPP." *Behavioral Sciences and the Law* 17 (1999): 7–27.

Baldwin, Marjorie L., and Rebecca M. B. White. "Workplace Accommodations That Work for Persons with Mental Illness." In *Perspectives on Disability and Accommodation*, edited by Kelly Williams-Whitt and Daphne G. Taras, 115–31. Victoria, BC: National Institute of Disability Management and Research, 2010.

Baldwin, Marjorie L., and Steven C. Marcus. "Labor Market Outcomes of Persons with Mental Disorders." *Industrial Relations* 46 (2007): 481–510.

———. "Perceived vs. Measured Stigma among Workers with Serious Mental Disorders." *Psychiatric Services* 57 (2006): 388–92.

Baldwin, Marjorie L., and William G. Johnson. "Labor Market Discrimination against Men with Disabilities in the Year of the A.D.A." *Southern Economic Journal* 66 (2000): 548–66.

Banks, Becky R., Jeanne Novak, David M. Mank, and Teresa Grossi. "Disclosure of a Psychiatric Disability in Supported Employment: An Exploratory Study." *International Journal of Psychosocial Rehabilitation* 11 (2007): 69–84.

Baron, Richard C., and Mark S. Salzer. "Accounting for Unemployment among People with Mental Illness." *Behavioral Sciences and the Law* 20 (2002): 585–99.

Bauer, Rita, Franziska Koepke, Linda Sterzinger, and Herman Spiessl. "Burden, Rewards and Coping—The Ups and Downs of Caregivers of People with Mental Illness." *Journal of Nervous and Mental Disease* 200 (2012): 928–33.

Beck, Hiroko, William E. Boden, Sushmitha Patibandla, Dmitriy Kireyev, Vipul Gupta, Franklin Campagna, Michael E. Cain, and Joseph E. Marine. "50th Anniversary of the First Successful Permanent Pacemaker Implantation in the United States: Historical Review and Future Directions." *American Journal of Cardiology* 106 (2010): 810–18.

Becker, Gary S. *The Economics of Discrimination.* 2nd ed. Chicago: University of Chicago Press, 1971.

Beers, Clifford Whittingham. *A Mind That Found Itself: An Autobiography.* Garden City, NY: Doubleday, 1965 (1st ed., 1908).

Befort, Stephen F. "An Empirical Examination of Case Outcomes under the ADA Amendments Act." *Washington and Lee Law Review* 70 (2013): 2027–71.

Behavioral Health Centers. "CMC Randolph: Annual Mental Health Report Mecklenburg County." Charlotte, NC: Carolinas HealthCare System, 2005.

Bell, Morris D., Wayne Zito, Tamasine Greig, and Bruce Wexler. "Neurocognitive Enhancement Therapy with Vocational Services: Work Outcomes at Two-Year Follow-up." *Schizophrenia Research* 105 (2008): 18–29.

Bernstein, Elizabeth, and Nathan Koppel. "A Death in the Family: Aided by Advocates for the Mentally Ill, William Bruce Left the Hospital—Only to Kill His Mother." *Wall Street Journal,* August 16, 2008.

Best, Lachlan J., Megan Still, and Grant Cameron. "Supported Education: Enabling Course Completion for People Experiencing Mental Illness." *Australian Occupational Therapy Journal* 55 (2008): 65–68.

Bleuler, Manfred. "A 23-Year Longitudinal Study of 208 Schizophrenics and Impressions in Regard to the Nature of Schizophrenia." *Journal of Psychiatric Research* 6 (1968, Supplement 1): 3–12.

Bogardus, Emory. "A Social Distance Scale." *Sociology and Social Research* 17 (1933): 265–71.

Bond, Gary R., and Robert E. Drake. "Predictors of Competitive Employment among Patients with Schizophrenia." *Current Opinion in Psychiatry* 21 (2008): 362–69.

Bond, Gary R., Michelle P. Salyers, Jerry Dincin, Robert E. Drake, Deborah R. Becker, Virginia V. Fraser, and Michael Haines. "A Randomized Controlled Trial Comparing Two Vocational Models for Persons with Severe Mental Illness." *Journal of Consulting and Clinical Psychology* 75 (2007): 968–82.

Bond, Gary R., Robert E. Drake, and Deborah R. Becker. "An Update on Randomized Controlled Trials of Evidence-Based Supported Employment." *Psychiatric Rehabilitation Journal* 21 (2008): 280–90.

Boyce, Melanie, Jenny Secker, Robyn Johnson, Mike Floyd, Bob Gove, Justine Schneider, and Jan Slade. "Mental Health Service Users' Experiences of Returning to Paid Employment." *Disability and Society* 23 (2008): 77–88.

Bruyère, Suzanne, William A. Erikson, and Sara A. VanLooy. "The Impact of Business Size on Employer ADA Response." *Rehabilitation Counseling Bulletin* 49 (2006): 194–206.

Burnham, John C. "A Clinical Alternative to the Public Health Approach to Mental Illness: A Forgotten Social Experiment." *Perspectives in Biology and Medicine* 49 (2006): 220–37.

Campbell, Kikuko, Gary R. Bond, and Robert E. Drake. "Who Benefits from Supported Employment: A Meta-Analytic Study." *Schizophrenia Bulletin* 37 (2011): 370–80.

Carpenter, William T. "The Facts of Schizophrenia: A Personal Commentary." *Schizophrenia Research* 128 (2011): 2–4.

Chaudoir, Stephenie R., and Jeffrey D. Fisher. "The Disclosure Process Model: Understanding Disclosure Decision Making and Post-Disclosure Outcomes among People Living with a Concealable Stigmatized Identity." *Psychological Bulletin* 136 (2010): 236–56.

Choe, Chung, and Marjorie L. Baldwin. "Onset of Disability, Job Matching, and Employment Outcomes." MPRA Paper No. 63805 (January 2015). http://mpra.ub.uni-muenchen.de/63805/.

Civil Rights Act of 1964, U.S. Code 42 (1964), §§ 1971 et seq.

Clarke, Diana, and Joanne Winsor. "Perceptions and Needs of Parents during a Young Adult's First Psychiatric Hospitalization: 'We're All on This Little Island and We're Going to Drown Real Soon.'" *Issues in Mental Health Nursing* 31 (2010): 242–47.

Cohen, Amy N., Shirley M. Glynn, Alison B. Hamilton, and Alexander S. Young. "Implementation of a Family Intervention for Individuals with Schizophrenia." *Journal of General Internal Medicine* 25 (2009): 32–37.

Collins, Wilkie. *Man and Wife.* Oxford World's Classics. New York: Oxford University Press, 1995 (1st ed., 1870).

———. *No Name.* London: Penguin Group, 1995 (1st ed., 1862).

———. *The Woman in White.* London: Penguin Group, 1994 (1st ed., 1868).

Concannon, James. "Mind Matters: Mental Disability and the History and Future of the Americans with Disabilities Act." *Law and Psychology Review* 36 (2012): 89–114.

Corrigan, Patrick W. "Mental Health Stigma as Social Attribution: Implications for Research Methods and Attitude Change." *Clinical Psychology: Science and Practice* 7 (2000): 48–67.

Corrigan, Patrick W., Amy C. Watson, Gabriela Gracia, Natalie Slopen, Kenneth Rasinski, and Laura L. Hall. "Newspaper Stories as Measures of Structural Stigma." *Psychiatric Services* 56 (2005): 551–56.

Corrigan, Patrick W., and Amy C. Watson. "Findings from the National Comorbidity Survey on the Frequency of Violent Behavior in Individuals with Psychiatric Disorders." *Psychiatry Research* 136 (2005): 153–62.

Corrigan, Patrick W., and Amy C. Watson. "The Paradox of Self-Stigma and Mental Illness." *Clinical Psychology: Science and Practice* 9 (2002): 35–43.

Corrigan, Patrick W., and John R. O'Shaughnessy. "Changing Mental Illness Stigma as It Exists in the Real World." *Australian Psychologist* 42 (2007): 90–97.

Corrigan, Patrick, Fred E. Markowitz, Amy Watson, David Rowan, and Mary Ann Kubiak. "An Attribution Model of Public Discrimination towards Persons with Mental Illness." *Journal of Health and Social Behavior* 44 (2003): 162–79.

Craddock, Nick, and Michael J. Owen. "The Kraepelinian Dichotomy—Going, Going . . . But Still Not Gone." *British Journal of Psychiatry* 196 (2010): 92–95.

Dalgin, Rebecca Spirito, and Dennis Gilbride. "Perspectives of People with Psychiatric Disabilities on Employment Disclosure." *Psychiatric Rehabilitation Journal* 26 (2003): 306–10.

DeLeire, Thomas. "The Wage and Employment Effects of the Americans with Disabilities Act." *Journal of Human Resources* 35 (2000): 693–715.

Dinos, Sokratis, Scott Stevens, Marc Serfaty, Scott Weich, and Michael King. "Stigma: The Feelings and Experiences of 46 People with Mental Illness; Qualitative Study." *British Journal of Psychiatry* 184 (2004): 176–81.

Dreyer, Barbara A. "Adolf Meyer and Mental Hygiene: An Ideal for Public Health." *American Journal of Public Health* 66 (1976): 998–1003.

Duckworth, Kendra M. "Employees with Psychiatric Impairments." Accommodation and Compliance Series: The ADA Amendments Act of 2008. *U.S. Department of Labor.* Last modified, December 17, 2008. https://askjan.org/bulletins/adaaa1.htm.

Easterly, William. *The White Man's Burden.* New York: Penguin Books, 2006.

Ellison, Marsha Langer, Zlatka Russinova, Kim MacDonald-Wilson, and Asya Lyass. "Patterns and Correlates of Workplace Disclosure among Professionals and Managers with Psychiatric Conditions." *Journal of Vocational Rehabilitation* 18 (2003): 3–13.

Fairclough, Samantha, Robert K. Robinson, Dave L. Nichols, and Sam Cousley. "In Sickness and in Health: Implications for Employers When Bipolar Disorders Are Protected Disabilities." *Employee Responsibilities and Rights Journal* 25 (2013): 277–92.

Farr, Clifford. "Benjamin Rush and American Psychiatry." *American Journal of Psychiatry* 151 (1994): 65–73.

Feldman, David B., and Christian S. Crandall. "Dimensions of Mental Illness Stigma: What about Mental Illness Causes Social Rejection?" *Journal of Social and Clinical Psychology* 26 (2007): 137–54.

Foldemo, Anniqa, Maths Gullberg, Anna-Christina Ek, and Lennart Bogren. "Quality of Life and Burden in Parents of Outpatients with Schizophrenia." *Social Psychiatry and Psychiatric Epidemiology* 40 (2005): 133–38.

Foussias, George, and Gary Remington. "Antipsychotics and Schizophrenia: From Efficacy and Effectiveness to Clinical Decision-Making." *Canadian Journal of Psychiatry* 55 (2010): 117–25.

Frank, Richard G., and Sherry A. Glied. *Better but Not Well: Mental Health Policy in the United States since 1950*. Baltimore: Johns Hopkins University Press, 2006.

Franks, Deborah D. "Economic Contribution of Families Caring for Persons with Severe and Persistent Mental Illness." *Administration and Policy in Mental Health* 18 (1990): 9–18.

Freuh, B. Christopher, Anouk L. Grubaugh, Anthony T. Lo Sasso, Walter J. Jones, John M. Oldham, and Richard C. Lindrooth. "Key Stakeholder Perceptions Regarding Acute Care Psychiatry in Distressed Publicly Funded Mental Health Care Markets." *Bulletin of the Menninger Clinic* 76 (2012): 1–20.

Gaebel, Wolfgang, Mathias Riesbeck, Wolfgang Wölwer, Ansgar Klimke, Matthias Eickhoff, Martina von Wilmsdorff, and Isabella Heuser. "Rates and Predictors of Remission in First-Episode Schizophrenia within 1 Year of Antipsychotic Maintenance Treatment." *Schizophrenia Research* 152 (2014): 478–86.

Gallagher, Sally K., and David Mechanic. "Living with the Mentally Ill: Effects on the Health and Function of Other Household Members." *Social Science and Medicine* 42 (1996): 1691–701.

Gianfrancesco, Frank D., Ruey-hua Wang, and Elaine Yu. "Effects of Patients with Bipolar, Schizophrenic, and Major Depressive Disorders on the Mental and Other Healthcare Expenses of Family Members." *Social Science and Medicine* 61 (2005): 305–11.

Gilmore, John H. "Understanding What Causes Schizophrenia: A Developmental Perspective." *American Journal of Psychiatry* 167 (2010): 8–10.

Giron, M., A. Fernandez-Yanez, S. Mana-Alverenga, A. Molina-Habas, A. Nolasco, and M. Gomez-Beneyto. "Efficacy and Effectiveness of Individual Family Intervention on Social and Clinical Functioning and Family Burden in Severe Schizophrenia." *Psychological Medicine* (2009): 1–12.

Glaeser, Edward L., David Laibson, and Bruce Sacerdote. "An Economic Approach to Social Capital." *Economic Journal* 112 (2002): F437–58.

Goffman, Erving. *Stigma: Notes on the Management of Spoiled Identity*. Englewood Cliffs, NJ: Prentice-Hall, 1963.

Goldberg, Susan G., Mary B. Killeen, and Bonnie O'Day. "The Disclosure Conundrum: How People with Psychiatric Disabilities Navigate Employment." *Psychology, Public Policy and Law* 11 (2005): 463–500.

Goldman, Howard, and Gerald N. Grob. "Defining 'Mental Illness' in Mental Health Policy." *Health Affairs* 25 (2006): 737–49.

Gomez, Rafael, and Eric Santor. "Membership Has Its Privileges: The Effect of Social Capital and Neighbourhood Characteristics on the Earnings of Microfinance Borrowers." *Canadian Journal of Economics* 34 (2001): 943–66.

Greenwood, Ronni Michelle, Ana Stefancic and Sam Tsemberis. "Pathways Housing First for Homeless Persons with Psychiatric Disabilities: Program Innovation, Research, and Advocacy." *Journal of Social Issues* 69 (2013): 645–63.

Grob, Gerald N. "Mad, Homeless and Unwanted: A History of the Care of the Chronically Mentally Ill in America." *Psychiatric Clinics of North America* 17 (1994): 541–56.

———. "Mental Health Policy in the Liberal State: The Example of the United States." *International Journal of Law and Psychiatry* 31 (2008): 89–100.

Gronfein, William. "Psychotropic Drugs and the Origins of Deinstitutionalization." *Social Problems* 32 (1985): 437–54.

Grover, Sandeep, Subho Chakrabarti, Munish Aggarwal, Ajit Avasthi, Parmanand Kulhara, Sunil Sharma, and Nitacha Khehra. "Comparative Study of the Experience of Caregiving in Bipolar Affective Disorder and Schizophrenia." *International Journal of Social Psychiatry* 58 (2011): 614–22.

Harcourt, Bernard E. "From the Asylum to the Prison: Rethinking the Incarceration Revolution." *Texas Law Review* 84 (2006): 1751–86.

Hartman, Patrick A. "'Interacting with Others' as a Major Life Activity under the Americans with Disabilities Act." *Seton Hall Circuit Review* 2 (2005): 138–73.

Hawthorne, Nathaniel. *The Scarlet Letter*. New York: Simon & Schuster, 2004 (1st ed., 1850).

Heinrichs, R. Walter. "Historical Origins of Schizophrenia: Two Early Madmen and Their Illness." *Journal of the History of the Behavioral Sciences* 39 (2003): 349–463.

Hemmens, Craig, Milo Miller, Velmer S. Burton, and Susan Milner. "The Consequences of Official Labels: An Examination of the Rights Lost by the Mentally Ill and Mentally Incompetent Ten Years Later." *Community Mental Health Journal* 38 (2002): 129–40.

Hollenbeck, Kevin, and Jean Kimmel. "Differences in the Returns to Education for Males by Disability Status and Age of Disability Onset." *Southern Economic Journal* 74 (2008): 707–24.

Howe, E. W. *Ventures in Common Sense*. New York: Alfred A. Knopf, 1919.

Hunter, Michael D., and Peter W. R. Woodruff. "History, Aetiology and Symptomatology of Schizophrenia." *Psychiatry* 4 (2005): 3–6.

Janssen, Paul. "The Social Chemistry of Pharmacological Discovery: The Haloperidol Story." *International Journal of the Addictions* 27 (1992): 331–46.

Jenkins, Janice Hunter, and Elizabeth A. Carpenter-Song. "Awareness of Stigma among Persons with Schizophrenia." *Journal of Nervous and Mental Disease* 197 (2009): 520–29.

Job Accommodations Network. "Accommodation Ideas for Addison's Disease." Accessed June 3, 2014. https://askjan.org/soar/Other/addisons.html.

Jones, Amanda M. "Disclosure of Mental Illness in the Workplace: A Literature Review." *American Journal of Psychiatric Rehabilitation* 14 (2011): 212–29.

Jones, Melanie K., Paul L. Latreille, and Peter J. Sloane. "Disability, Gender, and the British Labour Market." *Oxford Economics Papers* 58 (2006): 407–49.

Kaas, Merrie J., Suzanne Lee, and Carol Peitzman. "Barriers to Collaboration between Mental Health Professionals and Families in the Care of Persons with Serious Mental Illness." *Issues in Mental Health Nursing* 24 (2003): 741–56.

Kennedy, John W. "Phoenix Dream Center Opens Program for Foster Youth." *Pentecostal Evangel*, December 12, 2013. http://ag.org/top/news/.

Keshavan, Matcheri S., Henry A. Nasrallah, and Rajiv Tandon. "Schizophrenia, 'Just the Facts' 6. Moving Ahead with the Schizophrenia Concept: From the Elephant to the Mouse." *Schizophrenia Research* 127 (2011): 3–13.

Keshavan, Matcheri S., Rajiv Tandon, Nash N. Boutros, and Henry A. Nasrallah. "Schizophrenia, 'Just the Facts': What We Know in 2008 Part 3: Neurobiology." *Schizophrenia Research* 106 (2008): 89–107.

Kessler, Ronald C. "The Prevalence and Correlates of Untreated Serious Mental Illness." *Health Services Research* 36 (2001): 987–1007.

Killeen, Mary B., and Bonnie L. O'Day. "Challenging Expectations: How Individuals with Psychiatric Disabilities Find and Keep Work." *Psychiatric Rehabilitation Journal* 28 (2004): 157–63.

Koutra, Katerina, Sofia Triliva, Theano Roumeliotaki, Zacharias Stefanakis, Maria Basta, Chritos Lionis, and Alexandros N. Vgontzas. "Family Functioning in Families of First-episode Psychosis Patients as Compared to Chronic Mentally Ill Patients and Healthy Controls." *Psychiatry Research* 45 (2014): 486–96.

Kuipers, Elizabeth. "Family Interventions in Schizophrenia: Evidence for Efficacy and Proposed Mechanisms of Change." *Journal of Family Therapy* 28 (2006): 73–80.

Kvrgic, Sara, Marialuisa Cavelti, Eva-Marina Beck, Nicolas Rusch, and Roland Vauth. "Therapeutic Alliance in Schizophrenia: The Role of Recovery Orientation, Self-Stigma, and Insight." *Psychiatry Research* 209 (2013): 15–20.

Lebensohn, Zigmond M. "General Hospital Psychiatry U.S.A.: Retrospect and Prospect." *Comprehensive Psychiatry* 21 (1980): 500–503.

Lehman, Anthony F., Jeffrey Lieberman, Lisa B. Dixon, Thomas H. McGlashan, Alexander L. Miller, Diana O. Perkins, and Julie Kreyenbuhl. *Practice Guideline for the Treatment of Patients with Schizophrenia.* 2nd ed. Arlington, VA: American Psychiatric Association, 2010.

Lehman, Anthony F., Richard Goldberg, Lisa B. Dixon, Scot McNary, Leticia Postrado, Ann Hackman, and Karen McDonnell. "Improving Employment Outcomes for Persons with Severe Mental Illnesses." *Archives of General Psychiatry* 59 (2002): 165–72.

Link, Bruce, Jo C. Phelan, Michaeline Bresnahan, Ann Stueve, and Bernice A. Pescosolido. "Public Conceptions of Mental Illness: Labels, Causes, Dangerousness, and Social Distance." *American Journal of Public Health* 89 (1999): 1328–33.

Lopez-Munoz, Francisco, and Cecilio Alamo. "The Consolidation of Neuroleptic Therapy: Janssen, the Discovery of Haloperidol and Its Introduction into Clinical Practice." *Brain Research Bulletin* 79 (2009): 120–41.

Lowyck, B., M. De Hert, E. Peeters, M. Wampers, P. Gilis, and J. Peukens. "A Study of the Family Burden of 150 Family Members of Schizophrenic Patients." *European Psychiatry* 19 (2004): 395–401.

Lucca, Anna M., Alexis D. Henry, Steven Banks, Lorna Simon, and Stephanie Page. "Evaluation of an Individual Placement and Support Model (IPS) Program." *Psychiatric Rehabilitation Journal* 27 (2004): 251–57.

Lyons, Richard D. "How Release of Mental Patients Began." *New York Times*, October 30, 1984.

Macias, Cathaleen, Robert Jackson, Carolyn Schroeder, and Qi Wang. "What Is a Clubhouse? Report on the ICCD 1996 Survey of USA Clubhouses." *Community Mental Health Journal* 35 (1999): 181–90.

Magaña, Sandy M., Jorge I. Ramirez Garcia, Maria G. Hernandez, and Raymond Cortez. "Psychological Distress among Latino Family Caregivers of Adults with Schizophrenia: The Roles of Burden and Stigma." *Psychiatric Services* 58 (2007): 378–84.

Magliano, L., Andrea Fiorillo, Corrado De Rose, Claudio Malagone, Mario Maj, and the National Mental Health Project Working Group. "Family Burden in Long-Term Diseases: A Comparative Study in Schizophrenia vs. Physical Disorders." *Social Science and Medicine* 61 (2005): 313–22.

Magliano, L., G. Fadden, M. Economou, T. Xavier, T. Held, M. Guarneri, C. Marasco, P. Tosini, and M. Maj. "Social and Clinical Factors Influencing the Choice of Coping Strategies in Relatives of Patients with Schizophrenia: Results of the BIOMED I Study." *Social Psychiatry and Psychiatric Epidemiology* 33 (1998): 413–19.

Magliano, L., G. Fadden, M. Madianos, J. M. Caldas de Almeida, T. Held, M. Guarneri, C. Marasco, et al. "Burden on the Families of Patients with Schizophrenia: Results of the BIOMED I Study." *Social Psychiatry and Psychiatric Epidemiology* 33 (1998): 405–12.

Mann, Caroline E., and Melissa J. Himelein. "Factors Associated with Stigmatization of Persons with Mental Illness." *Psychiatric Services* 55 (2004): 185–87.

Marshall, Tina, Phyllis Solomon, Sara-Ann Steber, and Eddie Mannion. "Provider and Family Beliefs Regarding the Causes of Severe Mental Illness." *Psychiatric Quarterly* 74 (2003): 223–36.

Marwaha, Steven, and Sonia Johnson. "Views and Experiences of Employment among People with Psychosis: A Qualitative Descriptive Study." *International Journal of Social Psychiatry* 51 (2005): 302–16.

McDonell, Michael G., Robert Short, Christopher M. Berry, and Dennis G. Dyck. "Burden in Schizophrenia Caregivers: Impact of Family Psychoeducation and Awareness of Patient Suicidality." *Family Process Journal* 42 (2003): 91–103.

Michalak, Erin E., Lakshmi N. Yatham, Victoria Maxwell, Sandra Hale, and Raymond W. Lam. "The Impact of Bipolar Disorder upon Work Functioning: A Qualitative Analysis." *Bipolar Disorders* 9 (2007): 126–43.

Mitra, Sophie. "The Capability Approach and Disability." *Journal of Disability Policy Studies* 16 (2006): 236–47.

Möller-Leimkühler, Anne Maria, and Andreas Wiesheu. "Caregiver Burden in Chronic Mental Illness: The Role of Patient and Caregiver Characteristics." *European Archives of Psychiatry and Clinical Neuroscience* 262 (2012): 157–66.

Morrissey, Joseph P., and Howard H. Goldman. "Care and Treatment of the Mentally Ill in the United States: Historical Developments and Reforms." *Annals of the American Academy of Political and Social Science* 484 (1986): 12–27.

Mowbray, Carol T., Mary E. Collins, Chyrell D. Bellamy, Deborah A. Megivern, Deborah Bybee, and Steve Szilvagyi. "Supported Education for Adults with Psychiatric Disabilities: An Innovation for Social Work and Psychosocial Rehabilitation Practice." *Social Work* 50 (2005): 7–20.

Murray, Christopher J. L., and Alan D. Lopez, eds. *The Global Burden of Disease: A Comprehensive Assessment of Mortality and Disability from Diseases, Injuries and Risk Factors in 1990 and Projected to 2020*. Cambridge, MA: Harvard School of Public Health, 1996.

Murray, Christopher J. L., Theo Vos, Rafael Lozano, Mohsen Naghavi, Abraham D. Flaxman, Catherine Michaud, and Majid Ezzati. "Disability-Adjusted Life Years (DALYs) for 291 Diseases and Injuries in 21 Regions, 1990–2010." *Lancet* 380 (2012): 2197–223.

NC Division of Mental Health, Developmental Disabilities and Substance Abuse Services. "Exploring the Costs and Feasibility of a New Psychiatric Facility." Raleigh: North Carolina Department of Health and Human Services, 2013.

New Freedom Commission on Mental Health. *Achieving the Promise: Transforming Mental Health Care in America*. DHHS Pub. No. SMA-03-3832. Rockville, MD: 2003.

Nithsdale, Vicky, Jason Davies, and Paul Croucher. "Psychosis and the Experience of Employment." *Journal of Occupational Rehabilitation* 18 (2008): 175–82.

Noce, Robert H., David B. Williams, and Walter Rapaport. "Reserprine (Serpasil) in the Management of the Mentally Ill and Mentally Retarded." *Senate Interim Committee Report on the Treatment of Mental Illness* 20 (1956): 29–35.

Nordentoft, Merete, Trine Madsen, and Izabela Fedyszyn. "Suicidal Behavior and Mortality in First-Episode Psychosis." *Journal of Nervous and Mental Disease* 203 (2015): 387–92.

Norman, Ross, Deborah Windell, and Rahul Manchanda. "Examining Differences in the Stigma of Depression and Schizophrenia." *International Journal of Social Psychiatry* 58 (2012): 69–78.

Norman, Ross, Richard M. Sorrentino, Deborah Windell, and Rahul Manchada. "The Role of Perceived Norms in the Stigmatization of Mental Illness." *Social Psychiatry and Psychiatric Epidemiology* 43 (2008): 851–59.

Nuechterlein, K. H., Dawson, M. E., Ventura, J., Gitlin, M., Subotnik, K. L., Snyder, K. S., Mintz, J., & Bartzokis, G. "The Vulnerability/Stress Model of Schizophrenic Relapse: A Longitudinal Study." *Acta Psvchiatrica Scandinavica* 89 (1994): 58–64.

O'Brien, Gerald, and Melinda S. Brown. "Persons with Mental Illness and the Americans with Disabilities Act: Implications for the Social Work Profession." *Social Work in Mental Health* 7 (2009): 442–57.

Ochoa, Susana, Miriam Vilplana, Josep Maria Haro, Victoria Villalta-Gil, Franciso Martinez, Mari Cruz Negredo, and Pilar Casacuberta. "Do Needs, Symptoms or Disability of Outpatients with Schizophrenia Influence Family Burden?" *Social Psychiatry and Psychiatric Epidemiology* 43 (2008): 612–18.

Oxford English Dictionary. Oxford: Oxford University Press, 1970 (1st ed., 1884–1928).

Pachankis, John E. "The Psychological Implications of Concealing a Stigma: A Cognitive-Affective-Behavioral Model." *Psychological Bulletin* 133 (2007): 328–45.

Palmer, Brian A., V. Shane Pankratz, and John Michael Bostwick. "The Lifetime Risk of Suicide in Schizophrenia: A Reexamination." *Archives of General Psychiatry* 62 (2005): 247–53.

Pandya, Anand, Catherine Bresee, Ken Duckworth, Katrina Gay, and Michael Fitzpatrick. "Perceived Impact of the Disclosure of a Schizophrenia Diagnosis." *Community Mental Health Journal* 47 (2011): 613–21.

Parekattil, Sijo J., and Michael E. Moran. "Robotic Instrumentation: Evolution and Microsurgical Applications." *Indian Journal of Urology 26* (2010): 395–403.

Parks, Joe, and Alan Q. Radke, eds. *The Vital Role of State Psychiatric Hospitals*. Alexandria, VA: National Association of State Mental Health Program Directors, 2014.

Pescosolido, Bernice A., Jack K. Martin, J. Scott Long, Tait R. Medina, Jo C. Phelan, and Bruce G. Link. "'A Disease Like Any Other?' A Decade of Change in Public Reactions to Schizophrenia, Depression, and Alcohol Dependence." *American Journal of Psychiatry* 167 (2010): 1321–30.

Peterson, Debbie, Nandika Currey, and Sunny Collings. "'You Don't Look Like One of Them': Disclosure of Mental Illness in the Workplace as an Ongoing Dilemma." *Psychiatric Rehabilitation Journal* 35 (2011): 145–47.

Petrila, John. "Congress Restores the Americans with Disabilities Act to Its Original Intent." *Psychiatric Services* 60 (2009): 878–79.

Phoenix Dream Center. "About Us." Accessed June 3, 2014.http://www.phxdreamcenter.org/about_us.

Phoenix First Assembly of God. "Our Mission." Accessed April 14, 2014. http://www.phoenixfirst.org/about-us/mission-values.

Read, John. "Why Promoting Biological Ideology Increases Prejudice against People Labelled 'Schizophrenic.'" *Australian Psychologist* 42 (2007): 118–28.

Rinaldi, Miles, Eoin Killackey, Jo Smith, Geoff Shepherd, Swaran P. Singh, and Tom Craig. "First Episode Psychosis and Employment: A Review." *International Review of Psychiatry* 22 (2010): 148–62.

Roberts, Albert R., and Linda Farris Kurtz. "Historical Perspectives on the Care and Treatment of the Mentally Ill." *Journal of Sociology and Social Welfare* 75 (1987): 75–91.

Rollins, Angela L., Kim T. Mueser, Gary R. Bond, and Deborah R. Becker. "Social Relationships at Work: Does the Employment Model Make a Difference?" *Psychiatric Rehabilitation Journal* 26 (2002): 51–61.

Rose, Stephen M. "Deciphering Deinstitutionalization: Complexities in Policy and Program Analysis." *Milbank Memorial Fund Quarterly* 57 (1979): 429–58.

Rosensheck, Robert, Douglas Leslie, Richard Keefe, Joseph McEvoy, Marvin Swartz, Diana Perkins, Scott Stroup, John K. Hsiao, and Jeffrey Lieberman. "Barriers to Employment for People with Schizophrenia." *American Journal of Psychiatry* 163 (2006): 411–17.

Rudnick, Abraham, and Maya Gover. "Combining Supported Education with Supported Employment." *Psychiatric Services* 60 (2009): 1690.

Saks, Elyn R. "Successful and Schizophrenic." *New York Times*, January 27, 2013.

Salkever, David, Mustafa C. Karakus, Eric P. Slade, Courtenay M. Harding, Richard L. Hough, Robert A. Rosenheck, Marvin S. Swartz, Concepcion Barrio, and Anne Marie Yamada. "Measures and Predictors of Community-Based Employment and Earnings of Persons with Schizophrenia in a Multisite Study." *Psychiatric Services* 58 (2007): 315–24.

Salomon, Joshua, Theo Vos, Daniel R. Hogan, Mohsen Naghavi, Nazma Begum, Razibuzzaman Shah, and Muhammad Karyana. "Common Values in Assessing Health Outcomes from Disease and Injury: Disability Weights Measurement Study for the Global Burden of Disease Study 2010." *Lancet* 380 (2012): 2129–43.

Salomon, Joshua, Theo Vos, Daniel R. Hogan, Mohsen Naghavi, Nazma Begum, Razibuzzaman Shah, and Muhammad Karyana. "Supplement to Common Values in Assessing Health Outcomes from Disease and Injury." *Lancet* 380 (2012): 1–25.

Saunders, Jana C., and Michelle M. Byrne. "A Thematic Analysis of Families Living with Schizophrenia." *Archives of Psychiatric Nursing* 16 (2002): 217–23.

Schennach, R., S. Meyer, F. Seemüller, M. Jäger, M. Schmauss, G. Laux, H. Pfeiffer, D. Naber, L.G. Schmidt, W. Gaebel, et al. "Insight in Schizophrenia—Course and Predictors during the Acute Treatment Phase of Patients Suffering from a Schizophrenia Spectrum Disorder." *European Psychiatry* 27 (2012): 625–33.

Schomerus G., C. Schwahn, A. Holzinger, P. W. Corrigan, H. J. Grabe, M. G. Carta, M. C. Angermeyer. "Evolution of Public Attitudes about Mental Illness: A Systematic Review and Meta-Analysis." *Acta Psychiatrica Scandinavica* 125 (2012): 440–52.

Schulze, Beate, and Matthias C. Angermeyer. "Subjective Experiences of Stigma: A Focus Group Study of Schizophrenic Patients, Their Relatives and Mental Health Professionals." *Social Science and Medicine* 56 (2003): 299–312.

Schur, Lisa, Douglas Kruse, Joseph Blasi, and Peter Blanck. "Is Disability Disabling in All Workplaces? Workplace Disparities and Corporate Culture." *Industrial Relations* 48 (2009): 381–410.

Secker, Jenny, and Helen Membrey. "Promoting Mental Health through Employment and Developing Healthy Workplaces: The Potential of Natural Supports at Work." *Health Education Research* 18 (2003): 207–15.

Shah, Saleem A. "Legal and Mental Health System Interactions: Major Developments and Research Needs." *International Journal of Law and Psychiatry* 4 (1981): 219–70.

Silton, Nava R., Kevin J. Flannelly, Glen Milstein, and Margaret L. Vaaler. "Stigma in America: Has Anything Changed? Impact of Perceptions of Mental Illness and Dangerousness on the Desire for Social Distance; 1996 and 2006." *Journal of Nervous and Mental Disease* 199 (2011): 361–66.

Silveira, Celeste, Joao Marques-Teixeira, and Antonio Jose de Bastos-Leite. "More Than One Century of Schizophrenia: An Evolving Perspective." *Journal of Nervous and Mental Disease* 200 (2012): 1054–57.

Sin, Jacqueline, and Ian Norman. "Psychoeducational Interventions for Family Members of People with Schizophrenia: A Mixed-Method Systematic Review." *Journal of Clinical Psychiatry* 74 (2013): 1145–62.

Smerud, Phyllis E., and Irwin S. Rosenfarb. "The Therapeutic Alliance and Family Psychoeducation in the Treatment of Schizophrenia: An Exploratory Prospective Change Process Study." *Journal of Consulting and Clinical Psychology* 76 (2008): 505–10.

Spence, Michael. "Job Market Signaling." *Quarterly Journal of Economics* 87 (1973): 355–74.

Stain, Helen J., Cherrie A. Galletly, Scott Clark, Jacqueline Wilson, Emily A. Killen, Lauren Anthes, Linda E. Campbell, Mary-Claire Hanlon, and Carol Harvey. "Understanding the Social Costs of Psychosis: The Experience of Adults Affected by Psychosis Identified within the Second Australian National Survey of Psychosis." *Australian and New Zealand Journal of Psychiatry* 46 (2012): 879–89.

Steadman, Henry J., Fred C. Osher, Pamela Clark Robbins, Brian Case, and Steven Samuels. "Prevalence of Serious Mental Illness among Jail Inmates." *Psychiatric Services* 60 (2009): 761–65.

Stefan, Susan. *Hollow Promises: Employment Discrimination against People with Mental Disabilities.* Washington, D.C.: American Psychological Association, 2002.

Stone, Danielle, and Adrienne Colella. "A Model of Factors Affecting the Treatment of Disabled Individuals in Organizations." *Academy of Management Review* 21 (1996): 352–401.

Tandon, Rajiv, Henry A. Nasrallah, and Matcheri S. Keshavan. "'Just the Facts:' Meandering in Schizophrenia's Many Forests." *Schizophrenia Research* 128 (2011): 5–6.

Tandon, Rajiv, Henry A. Nasrallah, and Matcheri S. Keshavan. "Schizophrenia, 'Just the Facts' 4. Clinical Features and Conceptualization." *Schizophrenia Research* 110 (2009): 1–23.

Tandon, Rajiv, Henry A. Nasrallah, and Matcheri S. Keshavan. "Schizophrenia, 'Just the Facts' 5. Treatment and Prevention Past, Present, and Future." *Schizophrenia Research* 122 (2010): 1–23.

Tandon, Rajiv, Matcheri S. Keshavan, and Henry A. Nasrallah. "Schizophrenia, 'Just the Facts' What We Know in 2008. 2 Epidemiology and Etiology." *Schizophrenia Research* 102 (2008): 1–18.

Taylor, Pamela J. "Psychosis and Violence: Stories, Fears and Reality." *Canadian Journal of Psychiatry* 53 (2008): 647–59.

Teplin, Linda A., Gary M. McClelland, Karen M. Abram, and Dana A. Weiner. "Crime Victimization in Adults with Severe Mental Illness." *Archives of General Psychiatry* 62 (2005): 911–21.

Torrey, E. Fuller. *American Psychosis.* Oxford: Oxford University Press, 2014.

———. *Surviving Schizophrenia: A Manual for Families, Patients, and Providers*, 5th ed. New York: HarperCollins, 2006.

Tringo, J. L. "The Hierarchy of Preference toward Disability Groups." *Journal of Special Education* 4 (1970): 295–306.

Tsang, Hector W. H., Ada Y. Leung, Raymond C.K. Chung, Morris Bell, and Wai-Ming Cheung. "Review on Vocational Predictors: A Systematic Review of Predictors of Vocational Outcomes among Individuals with Schizophrenia; An Update since 1998." *Australian and New Zealand Journal of Psychiatry* 44 (2010): 495–504.

Tsemberis, Sam. *Housing First: The Pathways Model to End Homelessness for People with Mental Illness and Addiction*. Center City: Hazelden, 2010.

U.S. National Library of Medicine. "Diseases of the Mind: Highlights of American Psychiatry through 1900, Early Psychiatric Hospitals and Asylums." Last modified September 13, 2013. http://www.nlm.nih.gov/hmd/diseases/early.html.

Viana, Kristin. "People That Have Won." *Soundings East* 17 (1993): 9–12.

Vos, Theo, Abraham D. Flaxman, Mohsen Naghavi, Rafael Lozano, Catherin Michaud, Majid Ezzati, and Kenji Shibuya. "Years Lived with Disability (YLDs) for the 1160 Sequelae of 289 Diseased and Injuries 1990–2010: A Systematic Analysis for the Global Burden of Disease Study 2010." *Lancet* 380 (2012): 2163–96.

Walker, Elaine F., and Donald Diforio. "Schizophrenia: A Neural-Diathesis Stress Model." *Psychological Review* 104 (1997): 667–85.

Watson, Amy C., Frederick E. Miller, and John S. Lyons. "Adolescent Attitudes toward Serious Mental Illness." *Journal of Nervous and Mental Disease* 193 (2005): 769–72.

Weiner, Bernard, Raymond P. Perry, and Jamie Magnusson. "An Attributional Analysis of Reactions to Stigmas." *Journal of Personality and Social Psychology* 55 (1988): 738–48.

Weiner, Bernard. "On Sin versus Sickness: A Theory of Perceived Responsibility and Social Motivation." *American Psychologist* 48 (1993): 957–65.

Weiss, Marc Franchot. "Children's Attitudes toward the Mentally Ill: A Developmental Analysis." *Psychological Reports* 58 (1986): 11–20.

———. "Children's Attitudes toward the Mentally Ill: An Eight-Year Longitudinal Follow-Up." *Psychological Reports* 74 (1994): 51–56.

Westbrook, Mary T., Varoe Legge, and Mark Pennay. "Attitudes towards Disabilities in a Multicultural Society." *Social Science and Medicine* 36 (1993): 615–23.

Where Hope Lives. "Rescuing Victims of Human Trafficking." Accessed May 20, 2015. http://www.rescueprojectphx.org/index.php.

Whiteford, Harvey A., Louisa Degenhardt, Jurgen Rehm, Amanda J. Baxter, Alize J. Ferrari, Holly E. Erskine, and Fiona J. Charlson. "Global Burden of Disease Attributable to Mental and Substance Use Disorders: Findings from the Global Burden of Disease Study 2010." *Lancet* 382 (2013): 1575–86.

Wilk, Joshua E., Joyce C. West, Steven C. Marcus, Lisa Countis, Darrel A. Regier, and Mark Olfson. "Family Contact and the Management of Medication Non-Adherence in Schizophrenia." *Community Mental Health Journal* 44 (2008): 377–80.

Winchester, Simon. *The Professor and the Madman: A Tale of Murder, Insanity, and the Making of the Oxford English Dictionary*. New York: HarperCollins, 1998.

Wing, Victoria C., Ingrid Bacher, Kristi A. Sacco, and Tony P. George. "Neuropsychological Performance in Patients with Schizophrenia and Controls as a Function of Cigarette Smoking Status." *Psychiatry Research* 188 (2011): 320–26.

Wood, Lisa, Michele Birtel, Sarah Alsawyc, Melissa Pyle, and Anthony Morrison. "Public Perceptions of Stigma towards People with Schizophrenia, Depression, and Anxiety." *Psychiatry Research* 220 (2014): 604–8.

Wu, Eric Q., Howard G. Birnbaum, Lizheng Shi, Daniel E. Ball, Ronald C. Kessler, Matthew Moulis, and Jyoti Aggarwal. "The Economic Burden of Schizophrenia in the United States in 2002." *Journal of Clinical Psychiatry* 66 (2005): 1122–29.

Zwelling, Shomer S. *Quest for a Cure: The Public Hospital in Williamsburg: 1773–1885*. Williamsburg, VA: Colonial Williamsburg Foundation, 1985.

Index

About the Author

Marjorie L. Baldwin is a professor in the Department of Economics at the W. P. Carey School of Business, Arizona State University, and academic director for Public Health Programs in the College of Health Solutions at ASU. Professor Baldwin is a health economist who has devoted a major part of her career to studying work disability and disability-related discrimination, with a particular focus on persons with serious mental illness. She is the author or coauthor of more than fifth articles and book chapters and has been a principal investigator for major studies of labor market discrimination against persons with mental disorders sponsored by the National Institutes of Health. She is a member of the National Academy of Social Insurance, the American Society of Health Economists, the National Alliance on Mental Illness, and holds an adjunct faculty positon with the University of Minnesota School of Public Health.